REALIZING CAPITAL

REALIZING CAPITAL

Financial and Psychic Economies in Victorian Form

Anna Kornbluh

Fordham University Press

New York   2014

Library of Congress Cataloging-in-Publication Data

Kornbluh, Anna.

  Realizing capital : financial and psychic economies in Victorian form / Anna Kornbluh. — First edition.

     pages cm

  Includes bibliographical references and index.

  ISBN 978-0-8232-5497-2 (cloth : alk. paper)

   1. English literature—19th century—History and criticism. 2. Finance in literature. 3. Economics—Psychological aspects—England.

4. Economics and literature—England—History—19th century. I. Title.

  PR468.F56R43 2014

  820.9'3553—dc23

                                                              2013017377

Printed in the United States of America

16 15 14   5 4 3 2 1

First edition

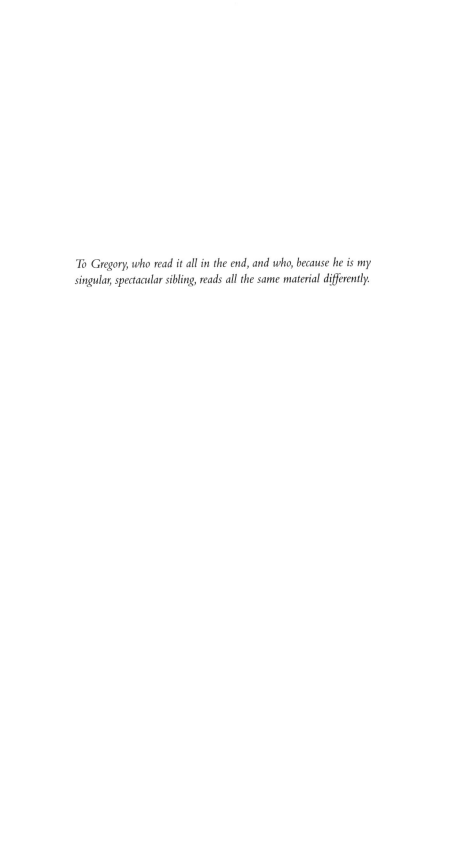

To Gregory, who read it all in the end, and who, because he is my singular, spectacular sibling, reads all the same material differently.

Contents

Mr. Casaubon had imagined that his long studious bachelorhood had stored up for him a compound interest of enjoyment, and that large drafts on his affections would not fail to be honoured; for we all of us, grave or light, get our thoughts entangled in metaphors, and act fatally on the strength of them. —*Middlemarch*

Acknowledgments

It would be unwise to commence a work about financial metaphors with a tally of debts, so I would say instead that many midwives delivered this book and many loved ones raised it. At the University of California, Irvine, the infant project was nurtured by Etienne Balibar, Natalka Freeland, Jayne Lewis, and Irene Tucker, and above all by the incomparably wonderful, impossibly brilliant Julia Reinhard Lupton. Kenneth, Hannah, Lucy, Isabel, and Eliot Reinhard made Southern California a home for me; Mia McIver, Benjamin Bishop, Craig Carson, Debra Channick, Patricia Goldsworthy, Kir Kuiken, Janet Neary, and Vanessa Osborne made that home warm. At the University of Illinois at Chicago, where The Institute for the Humanities provided indispensable support for the book's maturation, Jennifer Ashton, Nicholas Brown, Mark Canuel, Lennard Davis, Madhu Dubey, Stephen Engelmann, Chris Messenger, Walter Benn Michaels, and Mary Beth Rose set all the best ground rules, and my generous mentor Lisa Freeman helped me reframe them, while Sunil Agnani, Ainsworth Clarke, Rachel Havrelock, Nasser Mufti, and Roger Reeves formed a joyful cohort. Graduate students in my seminars "Symbolic Economies," "Freud and Victoria," and "Formalism and Its Discontents," especially Davis Brecheisen, Ryan Brooks, Heather Doble, Jim Nyenhuis, and Trevor Strunk, offered insight and cheer. Beyond institutional walls, Elizabeth Anker, Rick Barney, Eleanor Courtemanche, Jodi Dean, Dorit Geva, Eleanor Kaufman, Kiarina Kordela, Adam Kotsko, Leigh Clare LaBerge, Rob Lehman, Caroline Levine, Todd McGowan, Steven Miller, Anna Parkinson, Emily Rohrbach, Molly Anne Rothenberg, Eric Santner, Emily Steinlight, and Audrey Wasser were and are the sisters and brothers that sustain and inspire. Before there was even an inkling of a project, the infinitely talented, magnetically energetic Andrea, John, and Gregory Kornbluh, for whom words and ideas and books are the stuff of life, made every endeavor seem doable, every uphill adventure seem desirable. And after many things were in place, Ezra Friedman gave them luster and magic and a whole new order. Mira Blue Friedman gestated gently during final revisions, and slept sweetly during the production phase of this other baby.

A version of Chapter 3 first appeared as "The Economic Problem of Sympathy: Parabasis, Interest, and Realist Form in *Middlemarch*," *ELH* 77, no. 4 (Winter 2010); 941–67, copyright © 2010, The Johns Hopkins University Press. A version of Chapter 5 first appeared as "On Marx's Victorian Novel," *Mediations* 25, no. 1 (Winter 2011): 15-38.

Introduction   *"A Case of Metaphysics":*
                 Realizing Capital

> As we contemplated the fire, and as I thought what a difficult vision
> to realize Capital sometimes was, I put my hands into my pockets.

—Charles Dickens, *Great Expectations,* 1860

"To realize capital" is no mean feat. When Dickens's narrator glumly appraises the dim financial prospects of his naïve enterprising friend, the simple indicative clause "I put my hands into my pockets" effectuates a contrast between the materiality of hands and the ideality of vision, the physical gesture and the metaphysical realization. Beside the worldly difficulties of *acquiring* capital, such a contrast underscores, stand the philosophical difficulties of *realizing* capital, securing the status of "real" for something evidently ethereal. Ambitious naïfs and their generous friends—and every other player in the mid-Victorian economy—found themselves beset by these difficulties of the real as a result of the ascendance of capital propelled by "financialization," the transition to an economy in which the speculative begetting of money from money supersedes the industrial production and consumption of goods.[1] During the nineteenth century, shifts in what counted as "real" ignited considerable havoc: the era of financialization saw fiery debates and explosive volatility, chronic insecurity and—most surprisingly for anyone who shares Alan Greenspan's "shocked disbelief" at the financial catastrophe of 2008—regular, constant crisis.[2] From the 1830s to the 1880s, crises were rampant and recurrent. Financialization developed from rapidly paced legal innovation: every few years, new individual legal measures—like the 1833 Bank of England Charter Act, the 1844 Limited Liability Act, and the 1856 Joint Stock Companies Act—licensed the corporation, created the corporate person, and codified instruments like shares, futures, and derivatives. Each new act drew fierce contest, followed by yet another large-scale crisis.

To schematize this cyclicality: as soon as a century-old ban on corporations was repealed in 1824, a financial crisis erupted in 1825; pursuant to the 1833 Bank of England Charter Act's erasure of strictures on usury and authorization of paper banknotes, crises ensued in 1837 and 1839; the legalization of Joint-Stock Companies in 1844 resulted in the Railway Mania of 1845–1856 and subsequently stirred the 1847 financial crisis; Limited Liability was set in 1855 and Joint-Stock Companies further licensed in 1856; a crisis struck in 1857; and the 1860 repeal of Barnard's Act legalized futures and fomented the catastrophic 1866 crisis, collapsing Overend, Gurney, and Co. (the so-called "banker's bank").[3] Additional crises convulsed throughout the 1870s. The frequency and extremity of financial instability over most of the nineteenth century, in my reading, frames Dickens's observation that realizing capital posed some difficulties: how can one reliably go about "the business of getting on" if the bottom keeps falling out? Worse yet, how can something so manifestly tempestuous be moored in reality? Difficult to accumulate, capital is also difficult to stake as real. Traversing concrete and abstract, literal and figurative, Dickens's very phrase "to realize capital" crackles with irony—an irony that reverberates throughout the Victorian novel.

As the Victorians' preferred verb for financial genesis, "to realize" keys us in to the dynamic flux of the real in the epoch of financialization. According to Dr. Johnson's dictionary, when "realize" first came into financial usage in the eighteenth century, it meant, as we might expect from the idiom "real estate," "to convert money into land." The Victorian usage, by contrast, connotes the *conversion of land into money,* and more generally the conversion of assets, whether "real" estate or virtual futures, into the realer real of capital. To realize capital under financialization is a "difficult vision" because the real has crossed sides. How can something be made real if "real" itself is hard to pin down? Perhaps "a difficult vision" could regard "real capital" as something other than an oxymoron, but the vision of *Great Expectations* fully beholds these incongruities, pointing to the ontological instability and epistemological uncertainty of making something "real" when the real is on the make. No wonder it deems this predicament "a case of metaphysics."

Realizing Capital: Financial and Psychic Economies in Victorian Form analyzes this "case of metaphysics" of the mid-Victorian moment. It explores diverse mid-Victorian discourses—financial journalism, emerging psychology, political economy, and, above all, the realist novel—as they register these numerous difficulties in realizing capital. In these discourses we will encounter the idea of "fictitious capital" and its manifold significations, all at

[handwritten margin notes: "great def. of 'realism'"; "Capital isn't real ↓ Fictious Capital"]

base denoting the intuition that capital is not real—not only not material nor concrete, but not subject to the laws of time and space of this world, not possible to ground in ordinary logic. In nonfiction prose and through the literary conventions of realism (the aesthetic movement stirred by questions about the real), the Victorians trained their sights on the difficult vision of realizing fictitious capital. From the 1830s until the 1860s, Dickens was far from alone, and yet *Great Expectations* appears in retrospect to hail from the pivotal moment in history when capital did become real and the very idea of "fictitious capital" faded away.

Realizing Capital explores the rhetoric of this turn by which fictitious capital became a new kind of truth. In the sentence from Dickens with which we began, contemplating the difficulties of realizing capital prompts a gesture of inward retreat: "I put my hands into my pockets." I find this gesture emblematic of Victorian thought's struggle with fictitious capital and retreat to interiority. Confronting the manifest contradictions of realizing capital, Victorian thinkers looked inward to the capital of the self: the construct of "psychic economy," the idea that subjectivity is fundamentally economic and that the economy is fundamentally psychological, rose to prominence after the heyday of the idea of "fictitious capital."[4] Arguably one of the seminal metaphors of late modernity, this trope adopts "economy" as the preferred prism for understanding subjectivity and heralds desire as the motor of the macro-economy. The posited continuity that ensues from this metaphor—the characterization of capitalism as the natural issue of universal human psychology—has provided post-Victorian generations with the ultimate ideological alibi for a contingent mode of production: no matter that capital is speculative and ungrounded, for it is the manifestation of our nature. My book aims to account for this conceptual torsion, contextualizing the emergence of the fundamental trope for both psychology and political economy within the difficulties of realizing capital. It contends that "psychic economy" emerged as the new real estate of a disconcertingly liquid financial universe. Psychic economy realized capital.

The Victorian novel dexterously divulges this tropological movement. That modal realism abidingly defined by Georg Lukacs as the balancing of economic realities and psychic interiorities, social expansiveness and depth psychology, powerfully reveals the interpenetration of the intimate and the historical.[5] In addition, the self-consciousness of craft that effects this interpenetration calls attention to techniques of representation and to organizing metaphors while announcing the irony that rouses the realist literary project.

Particular tropes of irony, such as parabasis, and particular modes of irony, such as satire, will orient my analysis in the coming pages, so it is important to note at the outset that realism figures in this book as generally ironic, unrolling tropes, defamiliarizing realities, and exposing the rhetoric by which realities are constituted.[6] Thus, in the tradition of structuralist poetics most starkly formulated by Claude Levi-Strauss's "The Structural Study of Myth" and then taken up by dialectical literary criticism of both Marxist and psychoanalytic persuasions, I situate realism not as the determined reflection of established reality, but as the over-determined representation of unsolvable dilemmas that disrupt the integration of reality.[7] The particular dilemma that this book addresses is the historical process of financialization as it poses a profound set of questions about what is real, what is simulated, and whether there is any difference between the two. The realist novel works out this problem across its aesthetic registers (narratological, temporal, rhetorical, modal). In taking this "working out" to comprise neither closure à la false resolution of contradictions nor claims that could simply be made about "the" world, but rather the insightful framing of problems, I practice reading broadly informed by deconstruction. A deconstructive accent should also be heard in my argument's centralization of tropes—specifically, as I describe later, the tropes of personification and metalepsis—and the exchanges between tropes that enable the construction of worlds.[8] Realist fiction makes a world while highlighting the artifice of its making, in the process exposing the untenable opposition of real and made and the contingent fabrication of the life-worlds that parallel its own. This contrastive focus on the made world and the made real primes realist fiction to engage the paradoxes of fictitious capital. It is as fiction—the creation of excessive, aberrant, counterfactual realities—and not as documentary evidence—that realist literature is able to think the conditions of fictitious capital.

Fictitious Capital

Though now regarded as one of Marx's obscure whims, "fictitious capital" featured regularly in preeminent Victorian publications like the prominent weekly the *Economist* and the most famous daily newspaper, the *Morning Chronicle* (staffed by William Hazlitt, Henry Mayhew, John Stuart Mill, and Charles Dickens). Even if they ignored him, Marx's Victorian neighbors partially resembled him, detecting fictitious capital at the heart of the financial revolution and the astronomical growth of the credit economy. From the fourth principal participle of the Latin *fingere* (to form, to feign) "fictitious" meant feigned capital that alchemically precipitated real wealth) But the real could not be easily divested of feints. Credit instruments and the development of credit markets fomented a state of trade in which, as an 1840 House of Commons report held, "it is impossible to decide what part arises out of real *bona fide* transactions, such as actual bargain and sale, or what part is *fictitious, and mere accommodation paper*—that is, where one bill is drawn up to take another running, in order to raise a fictitious capital."[9] In the initial stride of this "running," credit instruments operate by deferring the completion of a sale. It is impossible to decide in the present tense whether that sale will be completed; only the future may finalize the sale. Any creditized transaction remains in a state of perpetual suspense respecting its *bona fides* until such moment in the future when its authenticity will have been confirmed. The advent of a market for the buying and selling of credit instruments simultaneously intensifies and alleviates the suspense of this temporal open-endedness. Once it is legal to purchase a futures contract it is technically feasible "to take another running"—to defer the completion of a sale by executing another sale in a different register, multiplying impossibilities in the guise of managing them.

As a market in credit, the London Stock Exchange enabled financial transactions and the generation of wealth in a purely speculative or proleptic way: all Victorian corporations, with the exception of the Bank of England, conducted IPOs *before* they commenced operations, utilizing the public stock market as their venture capital forum.[10] For example, if an entrepreneur wanted to build a railway, he would offer shares in a company with the promise that *eventually* he would indeed build the railway. The public would "subscribe" to buy shares, but payment for subscriptions would only be collected on the bimonthly "Accounting Day." Since, by the time of the Accounting Day, the price of a railway share might have fluctuated due to hype about subscriptions or to the availability of new information about the project, subscribers might exercise the option to further postpone payment until the next Accounting Day. This option was known as a "contango"— a fortuitous neologism that a Victorian etymology dictionary appraised "a corruption of *continue*." If, in the time lag between a subscription and Accounting Day, the price of a share had risen, an investor could "realize" a profit by immediately turning over his shares.

The essential thing to note about these credit protocols of investment is the case of metaphysics they pose, the difficult realities they commission: The "realized" profit differs principally from the profit of shareholder dividends, since the companies did not exist, and no labor had been performed, and it differs principally from the subscription that begets it, for the moment of realizing would be the only moment in the entire lengthy process at which actual money changed hands. "Fictitious capital" thus signifies the differential reality of a promise (the subscription) that profits (creating a new state of affairs, the actual money), a speech act whose eccentric felicity we could deem a "material event."[11] "Fictitious capital" brands these ontologically dubious profits; "fictitious" names this contrivance of finance, the futurity of "another running," the feigning of wealth that itself produces wealth, the power to make something out of nothing.

And yet. Profits reaped *within* the nexus of financial instruments/profits reaped *outside* this nexus; profits scored without an original outlay/profits scored with an original outlay: at some point it becomes "impossible to decide," as the House of Commons report warned, what part is real and what part is fictitious. The economist Henry Dunning Macleod stated the case plainly in 1855: "one is sometimes called real capital, and the other fictitious capital, but such a distinction leads to great confusion of ideas, because the results to the banker are absolutely identical in either case."[12] The case of metaphysics triggered by realizing capital through the Stock Exchange retroactively raises the specter that any valorized exchange is ontologically unstable, logically ungrounded—that is, even if critiques of financial artifice risk hypostasizing a "real economy" free of speculation, these critiques also open onto the unshakeable reality that all capitalist valorization is artificial.[13] Ultimately, "fictitious" signals not a firm classification, but rather the very impossibility of firm classification, the very violation of class—category, but also, for this matter, caste—incited by the financial revolution. In this sense "fictitious capital" is finally not a static concept, but a charismatic trope, the self-reflexive naming of the slippery problem of categorization in capitalism, which revolutionizes all categories (master and slave, general and particular, real and fictitious). The popular promulgation of the trope of fictitious capital goes some way toward helping us understand why, for the Victorians, realizing capital was such "a difficult vision." If capital in the throes of financialization was subject to a changing sense of the real, these changes might be said to have replaced an opposition "real-unreal" (land vs. money) with a dialectic of "real ← → fictitious" (money and its mutations in credit). In the sway of this new order, "to realize capital" is to advance that dialectic toward a synthesis in which the fictitious becomes the real.

Real fictitiousness, the fictitious real, realizing capital—these are the strange formulations barely grasped ("realized" in a more colloquial sense) at the moment of finance. As a Victorian observer Marx brilliantly explicated the implications of this discourse about fictitious capital, sublating the journalism he heartily consumed. For Marx the impossible indeterminacy noted by the House of Commons report (which he cites) opens onto the prospect that the fictitious cannot be isolated from the ordinary transactions, that capitalism is always already a machine of virtualizations, that something within all capital is fictitious. In the critical discourse around our present financial crisis, there is an unfortunate tendency to overlook this constitutive dimension, romanticizing the integral real of prelapsarian prefinancial capitalism.[14] By contrast, in his fluency with the Victorian fictitious real, Marx had no question that earlier periods of capitalism were inherently speculative.

This insight into the speculative core of capital comes early in *Capital*, volume 1, and composes one of Marx's greatest discoveries. Speculation takes place as soon as the most basic exchange relation is submitted to the very idea of formal equality in the name of "value," for equality between two qualitatively different goods, in two different spatiotemporal situations, is, as Marx put it, "in reality impossible." The very idea of "value" is this "makeshift," an abstraction that exceeds the exigencies of mere reality and conjures an ersatz grounding for the logical non-groundedness of exchange."[15] Speculation consists not only in this abstraction, but in the logicotemporal leap that realizes the abstraction: although parties in an exchange relation act *as if* the value of their objects already inheres before the sale, there is no possible guarantee of value ahead of the time of the exchange; only after a sale can value obtain. *Ex post facto,* value may be presumed to have grounded an exchange, but *ex ante facto* there are no logical grounds. Valorized exchange thus entails the conversion of *ex post facto* effects into *ex ante facto* causes.[16] Following Paul de Man's particular understanding of "metalepsis" as this substitution of effects for causes, we can see that the tropes and figures attributed to the stage of fictitious capital in fact condition the very possibility of capital at any stage.[17]

Immigrant in London, immersed in the mid-century financial press, Marx elicits the latent core of the Victorian discourse on finance, opening onto the ultimate difficulty of realizing capital: it is always already fictitious. Where there is value, there is fictitious capital; where there is money, there is fictitious capital; where there is credit, there is fictitious capital; where credit is bought and sold, as on the stock market, there is fictitiousness capitalized and intensified. Hence the opposition "fictitious/real" cannot hold in capitalism, when the fictitious *is* the real. In this sense "realizing capital" is not an ongoing action focused on an object, but a verbal adjective that modifies a subject: capital goes about realizing because capital's business is the incorporation of the virtual into the real.

The image of fictitious capital, circulated widely by the Victorian financial press and extrapolated by Marx, necessitates some revisions to prevailing New Historicist models of financialization and literature's role therein. Prominent genealogies of finance by literary historians, such as Mary Poovey's *Genres of the Credit Economy*, historicize the realization of capital as the triumph of "belief-producers," characterizing financial journalism and literary realism as accomplices in a project to normalize the instruments and culture of finance by familiarizing readers with economic facts and by constructing fiction as a regime of representation operating according to rules different than those of financial realities.[18] Viewing financial journalism through a less Foucauldian prism of discourse and discipline, epistemic breaks and teleological developments, and with more of a commitment to close reading, *Realizing Capital* uncovers the complexity and heterogeneity of Victorian conceptualizations of finance, gauging the uneven developments by which financialization evolved in tandem with widespread acknowledgment that its instruments were literally unbelievable. As my concentration on the actual representations of finance by Victorian journalists will bring to light, and as my readings of literary fiction's practice of irony and suspended disbelief will reveal, the institutionalization of finance emerged in the midst of the widespread conviction that there was nothing factual about it. Moreover, because the critical agency of literature inspires my analysis, I depart from those scholars like Poovey, Ian Baucom, and Sandra Sherman, who diagnose an "epistemological malaise" aroused by finance and then assuaged by literature.[19] My readings of the archive of financial journalism and of Victorian novels reveal that far from testifying to the accumulating reality of finance, journalists and novelists were actually obsessed with images of its evanescence. In taking stock of this obsession, my argument provides a richer, if more terrifying, account of the power of capitalism to perpetuate itself so as to render the question of belief in finance irrelevant. No tectonic knowledge revolution coerced the Victorians to, as Baucom puts it, "credit the existence of imaginary values"—they were not dupes inhabiting castles of sand that crumble in the hands of enlightened critics; *they simply acted as if it did not matter that everyone knew that capital values were imaginary.*[20] Rather than belief, it was this state of knowing very well, but nevertheless acting as if unknowing—the state that psychoanalysis terms "disavowal"—that secured the financial revolution.

Instead, then, of a historicism that solemnifies discourse as the arena in which power naturalizes itself, my argument heeds psychoanalytic and Marxist insights into the inconsistencies of ideology, mapping the displacements and condensations, the metonymies and metaphors, that structure social reality, and thereby tells the story of the displacement of "fictitious capital" by "psychic economy"—a displacement inscribed in the archive of Victorian financial journalism and early psychology, but interrupted and interpreted by the realist novel.[21]

From Fictitious Capital to Real Psyche

Despite the insights of Victorian financial journalists, and despite Marx's advancement of those insights—despite, that is, commanding evidence from the moment of financialization that capital is fictitious—the ideological normalization of finance from that moment to our own bespeaks a counteroffer: capital is real. In the Dickensian idiom with which we began, realizing capital involves putting hands into pockets, reaching inward to a wealth of affect capable of endowing particular fortunes (as Pip does for Herbert) and stabilizing the very idea of financial fortune. Likewise, as the Victorians encountered the virtual reality of capitalism—and indeed, as capitalism exposed itself as a metaphysical system capable of deflecting the question of its groundlessness—reaching inward touched a substitute ground: a psyche whose intrinsic economy of unlimited desires and unpredictable vacillations could be located as the final cause of a volatile economy. I maintain in this book that this personification of capital preoccupied journalists, political economists, psychologists, and novelists with different degrees of sagacity: while prose writers proliferated this displacement, novelists probed many of its effects. I explore the pervasive image of "psychic economy" as it congeals the mutually grounding relationship between psychology and economics in Victorian intellectual traditions. Beyond its literal iterations, "psychic economy" sustains the conceptual infrastructure of numerous discourses, consolidating the imaginary continuity of the financial economy and the psychological subject—the continuity first conceived in the Victorian era and bequeathed to us as one of its most enduring legacies. As such, it encapsulates the ideological operation called "psychologism": naturalizing contingent relations as innate.[22]

To understand why the rhetoric of psychic economy assumed the function of naturalizing the economy precisely at the moment when the economy was coming to seem most artificial, it is helpful to recall not only the momentous Victorian shift toward a secular ontology "in which human subjectivity seems to become the foundation of all things," but also the strategic invocation of this foundation in the rhetorical traditions around capitalism from the seventeenth century onward.[23] In focusing on this economic work of the idea of psychic economy in the Victorian period, I extend the insights of historians of those traditions of personal and characterological rhetoric. Albert O. Hirschman formidably established that early modern political debates over capitalism were won through appeals to "interests" as the taming of the passions.[24] J. G. A. Pocock's seminal argument that financial instruments like credit ordained a "new image of social personality" has been elaborated by *dix-huitièmists* Deidre Lynch, Margot Finn, and James Thompson into an account of the importance of individual character to the basis of credit. Economic historians deem the credit economy "reputationally intensive" because exchange relations stabilized themselves by reference to character and by establishing chains of acquaintance across social distance.[25] Poovey helpfully describes the mode of knowledge that this connection between character and credit entailed:

> Before the nineteenth-century development of extensive banking and bill-broking systems, an individual could typically judge the value of a particular credit instrument—say, a merchant's bill of exchange or a neighbor's promissory note—by personal knowledge of the individual who offered it.[26]

As Poovey herself acknowledges, the Victorian era's sophistication of credit occasioned a reorientation of this social epistemology. Poovey characterizes that shift as one from knowledge of "an individual" to knowledge of "an instrument itself," and much of her impressive oeuvre examines the development of technical expertise as it factualized finance. I pursue a different, complementary possibility in this book. I argue that this shift could equally be understood as a transition from knowledge of an individual in the particular to knowledge of an individual in general: instead of the comportment of a character, one deals in characterology. When distances in time and space made intimate knowledge of trading partners untenable, technical knowledge of trading instruments surely compensated—and, I assert, so too did knowledge of intimacy itself—generalizations about character, subjectivity, and interiority.[27] Early psychology, a discipline steeped in economic language, cultivated theories of the ways and means of desire that could reassure economic agents. "Psychic economy," the crowning personification of the economy, is the figurehead of this assurance, a trope whose universal heuristic value was taken to the bank.

Reading Fictitious Capital

A curious sentence from Dickens begins this book, a renowned moment from Eliot stands as epigraph, and throughout, the rhetoric of the novel guides my analysis. My argument that finance gained traction in part through the economic metaphors in psychology is inspired by the realist novel's nuanced exploration of the power of metaphor. In line with Louis Althusser's famous position that art "gives us to see (*nous donner à voir*) something which alludes to reality," *Realizing Capital* contends that the realist novel gives us to see the metaphors of modernity.[28] Realism commences from the premise that reality is not self-evident—that the structuring metaphors of the world merit and indeed require elaboration of the sort uniquely afforded by literature.[29] To appreciate this interrogation of the real requires setting aside the new historicist orthodoxy that literary texts reiterate the (supposedly coherent) sociopolitical networks that determine them. Only by honoring realism's innate desire to defamiliarize reality may we encounter the full force of realism's astonishing capacity to, in the words of J. Hillis Miller, "bring into the open the imaginary quality of reality"—to contravene the givens of the cultural symbolic world and invite new gifts.[30]

My readings build upon this understanding of realism as a destabilization of reified reality, taking it as the foundation from which the Victorian novel launches its investigation into financial capitalism's parallel destabilizations. In discerning the specific ways in which the novel form intermeshes with economics, I thus diverge from the traditions of both the history of novel criticism and orthodox Marxist literary analysis, for I see the realism of capitalism not as a matter of mimetic recording, but rather of aesthetic mediation. Literary historians have often hypothesized a preference for mimesis over metaphor that positions realism as an epistemological guarantee for capitalism. By virtue of what Ian Watt describes as "a language (that) is much more largely referential" than other literary modes, realism adheres to laws of time, space, probability, and plausibility, and ultimately achieves, Patrick Brantlinger pronounces, a "reification of the status quo."[31] The most insidious result of this reification, John Vernon argues, is that realist language underwrites paper money: it secures referentiality in a way that guarantees money's claim to refer to value.[32] In these histories capitalism launches a "system-wide determination to credit the existence of imaginary values," deputizing literary realism to "produce belief."[33] Realism thus appears a determined appendix to a preexisting reality, a dependent superstructure unidirectionally flowing from the base. Orthodox Marxist literary criticism, often accused of exactly such vulgar determinism, has surprisingly been more willing to grant realism a critical rather than reifying function in its potential to achieve a cognitive map of the totality of social relations.[34] Although these two trends in criticism thus seem locked in opposition, they share the underlying assumptions that realist referentiality comes at face value and that our relationship to capitalism is primarily *epistemological*—either we believe in financial value or we don't; either we can cognitively map capital's organization of the social or we cannot. I have already begun to demonstrate, based on the archive of the idea of "fictitious capital" and the insights of psychoanalysis, that our relationship to capital more likely sidesteps entirely the question of what we know and what we believe, instead finding its stride in what we do. Victorian thought about the mediated, figurative, and unreal prowess of capital highlights this irrelevance of the epistemic problematic. Moreover, the presence of the discourse of fictitious capital necessarily complicates our understanding of the economic facts the realist novel is said to report. In short, the realism of capitalism queries whether or in what sense capital is real; the Victorian pinnacle of literary realism coincides with a pervasive and powerful conception of capital as unreal—ethereal, virtual, imaginary.

Furthermore, this archive equally necessitates complicating our understanding of the mode of realist representation. The prevalent notion of fictitious capital capaciously captured the ungroundedness of capital and the financial economy's traffic in figurative language. Where the industrial economy traded goods, the financial economy exchanged representations of value—representations that the Victorian financial press expressly likened to metaphors, to figural language, and, indeed, to poetry. "The poetry of banking," we will learn in the coming pages, evoked both Plato's restricted sense of imagistic language and his general sense of making something out of nothing. The reality of capital is poetic, unreal, and fictitious; realist depiction of it must therefore involve feigning and forming.

And here we come to another signification of realizing capital: to "realize" in a linguistic sense is to express "in a particular phonetic, graphic, or syntactic form." In the form of the word "dreamed," for instance, *-ed* realizes the grammatical morpheme {past}. To realize capital is to express capital graphically, rhythmically, structurally—to craft language so as to crystallize or perform the figurative, fictitious agency of finance. The case of metaphysics posed by capital's oscillations between real and fictitious finds its strongest record not in referential depiction, but rather in aesthetic disclosure. This opposition between reference and form comprises the core of *Realizing Capital;* on the model of Lukacs's remark that "the truly social element in literature is the form," I suggest that the truly financial element in realism is the form.[35] The realist novel engages economics neither via reference to economic content nor through its production and consumption in the market, but in its narratological, rhetorical, and temporal structures and the resonance, smooth or sticky, intensive or ironic, across those structures. For example, to read *Middlemarch's* ideas about finance, I look not for portraits of bankers, but to that novel's remarkably odd, recurrent topos of metanarrative intrusion. As formal elements in which the narrator excessively worries her own distribution of narrative "interest," these self-reflexive structures perform the self-referential morphology of financial interest, money begotten by money. In a novel conspicuously set during the run-up to the Bank of England Charter Act's revolutionary repeal of bans on usury, deliberating forms of interest take place through imagistic structures of interest.

When historicist critics define realism as an endeavor to mimetically capture or account for capitalism, when they presume that the novel primarily incorporates capital indexically (by directly referring to economic facts in the world), they overlook the historically specific fact that, for the Victorians, capital was no simple referent amenable to mimetic index.[36] The rendering of capital in realism therefore entails less reference—to brokers, to laws, to new instruments readers must learn about—and more aestheticization, crafting forms that engage the formal logic of capital. In turn, the criticism of realism requires less what Michel de Certeau terms "tirelessly restoring referentiality" and more *reading.*[37]

"Reading" I employ here in a highly specific sense: attending to the aesthetic material of literary language. To the historicist's reduction of literature to discourse, I oppose deconstruction's insistence on the irreducibility of tropes to intuitive ideas, and I work instead to encounter the material and process of literary thinking.[38] The book's animating protocol is thus to encounter this material through close, tropological reading, but my stress on "thinking" is not strictly deconstructive in a de Manian sense of revealing the autonomy of language from logic or meaning.[39] It is rather owing to Marxist and psychoanalytic materialisms that mind inescapable problems in human experience (antagonism and its displacement in representation) and register formulations, incarnations, articulations, and distortions of those problems in aesthetic production. The distinction between materialism and hermeneutic is crucial here: Marxism and psychoanalysis are often pilloried for their apparent procedures of excavating hidden meanings, but such caricatures are entirely inconsistent with the core commitments to structural analyses of forms that organize these endeavors.[40] As the energetic, self-reflexive interrogation of *method* in both of these traditions indicates, these materialisms have neither predestined conclusions nor a priori concepts at which their readings must arrive—they have only the point of departure of insuperable antagonism and the purely formal tracks of mediation and overdetermination.

In privileging *reading* thus balanced on the touchstones of deconstruction, psychoanalysis, and Marx, this book breaks not only with "the new economic criticism," but with much of current scholarship on Victorian literature and culture, finding common ground with the exceptional reconceptualized formalism lately practiced by Caroline Levine and Alex Woloch.[41] While Levine is far more explicit about her methodological innovation, authoring a manifesto "toward a new method," she is joined by Woloch in a commitment to modifying existing formalisms so as to underscore neither the intrinsic unity of a work nor its unredeemable disunity, but rather the friction within and between forms, the way a work calls attention to the under- and overlap between itself and the social world.[42] Thus Levine urges surrendering the conviction that literary forms "fit" the social, and Woloch insists on the possibility that literary form might work as "a representation of, rather than simply a derivative reproduction of, this (social) structure."[43] The ill fit between the literary and the social—the asymmetries, the chafing, the strained seams—delineates those spaces of irritation through which literature may ultimately ironize the social regimes it mobilizes.

The method I propose follows the lead of Levine's "strategic formalism," a kind of "social close reading" blending deconstructive techniques and the best historicist impulses to explore the intellectual and political force of literary forms that do not reiterate a preexisting world, but rather limn, ironize, and even unmake forms of worlding.[44] One might call this reading "financial formalism" to feature its situatedness: a formalism that reads literary form's critical thinking about the historically specific material and conceptual question of finance. Financial formalism esteems figurative language as a mode of thinking about finance, tracking the labyrinth of aesthetic responses to intellectual pressures situated in history, but irreducible to it. Emphasizing what literature mints, financial formalism uncovers texts whose financial intelligence is discounted by historicism: texts whose plots do not depict financial crises or bank failures, whose pages do not feature financiers or stockbrokers. While the historicist expects evidence of financialization in texts like *Hard Cash, The Game of Speculation, Cranford,* and *Hester,* as most recent studies of economics in Victorian literature do, the financial formalist has greater expectations of literary form.[45] Instead of reducing literature to false resolution of systemic contradictions or to flat-footed iteration of a putatively prior and already fixed discourse, this book's method foregrounds the contemplative agency leveraged by literature.[46] My readings affirm formal structures of literary self-reflexivity such as irony and satire as modes of critical inquiry that convey not just the mechanics of their tropes, but their effects in any world. That is, where some versions of deconstructive literary criticism might circumscribe the functions of language within the context of a given reading, or of a text reading itself, it strikes me as necessary, in the case of the realist novel (the aesthetic mode whose specificity is its mediation of realities and of worldliness; the aesthetic mode less commonly studied by deconstructive critics), to attend to the ways that realism strategically reveals the work of tropes in worlds.

Marking the aesthetic verve with which literature thinks, I invite a reappraisal of Victorian literary realism that foregrounds what John Ruskin called the "imaginative power" of Victorian thought, acknowledging the creativity with which literature interrogated (rather than simply promoted) pivotal contemporary events like financialization.[47] This crucial critical faculty guarantees that an aesthetic work opens portals onto not only what *is,* but also what *could* or *should be.*[48] Literary thinking elucidates problems in different registers, reframes concepts so that other ideas may emerge. Literary language—even in the high realist novel—works not instantiatively, but performatively. Literature is a mode of thought structured by juxtaposition and condensation, by sensuous synthesis and syncretic sedimentation. To read literature, to be open to how literature thinks, is to pose that quintessential Dickensian question, "what connexion can there be?": what connection exists between the voices, plots, motifs, temporalities, and images that are mobilized within one bounded work? Form, as forum for these elective affinities and flattering contrasts, wields a conceptual agency—an agency for assembling concepts while simultaneously defamiliarizing them—for relating without reifying, for weaving a loose and gossamer web.[49] Literary form seeks out connections where there were none, charts dislocations where there were destinations, re-presents what has been all too present. When literature thinks, it asks us to cock our heads and think with it, to think in a distinctive and oblique mode, to perambulate the web rather than toeing the line. The principles and principals of the novel's *own* world—its counterfactuality, its creativity, its standing-in-excess of what *is,* its tropes, its strophes, its syntax, its purr—impel its elucidation of the world outside its world.

❧

This argument unfolds in three stages: unpacking the tropes of personification and metalepsis at work in the discourses around finance and psychology; illustrating the novel's critical engagement with these tropes; and showing how the major analysts of modernity inherit this novelistic concern. Chapter 1, "Fictitious Capital/Real Psyche: Metalepsis, Psychologism, and the Grounds of Finance," establishes the broad contours of the coincidence between financialization and the psychic economy metaphor. Drawing on the financial press and literary periodicals, I explore the analysis of fictitious capital propounded by leading Victorian intellectuals, with particular mindfulness of the close association of fictitious capital with figurative language, or "the poetry of banking." Through close reading of works by Walter Bagehot, a founding editor of the *Economist,* and David Morier Evans, an acclaimed and best-selling financial journalist, I heed the disoriented tenor of this discourse as it plumbed the vortex of finance and surveyed the calamities of recurrent financial crises. Just as I do not reduce literature to the referential function of language, I do not treat nonfiction prose as pure deixis, working instead to orbit the figurative trajectories of financial journalism.[50] I find a curious reversal in the 1860s: psychological *effects* of financialization began to appear as *causes* of financial events. By way of this metaleptic substitution of cause for effect (a particular case of the general definition of metalepsis as "the substitution of one trope for another"), the discourse of fictitious capital dissolved and the construct of psychic economy solidified.[51] An ingot in the menacingly abstract financial vortex, this trope offered itself as the anchoring cause of crisis and the anchoring signifier for the emergent discipline of psychology.

At the center of the book are novel readings. I show how three major texts spanning the heyday of Victorian realism, from the late 1850s through the late 1870s, all engage formally, narratively, and imagistically—in addition to thematically—with the financial economy, the problematic of realization, and the construct of psychic economy. My choice of canonical texts supports my emphasis on the heterogeneity of Victorian discourses, for even these most Victorian of Victorian novels will be seen to investigate, rather than disseminate, those ideas we now take to be reigning ideologies. Canonicity, my selection of texts implies, is an internally riven sphere in which literature both subtends and transcends the state of ideas in which it takes shape. The tendency to reduce majority to hegemony not only oversimplifies the operation of ideology; it also, as Harry Shaw points out, aggrandizes the critic-qua–anatomist of discipline infinitely wiser than lay readers at whom the ruses of power are directed.[52] My arguments activate the critical agility of literary form, finding in the astuteness of major texts an alternative basis for their ongoing resonance with generations of readers.

Chapter 2, "Investor Ironies in *Great Expectations*," reads Dickens's unusual use of first-person narration as a reflection on the logics of personhood and tropes of personification that accompany financialization. Attending to unanswered questions, haunting images, and unreliable narration, I read figural and narrative irony as engagements with financial temporality and personified economies. Linking the novel's investment plot to both the Limited Liability Act of 1855 and the birth of the corporate person in 1856, I argue that the radically unreconciled temporal structure of the narrative and the conspicuously problematized images of psychic economy simultaneously undermine the narrator's supposed moral development and inflect the novel's thinking about both the unaccountable persons of limited liability and the relentless futurity of financial investment. Chapter 3, "The Economic Problem of Sympathy: Parabasis and Interest in *Middlemarch*," details the strange narrative gesture of parabasis (moments at which the narrative "stands beside" itself) as it performs the self-reflexive topos of financial interest, disclosing the artifice of finance. Examining Eliot's commingling of financial form and affective content in her famed philosophy of sympathy, I argue that *Middlemarch* directly casts aspersions on psychic economy as the prime instance of "thoughts entangled in metaphors." Chapter 4, "'Money Expects Money': Satiric Credit in *The Way We Live Now*," considers the remarkable fact that this novel, widely celebrated as the most vitriolic satire composed in the Victorian period, actually abandons its satire for its last two hundred pages. Reading this modal crisis as an allusion to financial crisis, I argue that the novel's satire implodes when it realizes that satirizing finance is logically inconsistent. It is not possible to coherently critique the circulation of exaggerated tropes (i.e., to critique fictitious capital) if the means of critique is satiric hyperbole, the circulation of exaggerated tropes. The modal conversion stemming from this hypocritical collusion compels Trollope to put down "the whip of the satirist," resulting in a conventionally realist focus on interiority and intimacy as hypothetically less figurative (more real) subjects of narration. If the novel thus performs that very recursive grounding of the financial economy in the inner economy of the psychological individual that I argue permeates Victorian discourse, it also critically destabilizes this gesture through the many ironies at work in this last quarter of the text.

These novels share three features. They model their narrative frameworks on various financial instruments whose legal ratification they observe, showcasing the figural artifice of finance; they mobilize, thematically and within the narrative discourse, the rhetoric of psychic economy; they are peculiarly riven by ironies that deform their narratives (Eliot's intrusions, Dickens's undermined first person, Trollope's deflated satire). My analysis reads the coincidence of these three stylistic features (tropes of psychic economy, narrative modalities of finance, formal ironies) as illuminating the connections between textual economy, financial economy, and psychic economy. In explaining these three interlinking registers, I argue that *Great Expectations, Middlemarch,* and *The Way We Live Now* eloquently engineer a critique of the power of the image of "psychic economy" to ideologically ground finance in the psyche. Reciprocally, I maintain that this historically specific intellectual context of constellating finance and the psyche provides an indispensable aperture onto the contemplative agency of these texts: only if we apprehend the great stakes of the many conceptual problems provoking these novels can we adequately appreciate their adroit aesthetics. Toward that appreciation, my readings consider not merely theme or plot, but metaphorical, modal, narrative, and temporal layers as they bisect and enfold one another, aiming to suggest answers to perennial questions about the form of these novels: Why is *Great Expectations* temporally out of joint? What does that middling narrator of *Middlemarch* want? Why does *The Way We Live Now* abandon its satire?

Realizing Capital premises its valorization of literary thinking upon the contrast between the nonfiction prose in Chapter 1 and the novels in chapters 2, 3, and 4, ultimately drawing a distinction between the order of discourse and that of literature. Though Victorian discourse eventually resolves its own critique of fictitious capital into its embrace of the rhetoric of psychic economy, the novels preserve a critique of financial ungroundedness and reject psychic economy. In the third and final section of the book, I alter the terms of this contrast between fiction and nonfiction, taking up Marx's *Capital* and Freud's economic hypothesis as nonfiction interventions into both the artifice of finance and the vicissitudes of psychic economy, but as interventions that come into greatest relief when we approach these texts through figural readings—that is, when we read them as we read novels. Psychoanalysis and Marxism drive the book's method, but in this final section major texts of Marx and Freud are encountered less as handbooks of method than as aesthetic works meriting their own close treatment and magnifying the lasting critical project of the Victorian novel.

Chapter 5, "London, Nineteenth Century, Capital of Realism: On Marx's Victorian Novel," rethinks Marx's critique of political economy as a companion instance of the Victorian novel's meditations on realizing capital. Taking a cue from the literary thinking of *Great Expectations, Middlemarch,* and *The Way We Live Now,* I read the first volume of *Capital* as a Victorian novel in order to approach anew its insights into finance capital. Focusing on the structuring role of the tropes of personification and metalepsis, I suggest that a number of Marx's most significant ideas about capital find their strongest expression performatively rather than instantiatively. Those ideas, I submit, pertain to the ungroundedness of capital (much in line with the Victorian discourse of fictitiousness in which Marx was immersed) and to the drive of capital (the metaphor of psychic economy traversed, brought through the looking glass). Like Walter Bagehot, David Morier Evans, and others, Marx criticized the artifice of capital; like those of Dickens and Eliot, his ideas took shape aesthetically, and he disdained the ideological project to impute capital to "the innermost life"; however, he went beyond all these thinkers when he began to articulate a version of the psychic economy metaphor in which the psychological subject in question is not *homo economicus,* but capital itself. In Marx's great Victorian novel, the protagonist is the title character.

Chapter 6, "Psychic Economy and Its Vicissitudes: Freud's Economic Hypothesis," approaches Sigmund Freud's oeuvre with the same method of figural interpretation employed in the other chapters. Though language, geography, and, eventually, time separate Freud from the Victorian context of the other chapters, profound and unexpected conceptual affinities span this distance. In his conspicuously cautious exploration of the metaphor of psychic economy, Freud thus stands heir to Victorian novels rather than to Victorian psychology. Present-day discourse in both popular and scholarly arenas widely employs the construct of "psychic economy" as an explanatory principle, generally crediting Freud with its discovery. As a complement to my analysis of the concept's emergence long before Freud, I disrupt facile attributions of the concept to him by showing how psychic economy is anything but a simple, unified notion within his project. Following his caution that economic language "leads us to one of the most important, but unluckily also, one of the most obscure, regions of psychoanalysis," and closely reading his language, I argue that Freud's various formulations perform the essential deferral of the grounding of economy: *there is no given economy*; no hypostatized, orthographically capitalized "Economy." This—and no ideological naturalization of capitalism—is what defines Freud's economic thought, and what makes him, as he himself claimed, a product of Victorian novels, even as he revolted against Victorian psychology.

Finally, the brief Epilogue concludes with reflections on the psychic economy trope in the discourse around the global financial crisis of 2008. In finance and in crisis, in organizing structures and defining metaphors, we are far more Victorian than either millennial fundamentalists or historicist critics would maintain. But just for that reason, we might take a page from Victorian novels and defamiliarize the metaphors we live by.

⤳

Practical difficulties, metaphysical difficulties, aesthetic difficulties—"what a difficult vision to realize capital sometimes" is. It has perhaps become clear that a spiral of interlocking considerations anarchically governs *Realizing Capital*: that realist form is an economically astute mode of thinking; that the Victorians were more sophisticated in their relation to finance than many historicists would have us believe; that the critique of fictitious capital evidencing that sophistication was eventually eclipsed by the trope of psychic economy; that this trope crystallizes one of the pivotal ideologies of modernity; that questioning this trope inspired Dickens, Eliot, and Trollope, as well as Marx and Freud; that any possible union of psychoanalysis and Marxism rests in the same questioning and problematizing, rather than reifying, "psychic economy." If this spiral is at times dizzying, that will have been, I hope, the performative effect of the metaleptic maelstrom inducing the vertigo of finance.

I. *Fictitious Capital / Real Psyche*

Metalepsis, Psychologism, and the Grounds of Finance

In 1859 David Morier Evans, London's premier financial journalist, published a book of "History" promising to "link" the country's most recent financial crisis, in 1857 and 1858, to "the several similar dread visitations which have occurred since the remarkable epoch of 1825."[1] Evans, whom contemporary scholars regularly regard as the primary source par-excellence for Victorian thought about finance, edited the *Banker's Magazine* and published several books on the financial economy that found wide popular readership.[2] By the time of this 1859 "History," Evans's copious output could, he unabashedly declared, "afford more combined information in relation to financial and commercial progress than has hitherto been published" (vi). He took a "retrospective glance" at the crises of 1825, 1837, and 1847 and used his history to advance a systematic explanation of the causes of financial crises. Twenty-first-century readers will likely marvel that this confident, experienced authority blamed neither greedy investors nor lax regulators, but "the deep-rooted system of fictitious credit . . . so thoroughly expanded through all branches of business" (30). The total "system of fictitious credit" resulted in an economy that "existed on a false basis," a castle of sand perched precariously atop "an unstable foundation."[3] Crisis therefore belonged to the structure of finance, a structure whose artifice, Evans maintained, bested the imagined horrors catalogued by fiction: "all the ingenious fictions of Dumas and George Sand sink into insignificance when compared with the realities" of contemporary crisis.[4]

With a constancy that should compel us to refine the common historicist depiction of financial journalists as "apologists for the credit economy" who generated discourse to instill comfort with finance, Evans and other journalists astutely gauged the structurally "unsound" base of the financial economy.[5] From the moment of the 1833 watershed in financialization—the Bank of England Charter Act's repeal of bans on usury, which the *Morning Chronicle*, the *Charter*, and the *Economist* all deplored for having "introduced a new element, that of fictitious capital" into daily life—to the century's largest crisis, when the *Economist* pronounced that "the crisis of 1866 is in its essential character . . . a malady of credit arising from causes inherent in such credit"—"fictitious capital" was an irrefutable, systemic explanation for crises.[6] "In the end," the *Economist* concluded memorably, "fictitious credit always breaks down."[7]

The ubiquity and conviction of these prescient critiques of fictitious capital make it all the more striking that the idea is so rare today—rare both in scholarship on Victorian finance and in general appraisals of capital. The idea of fictitious capital has largely been lost to us, impoverishing both our understanding of present-day finance and our scholarly account of the cultural discourses attending the birth of finance. In this chapter I aim both to excavate the discourse of fictitious capital, an extraordinary layer in the historical sedimentation of economic thought, and to offer an explanation for its occlusion. I pinpoint the late 1850s as a pivotal period in the history of finance and of psychology—a moment when the cumulative historical awareness of crisis as a systemic feature of capitalism peaked and when psychological discourse boomed. Linking these two discursive developments, I find that analysis of the structural dimensions of financial crisis was subsumed by fascination with its psychological dimensions. The critique of fictitiousness disappeared when the construct of an inner psychic economy realized capital.

Through close readings of Victorian journalism, including Evans, his peer Walter Bagehot, and others, alongside the writings Karl Marx composed as a Victorian correspondent, I explore the "difficult vision" of grounding finance logically. The financial economy depended for its development on disavowing the inherent fictitiousness of all credit. Crises were junctures at which it was no longer possible to act as if the leap of credit would succeed; the truth of the system irrupted and forced traumatic confrontation. As the scope of the financial economy broadened, the gravity of such confrontations became a topic of concern independent from the analysis of fictitious capital, with financial journalists growing obsessed with the psychological predicament of investors. Eventually these predicaments came to be perceived less as effects of financial instability and more as causes. I will be arguing that this substitution of effect for cause forms the central trope of Victorian financial discourse. In describing this logical maneuver as a trope and specifically naming that trope "metalepsis," I draw upon a tradition of thought first introduced by the rhetorician Quintilian and more recently associated with Gérard Genette's narratology and Harold Bloom's theory of reading.[8] For Genette metalepsis evokes a "transgression" of "changing level" within narrative discourse that can "disturb the distinction between levels"; Bloom defines metalepsis as "the trope of a trope, the metonymic substitution of a word for a word already figurative."[9] Common to both of these usages, as to Quintilian's original emphasis on metalepsis as "an intermediate step, signifying nothing in itself, but affording a passage to something," is the importance of a *succession* of figures, the movement of a series.[10] Through the motion of substituting psychological effects for causes, psychologism came to supplant the structural critique of finance that had predominated in the mid-Victorian period. The critique of an unsound system dissolved in "animal spirits"; the very idea of "fictitious capital" was replaced by that of fickle subjects.[11] My reference here to our contemporary notion of "animal spirits," popularized by the Yale economist Robert Shiller, may begin to indicate the extent to which the legacy of this metalepsis continues to organize much thought about financial economics today. Instead of calculating leverage, we lament flagging confidence; instead of legislating regulation, we prescribe therapy.

The metalepsis by which psychologism takes hold is crystallized in the metaphor of "psychic economy." The work of this chapter establishes some rhetorical conditions of possibility for the emergence of this notion, tracing within Victorian financial journalism both the vertigo of analyzing fictitious capital and the lure of psychological investigation as guardrail against that free-fall. My discussion of financial journalism will also touch on parallel developments in psychology and political economy, aiming to establish the circulation of ideas encompassing Dickens, Eliot, and Trollope as explored in the middle portion of this book. Victorian financial journalists like Evans and Bagehot, I conclude, put their fingers on the very real problem of finance's absent foundations, but they ultimately displaced that problem by founding the idea of psychic economy, an inner basis of economic transactions. The contrivance of this displacement, I maintain in coming chapters, provoked Victorian novels to elaborate on the shifting grounds of financial and psychic economy.

Capital Poetics

To understand how the putatively natural foundation of psychic economy compensated for the unfounded artifice of fictitious capital, it is first necessary to examine in greater detail precisely what "fictitious capital" signified for financial journalists in the mid-Victorian moment. On the rare occasions in rarified circles when we think of the concept today, it is only as the obscure topic briefly discussed in volume 3 of Marx's *Capital*. During our own twenty-first-century crisis, to which "fictitious capital" once again seems fiercely apt, critics have lamented that this idea hangs tenuously threaded in Marx's writings. But arguably, he may not have extensively defined the notion because he found it already widely theorized by Victorian journalists, whom he credited when introducing the concept.[12] When Marx arrived in London in 1848, he quickly obtained a reader's ticket to the British Library, where, alongside Carlyle, Ruskin, and Dickens, he immersed himself in British governmental reports and Parliamentary proceedings, in English literature, and in the London press. He devoted his first three months to reading all extant back issues of the *Economist,* the ambitious weekly that had begun printing in 1843, and whose pages afforded not just fodder for his analysis of the capitalist mode of production, but also an analytic framework in the concept of fictitious capital.

As argued in every publication from the *Economist* to Charles Dickens's *Household Words* to Parliamentary reports, "fictitious" announces a feigning of wealth that itself produces wealth, the capacity of a stock certificate or even a promise to precipitate substantial value. The remarkably proleptic credit protocols of the London Stock Exchange, the system of subscription and contangos I described in the Introduction, allowed investors to realize profits within the network of the Stock Exchange itself, independent of labor or company dividends, and of what Evans called "actual money."[13] Capital could be realized without the input of real or actual money, issuing merely from the quasi-material event of the promise and the representational nexus of meta-promises extended by financial instruments.[14] "Fictitious capital" denominates this contrast between the actual and the represented, a kind of value intrinsically tainted by representation. The *London Review* succinctly defined "fictitious" as "a matter of figures representing as existing that which has no real existence."[15] Since the very idea of fictitious capital is therefore emboldened by that opposition between "representing" and "real" at the heart of every attack on artifice dating from Plato's banishment of the poets, it is perhaps to be expected that Victorian journalists frequently employed a synonym for "fictitious capital": "the poetry of banking."[16]

"And what has poetry to do with banking?" A piece in the inaugural run of Evans's the *Banker's Magazine* answered the question begged by its title— "The Poetry of Banking"—"many of the objects and events of ordinary life are in their nature highly poetic. Like Molière's character who had been speaking prose for forty years without knowing it, we talk, and think, and act poetry, without being at all conscious of the fact."[17] Unbeknownst to us, poetry is the medium of financial life, the essence of the financial mode of production, making things with words. In this idiom "poetry" deepens the connotations of "fictitious" that we have begun to trace. It brands the exotic argot of bankers, a lingua franca "perfectly unintelligible to those who had not been brought up to talk Stock Exchange fluently."[18] The native speakers of finance, "men of imagination, the men whose temperament is of the species called poetic," were "gentlemen endowed with an extensive command of language and metaphor."[19]

Metaphoric substitutions, metonymic displacements, and ultimately the dynamic shuffling of one figure into another figure named by the meta-trope of metalepsis organize the whole financial industry: as journalists frequently explained, money stands as "the general representative of value"; paper money extends this representative chain, minting "merely the representative of a representative"; and "shares" in turn distend the chain, totaling the representative of a representative of a representative.[20] Figures exchange themselves for more figures in an indefinite arc never arrested by "the vulgar device of payment" and propulsively unfurling "by recourse to further financial operations."[21] Credit instruments are "pieces of paper, lines in books, mystic words uttered in bank parlors" that become paradoxically effective "omnipotent nothings."[22] Through these trope machines, the figurative enterprise of finance achieves "a work of imagination of the highest order," "mak(ing) something out of nothing."

"Poetry" is thus this imaginative making at which epic plumes succeed while money men excel:

> Our bankers, rightly considered, have contributed a series of *Lalla Rookhs*
> (Thomas Moore's epic poem). As imagination bodies forth the form
> of things unknown, the banker's pen turns them to shape, and gives to
> airy nothings an alarming amount of credit. . . . Can the poetic faculty
> further go?[23]

Bankers *are* poets because their techniques "body forth the form of things unknown,"—effectuate in present material form things heretofore unembodied and unknown. Imaginative presentation of things inaccessible through knowledge or logic: the "poetry of banking" detects in finance the same conundrums that we earlier saw Dickens label the "case of metaphysics." For the essence of finance is an uncognizable jump, a logic-defying leap that cannot be consciously grounded. Take just three financial definitions: first, "derivative," an assetized prediction about an asset one does not own. Next, "leverage," investing money one does not own. And third, "shortselling," selling stock one does not own. In all three cases, one abuts the paradoxes of financial instruments. "Does not own" is in the present tense; a financial instrument, what Evans and other journalists often deemed a "time bargain," breaks out of the fetters of time and rallies a future in which the formalities of mere possession dissipate under the momentum of accumulation.[24] I do not own corn now, but if there comes a time when corn prices surge, I *will have* wanted to own corn so that I might sell it profitably—that future anterior tense supplying the logic for naming the instrument that would allow me to do so a "futures contract." The velocity of this futurity is embossed in the very connotations of "finance." Etymologically entwined with *fin,* the end, "to finance" originally meant "to pay off a debt," "to bring a transaction to a close." But the flourishing of financial transactions and innovation of financial instruments powerfully deferred this sense of closure into the future. Finance designs an economy in which the ends precede the means as predictions about the future supersede production in the present. Symbolic sublimations of time, financial instruments mobilize figurative language to realize in the present what will have been the future. The "poetry of banking" then finally heralds this sublimation, this process of imaginative making in creative language whose product was fictitious capital, value of a purely imaginary ontology.

Later I will have more to say about the consequences for literary form that arose from this association of poetry with finance.[25] But for now let us underscore that the Victorian financial press's equation between fictitious capital and the poetry of banking can stimulate some illuminating connections between Marx's allusive formulations about fictitious capital and his remarks elsewhere about money, language, and imaginative making. While the Victorian press might suggest that financialization is the only poetic phase of capitalism, Marx reveals that the advent of money is already a poetic estrangement. He insists that money must not be analogous to language in

general, but to language in the sway of becoming-foreign (a good definition
of poetry):

> To compare money with language is . . . erroneous. . . . Ideas which have
> first to be translated out of their mother tongue into a foreign tongue in
> order to circulate, in order to become exchangeable, offer a somewhat bet-
> ter analogy; the analogy is then not with language, but with its foreignness
> (*fremdheit*).[26]

As a kind of representation that makes a claim to value, a claim to represent an abstraction that lacks ontological positivity, money contrives to
effectuate the concrete existence of that abstract substance. Such a contrivance is aligned not with language in its quotidian or referential function, but
with language in its defamiliarizing tropological character. Just as the "time
bargains" of finance raise the specter of cheating time, bucking the very
imperviousness to human manipulation that defines temporality as such,
all monetized transaction involves temporal suspense that is performatively
overcome. Finance operates in the future anterior tense, but in so doing it
merely punctuates the logic of futurity and deferral already betokened by
money, itself always already a credit instrument. As Marx notes, "'I promise
to pay' is the usual formula for English banknotes," and is printed on the
paper, still to the present day.[27] Note here that the paper voices itself as "I"—
the promise issues from the paper, not the holder—an agency that alludes to
paper money's power to create a fact or state, what J. L. Austin would demar-
cate as its performative dimension: the promise will only be fulfilled with the
coming of the future, but the very enunciation of the promise *presents* this
future in the now. The paper declares "this bill is legal tender for all public
and private debts," and the declaration makes it so.[28] The resonances of the
"poetry of banking" in the Victorian press coverage of fictitious capital may
therefore help us to read the "poetry of money" in Marx's critique.

Even more fundamentally, logically prior to the valorization of labor by
money, labor itself, Marx's formulations suggest, is already bound up with
poetry, with this same foreign representation. Making out of illusion is the
condition of all human making:

> Labor is, first of all, a process between man and nature, a process by which
> man mediates. . . . We understand labor in a form that stamps it as exclu-
> sively human. A spider conducts operations that resemble those of a weaver,
> and a bee puts to shame many an architect in the construction of her cells.

But what distinguishes the worst architect from the best of bees is this, that the architect raises his structure in imagination before he erects it in reality. At the end of every labor-process, we get a result that already existed in the imagination of the laborer at its commencement. He not only effects a change of form in the material on which he works, but he also realises a purpose of his own.[29]

While the bee fulfills needs by changing the form of natural materials, man forms an idea, an imaginative projection, of both needs and their fulfillment. Labor for Marx, Jennifer Bajorek notes, must thus be defined as the mediation of material and ideal.[30] Crucial affinities therefore entwine labor and language (especially language conceived of as inherently imaginative)—which is why, in defining human nature, Marx lit upon Milton: "Milton produced *Paradise Lost* in the same way that a silkworm produces silk, as the activation of his own nature."[31] Marx chooses literary production as the exemplar of natural production: literary making is natural making. Finance must thus be understood as the consummation, rather than the invention, of this material idealization.

While Evans and Bagehot did not go as far as Marx in theorizing this continuity between fictitious capital and capital as such, they and other members of the Victorian press did broach the difficulties of identifying where "real" capital ended and fictitious began. Indeed, Marx's very first introduction of the phrase "fictitious capital" into his own writing came as a citation of a Yorkshire banker's House of Commons report warning that it was becoming "impossible to decide (between) real *bona fide* transactions . . . and *fictitious*" (italics original).[32] The *Economist* likewise caught this difficulty, printing a special advisory, "To Readers and Correspondents," attempting to alleviate it: "*fictitious capital* is generally applied to capital raised or borrowed on credit and not on bona fide securities; for example, capital borrowed on an accommodation bill, which, though it purports to represent real value, does not do so."[33] Because fictitious capital named the credit extended through financial instruments (starting with stock certificates for companies that did not yet exist and advancing through futures contracts for hypothetical value fluctuations), the *Economist* concluded it was the "necessary accompaniment" of "the mechanism of the stock exchange."[34] The *Morning Chronicle* summed up this pervasiveness:

If the capital is fictitious so are the dividends—if the dividends are fictitious so is the currency that represents them—if the currency is fictitious, all prices valued in that currency must be fictitious also. In fiction, therefore, we move, live, and have our financial being. When will this fiction end?[35]

This sense of endlessness registers the absent end, the *fin* of finance, the presupposition of financial transactions that ultimately subtracts that end from any moment of present reality.

Presenting the future in the now, realizing capital through speech acts— these problematics of finance that strain logic and time, as elaborated by Marx and his brethren Victorian financial journalists, chart a necessary leap—not a leap of faith on the part of investors, but a leap against and across present actuality by the metaphysical system of capital itself. "Fictitious capital," one of Marx's more allusive formulations holds, is "purely illusory, yet it has its own laws of motion for all that." Through this motion, the illusion produces material effects, subverting any easy opposition between the material and the illusory, the real and the fictitious. This precipitous leap from immaterial to material prompted Marx to esteem fictitious capital "the most complete fetish," for in it the leap of the commodity (its *salto mortale*) and the leap of money (what he highlights in the *Grundrisse* as its promissory performative dimension) find their consummation. In adumbrating material illusions and impossible distinctions, fictitious capital illuminates the fictifying of all valorized exchange.

So much has been a problem since the beginning of *Capital,* volume 1, in which, citing Aristotle, Marx elaborates the "real impossibility" of commensurate exchange. Value provides a "makeshift" grounding of the logical nongroundedness of exchange—a hypostasis of an abstraction that exceeds the exigencies of mere "reality." As the philosopher Kojin Karatani has illuminated, the abstraction "value" can only be confirmed after the fact: there is no possible guarantee ahead of time—only after a sale can value obtain, even though the parties to a sale act as if value already inheres before the sale.[36] *Ex post facto,* value may be presumed to have grounded an exchange, but *ex ante facto,* exchange is logically nongrounded. Every act of exchange thereby involves this leap of faith; Marx returns again and again to the figure of the leap to illustrate this insurmountably speculative dimension of all valorized exchange. The moment of finance capital as such merely piques to "the most complete" intensity this temporal retroaction. As the "most complete fetish," fictitious capital only punctuates the logico-temporal leap that galvanizes all capital. In the words of David Harvey, "the category of fictitious capital is in fact implied whenever credit is extended in advance."[37] For this reason we must rigorously refrain from romanticizing the nonfictitious "reality" of earlier capitalism when talking about finance. Our current preoccupation with the extremes in the apparently brave new world of finance risks forgetting Marx's revelation that every stage of capital is fictitious. Although empirically speaking the past did not *fully* concretize the universal structure of capital, structurally speaking this fictitious virtuosity has always been with us.[38] Ever since the regime of value ascended, "without knowing it, we talk, and think, and act poetry, without being at all conscious of the fact."

Our lack of conscious awareness of the poetry of banking is less the obstacle to financialization than its condition of possibility. Fictitious capital is "so intricate and complicated," as Evans concluded, it would be "no easy matter intelligibly to describe it."[39] Fortunately, then, for the flourishing of the Stock Exchange, understanding finance, if such a thing were possible, was unrelated to participating in the market. Already by 1846 a House of Commons report compiled data on the popularity of investment, filing such a "curious collection of the names, addresses, and amount of interest of every investor" that "it defies all notions of analysis." Indeed, the report tallied a comically wide social strata of investors:

> a combination of peers and printers, vicars and vice-admirals, spinsters and half-pays, M.P.s and special pleaders, professors and cotton spinners, gentlemen's cooks and Q.C.s, attorney's clerks and college-scouts, waiters at Lloyd's, relieving officers and excisemen, barristers and butchers, Catholic priests and coachmen, editors and engineers, dairymen and dyers, braziers, bankers, beer-sellers and butlers, domestic servants, footmen, and mail guards; with a multitude of other callings unrecorded in the Book of Trades.[40]

Evans directly explained that this diversity of investors in no way evidenced popular understanding of the mysteries and puzzles of finance: though "the stock exchange, and the business therein transacted, seem always to have been a mystery to the public," "the farmer is now as deep in railway shares as the merchant, the merchant as the banker; and the whole circle of society is so entangled in the mania."[41]

Such general ignorance may account for the peculiar fact that while the financial press regularly attributed recurrent crises to the structure of finance itself, investors just as regularly renewed their enthusiasm for investment; each new crisis was followed by a new boom. However incisive the Victorian critique of fictitious capital was, the ultimate trick of finance was that its artifice did not gainsay its effectivity. The critique of fictitious capital yielded only diminishing returns, for the mere exposure of ungroundedness does not interrupt figurative circulation. Again, Marx points to the objective efficacy of fictitious capital: "fictitious capital is illusory . . . yet it has its own laws of motion for all that."[42] Through such laws of motion, a metaphysics that performs anew the physical world, fictitious capital signifies an illusion that has material effects, a *material illusion*. If this objective independence from subjective attitudes invites some refinement of the prevailing arguments about finance as an epistemological problem (how to believe in it, how individuals can "credit" transactions) such that we can see instead the problem's non-epistemological dimension (how what matters is not belief on the part of the subject, since objective reality itself believes in the subject's place, but rather acts), then this importance of acting without belief—of what psychoanalysis terms "disavowal"—may also explain why finance apparently demanded psychological investigation.

Nightmare on Lombard Street

Where Marx pursued the logical consequences of the critique of fictitious capital into a structural account of the capitalist mode of production, the Victorian journalists who inspired his investigation turned their attention toward the subjective experience of a system propelled by the paradoxical realities of fictitiousness. This phenomenological and ultimately psychological lens eventually replaced the politico-economic systemic one. Having investigated the causes of crises, journalists became preoccupied with their effects. In part this shift may be owing to the regularity of crises, something like the snuffing of the burning question of whence they came. By the late 1850s it required only short-term memory to foster a public sense of crises as rhythmically recurrent. Already before the century's most calamitous crisis, the 1866 failure of Overend, Gurney, and Co. (the so-called "Banker's Bank"), crises had become expected and anticipated.

This sense of regularity and inevitability, however, did not mean that crises were taken lightly. On the contrary, crisis registers across diverse publications as traumatic. For instance, in both of his books on crises, Evans documented the "intensity of alarm," averring that "terror will long linger in the remembrance of those who witnessed its career . . . so great was the madness of all classes that, from peer to peasant, few ultimately escaped unscathed."[43] In an academic report on "The Sad Intensity of Modern Life," the *Quarterly*

Review of Social Science lamented that such lingering terror drove many men "to break off or break down in mid-career, shattered, paralyzed, reduced to premature inaction or senility."[44] In point of fact, The Commissioners on Lunacy, which tracked occupations of patients admitted into asylums in England and Wales in the 1850s, found that "persons who buy or sell, keep or lend money (merchants, bankers, and so forth)" ranked second only to military personnel.[45] "Shadowless Men," a *Household Words* piece on the aftermath of 1856, graphically documented the psychological imprint of crises:

> if they do not dash the brains of their victims out at once with blows, they fill them with the hot coals of grief until they consume them with fire. . . . It is indeed frightful to think how they fill churchyards and lunatic asylums. . . . When the risks came into play they found themselves engaged in business which they did not understand and which they found decidedly hazardous. They were sleeping partners with hideous nightmares and dreadful awakenings.[46]

Journalists interested in the traumatic experience of crises often fixed on images of death. In a common sentiment, the *Chambers Journal* archived "the wear and tear, the amount of excitement that such a man must often experience, is sometimes so overpowering as to lead to calamitous consequences— ruin to himself, wife, and family, social degradation, and occasionally even suicide and death."[47] After a crash, The City is a zombie-land of "hideous nightmares," a ghost town "silent and awful as the city of the dead; silent as the grave of sunken capital should be."[48] Death is at once the only final resting place of finance's propulsive futurity and the product of those arrested propulsions.

Evans's career came to a strange end, perhaps capitulating at a different level the insuperable traumas he investigated. His last published work was extremely peculiar, proffering mentally unstable reflections on the horrors of the stock exchange. Shattered grips on reality, shadowless men, hideous nightmares, and fateful death all bristle in the titular metaphysical ambivalence of that final work, *Speculative Notes on Speculation: Ideal and Real* (1864). There Evans confronts the enigma of why, burned by previous crises and tormented by the prospects of future crises, average people continue to participate in the financial system: "Old and young, rich and poor, have I seen drawn into this inextricable vortex, each struggling with his own particular views to obtain the one grand object, but never in reality getting it; and when disappointed and heartbroken, sinking into decrepitude, and at last the grave."[49] Marveling at this gravitational pull of finance, *Speculative Notes* compiles a motley dossier of ruined investors, a chronicle of addicts for whom "speculation is like snuff-taking or smoking—a habit which, when once acquired, it is difficult to shake off; and people who are afflicted with the mania will go on speculating as long as they (can)."[50]

As if reporting these stories irreversibly alters the reporter, documenting such psychic strain discomposes the journalist's authoritative voice, leading to episodes like "Dark Somber Morning, Bright Glowing Eventide," which waxes totally psychotropic as it dramatizes the temporal dysphoria of financial future anteriority. In trying to recollect the crisis of 1857 under the penumbra of a possible new crisis, Evans's past-tense narrative vacillates between "ideal and real," lurching into an out-of-joint present:

> with the future I will not attempt to deal; but of the past I may freely speak, and, in the character and under the guise of a vision, tell of what I then heard and saw. It is the year 1857. . . . Things in general . . . are bad indeed . . . unless the Bank . . . interferes, the crash will be dreadful. This comes upon me with more amazement than anything else I have heard during this portentous crisis. . . . I return home, restless and uncomfortable. . . . I endeavor to sleep, but all my efforts are unavailing, and in a feverish dose my mind wanders, and combining the progress of events with a little fanciful illusion, presents a sketch not far removed from stern reality.[51]

In this twilight time zone when past narration lurches into present tense, a phantasmagoria unfolds; a "vision" envelops "a little fanciful illusion." Evans tallies the cognitive and psychological costs of living in a fictitious world, a world in which overwhelming emotions merit gargantuan personification:

> Gaunt panic, with uncertain gait and distorted visage, stalks hurriedly through the land. Like the leper of old, downcast in mien and paralysed in limb, his presence is the signal for immediate apprehension, lest his contagious touch should strike with disease sound constitutions and bleach white the bones of living men.[52]

This hyperbolic personification embodies the trepidation around the precarious financial system in the image of unattributed emotion. To portray the intensity of crises, Evans confabulates aberrantly vivid language, whose disorienting eccentricity captures the true distortion of material illusions. For all of his focus on psychological dynamics, he remains clear that these dynamics are the effects of engaging with the financial system; the system preexists the unstable psychology it wreaks. The psychological dimension of crisis is here *not a cause,* but a reverberation: the abyss of finance reflected back in the unmoored psyche.[53]

The prolific Evans set aside his pen after *Speculative Notes,* continuing to work as an editor, but living for another decade without writing another text. The hallucinatory summit to which he ascends in *Speculative Notes* may have left little else to say. When he retired from writing, the mantle of first reporter of finance, especially for coverage of the enormous 1866 crisis, fell to Walter Bagehot, a founding editor of the *Economist* and author of numerous volumes of essays on finance and political economy.

In Bagehot's discourse we can encounter the psychic aftershocks of finance: shell-shocked from crises, consumed with chronicling psychological states, and adrift in the "inextricable vortex" of fictitious capital, financial journalists began to perceive the outsize psychological *effects* of the unstable financial system as *causes* of its very instability. This substitution of effect for cause, the trope of metalepsis, surfaced atop the riptide of financial derivation—and flowed into twentieth-century economic wisdom. In *Lombard Street* (1874), Bagehot's essay collection about London's Wall Street, which continues to be approvingly cited by economists today, the metalepsis slips in.[54] An investigator of the "case of metaphysics" of realizing capital, Bagehot opens his treatise with a sharp distinction between "very abstract words" and "concrete realities."[55] He promises to explain the dynamics that polarize this opposition. The pace and rhythm of his text toe along the fulcrum of structural causality and psychological foundationalism in Victorian financial thought until it tilts decidedly to one side.

As an example of such an opposition between the structural and the psychological, let us take Bagehot's self-consciousness about the paradoxical nature of the Bank of England's reserve. The year 1844 had seen the passage of Sir Robert Peel's solution to the problem of fictitiousness via the regulation of the reserve. Unlike the United States or the Continent in the nineteenth century, England after Peel favored a flexible over a fixed assets–leverage ratio. The essence of Peel's Act was to centralize the calculations of this ineffable "point of value" in the Bank of England by greatly reducing the right of issue of banknotes by country, private, and joint stock banks. In turn the Bank of England would divide its issuing department from its banking department and clearly publicize the banking department's balance sheets of assets and liabilities. The dissemination of information about the reserve ratio would, the thinking went, assure the public at large that notes were backed and thereby ensure against claims for that backing. With its reinforced, centralized standing, the Bank of England became "the banker's bank," holding the reserves of companies, capitalists, and many other banks, which amounted to approximately fifty percent of its deposits.[56] Peel's Act did not fix a ratio of reserve to leverage, but rather legislated "flexibility," promoting a psychological orientation in which the soundness of banking was not a mathematical question, but a symbolic one—a question to be solved by the symbolic means of reputation and respect. The Bank was anointed the safe central reserve and would perform rituals of transparency and accountability, and in return its foundations would appear sufficiently sound to the public to overcome fictitiousness. Rather than conforming to mathematical rules or to principles of a financial science, the Bank represented itself as transparent and counted on the emotional effects of such storytelling.

Even after it had been in effect for three decades, Peel's Act had achieved so convoluted a ground for finance that reserve policy continued to generate debate. In *Lombard Street* these debates take the form of identifying the reserve as one of the key paradoxes of financial metaphysics. Elaborating at length that this reserve fund authorizes and authenticates the majority of financial and commercial transactions in Britain, Bagehot acknowledges the oddity that this authorizing function must, at a certain point, directly contradict itself. In order to secure the financial system as a whole, the Bank *holds* a reserve, but, at intervals of distress, in order to secure the financial system as a whole, the Bank must *release* that reserve:

> As has been already said—but on account of its importance and perhaps its novelty it is worth saying again—whatever bank or banks *keep* the ultimate banking reserve of the country must *lend* that reserve most freely in time of apprehension (64).

The very source of solidity in times of security must be itself liquidated in times of insecurity.

It is on account of paradoxes like this that Bagehot stressed that the structural unsoundness of finance could be overcome by the magnetic force of common action. "In exact proportion to the power of this system is its delicacy—I should hardly say too much if I said its danger. Only our familiarity blinds us to the marvelous nature of the system" (17). Powerful and dangerous, mighty and delicate, fictitious and marvelous, finance finds its center, Bagehot opines, in the blindness of habit. The "rough and vulgar structure" of English finance, if perceived directly, would surely be calamitous—not only for economic transactions, but for the mental stability of folks going about their business blissfully unaware of the sinkhole beneath their feet:

> There is no country at present, and there never was any country before, in which the ratio of cash reserve to the bank deposits was so small as it is now in England. So far from being able to rely on the proportional magnitude of our cash in hand, the amount of that cash is so exceedingly small that a bystander almost trembles when he compares its minuteness with the immensity of the credit which rests upon it (18).

It is this condition of trembling, of awe before the fragile edifice, that defines the financially savvy. Greater understanding leads not to greater profit, but to greater unease. Fortunately, then, for the market itself, most financial agents subsist in ignorance. While "a person who takes care of his mind will keep up the perception" that finance is unstable, the mass of financial actors, according to Bagehot, little appreciate the delicacy of the system, and for that reason, the system's delicacy is kept in check.[57] Investors and depositors act as if the system of fictitious credit were stable, and their acting makes it so. Bagehot links this logic of the collective disavowal to what later goes by the name of "ideology" chez Althusser, by explicitly analogizing participation in the financial system to political cohesion:

> Queen Victoria is loyally obeyed—without doubt and without reasoning—by millions of human beings. If those millions of people began to argue, it would not be easy to persuade them to obey Queen Victoria, or anything else. Effectual arguments to convince the people who need convincing are wanting. Just so, an immense system of credit, founded on the Bank of England as its pivot and its basis, now exists (69).

The retroactive effect of disavowal, its agency in securing contracts financial and social ("I know I did not agree to obey the Queen, nonetheless I will act as if I agreed"/"I know credit is non-grounded; nonetheless I will act as if it is sound") extends Bagehot's insights that "in true metaphysics . . . unbelief far oftener needs a reason and requires an effort than belief . . . the mere presentation of an idea . . . makes us believe it. . . . The belief of the money-market . . . is as imitative as any belief."[58] Through a psychological prism, Bagehot broaches the structural dynamic Marx terms the essential "leap of credit."[59] As Bagehot puts it, "credit is a power which may grow but cannot be constructed"—a lurching into effectivity that we have seen to define the structure of capital (69). In the effects are to be found the cause, and thus Bagehot identifies "the immense system of credit" as auto-grounding: "every banker knows that if he has to *prove* that he is worthy of credit, however good may be his arguments, in fact his credit is gone: but what we have requires no proof. The whole rests on an instinctive confidence generated by use" (69). Butting up against the plain fact that the Bank of England's reserve is too small to function as effective guarantee, Bagehot muses on the disjunction between plain facts and everybody's feelings: "Instant payment, in the years I speak of, the Bank of England certainly could not have made. But no one in London ever dreams of questioning the credit of the Bank, and the Bank never dreams that its own credit is in danger. Somehow everybody feels the Bank is sure to come right" (40). Habit, use, effectivity involute into feeling, confidence, and causality. These are Bagehot's psychologistic versions of Marx's insight that in capitalism "effects become causes in their turn . . . and the whole process . . . always reproduces its own conditions."

But where Marx emphasized the objectivity of these metaleptic effects become causes, Bagehot grew distracted by the subjectivity of it. Even as he arrived at insights into the opacity and precarity of the financial system, he began to replace these systemic assessments with psychological evaluations. Credit, as *Blackwoods Magazine* argued, is a "peculiarity" that "even the philosophical mind finds it hard to answer," and Bagehot seems to have become mired in probing the mindsets that could brook such peculiarity.[60] He thus eventually laid aside his own analysis of the reserve problem and began to explain crises as "the madness of modern overtrading," transposing the structural instability of fictitious capital to the fickle unreliability of the psychic economy.[61] "A panic, in a word, is a species of neuralgia," goes Bagehot's famous formula (resurgent in the financial press after 2007), which medically specifies that panic is not the result of outside stimulus, but is rather precipitated internally.[62] To prevent this psychic state of affairs, it seems a psychologically adroit financial policy is necessary. Bagehot thus endeavors to resolve the decades-long debate on fixed and flexible reserves by proposing a new rule, a quasi-flexible baseline called "the apprehension minimum," pegged to the psychological standard:

> A panic is sure to be caused if (the Bank) reserve is, from whatever cause, exceedingly low. At every moment, there is a certain minimum which I will call the "apprehension minimum" below which the reserve cannot fall without great risk of diffused fear; and by this I do not mean absolute panic, but only a vague fright and timorousness which spreads itself instantly, and,

as if by magic, over the public mind. Such seasons of incipient alarm are exceedingly dangerous, because *they beget the calamities they dread*. . . . There is
no "royal road" to the amount of the "apprehension minimum": no abstract
argument, and no mathematical computation will teach it to us. And we
cannot expect that they should.[63]

As with Evans's "gaunt panic," Bagehot emphasizes a disembodied atmo-
spheric emotion, "a season," in which an emotion "diffused" and "vague,"
self-spreading "as if by magic," preexists "the public mind" it incorporates.
Spinning in the eddy of "whatever cause," drowning in the metaleptic sway
of fears that "beget the calamities they dread" (the effects become the cause),
Bagehot clings to a life raft and grasps only an oxymoronic ratio that "no
mathematical computation" can designate.[64] Floating this new hybrid concept, Bagehot contrives a fishtailing mutual grounding between economics
and psychology.

In *Lombard Street* and elsewhere, Bagehot fully adopts psychologism,
forgoing analysis of financial logic in favor of generalizations about investor emotions. Where once crisis had been explained with references to the
delicacy and unsoundness of the financial system, the late writings blame a
poorly managed economy of desire and stimulation:

> every mania is caused by the impossibility to get people to confine them-
> selves to the amount of business for which their capital is sufficient . . . this
> is caused by the wish to get rich, but in a considerable degree too, by the
> mere love of activity. There is a greater propensity to action in such men
> than they have the means of gratifying. Operations with their own capital
> will only occupy four hours of the day, and they wish to be active and be
> industrious for eight hours, and so they are ruined. If they could only have
> sat idle for the other four hours, they would have been rich men.[65]

In presenting the depth psychology of crisis, Bagehot posits "the unconscious organization of capital," a continuity between the macro-economy
and "the economy of man's nature"—a continuity that comes to explain
not only crises, but normal economic functioning, as well.[66] Psychic energy is governed by laws of economic expansion and contraction ("if you
spend nervous force in one direction, you will not have as much to spend
in another"), and by extension "desire" becomes "a vital element in every
market" because "the principle way in which capital increases in England

now, is by abstinence from enjoyment."[67] Bagehot's commitments to a rubric of psychic economy clearly come down on the side of moderated desire: economic growth will stem from keeping in check the libidinous tendencies that lead to economically imprudent "feverish and irrational excitement" over investment opportunities.[68]

While such ideas of moderation support both the archetype of Victorian corseted desires and the thesis of Max Weber, it is important to note that the psychological explanations of economic phenomena have the effect of suggesting a mode of regulation that is psychological and libidinal rather than legal or infrastructural, an "apprehension minimum" rather than a fixed policy on leverage. Economic actors need "only sit idle," and the calamities of crashes and instabilities of finance will be smoothly controlled. This effect brings with it an obverse: economic events are not available to political determination, but rather follow their own autonomous course. The rhetoric of psychic economy comes thereby to work in two dimensions, auguring the economic foundation of the psyche and the psychological basis of the economy. As a result of this work, the economy itself resembles an amalgamated psychological subject. Hence the psychological tropes for economic phenomena, ranging from Lord Overstone (who authored the 1844 Banking Act) to Paul Krugman (the Princeton University professor and columnist for the *New York Times*): references to "confidence," "excitement," "distress" culminate in such avowals as "the stock market is manic-depressive."[69]

The Financial Mind

Though posterity receives Evans and Bagehot as the spokesmen of financialization, the bulk of their works approach finance not as a set of tools or rules whose usage can be effectively mastered, but as a set of intractable paradoxes: time bargains, apprehension minimums, and the quicksand of fictitiousness. Somewhere in the process of elaborating these paradoxes, between the 1850s and the 1860s, the charge of fictitiousness lost its force, and attention turned to the subjective experience of financial ungroundedness. I have been arguing that this shift, from probing financial logics to pursuing psychological perspectives, comprises a problematic psychologism: systematic analysis of the "case of metaphysics" was displaced by impressionistic exploration of affect. Where fictitious capital made the financial economy inexplicably complex, defiantly elusive of exposition, the psychic economy realized capital, domesticating the economy as the natural issue of interiority. I want now to briefly examine a complementary development that also contributed to this paradigm shift.

The emergence of what we now recognize as the discipline of psychology nurtured financial journalism's turn toward psychological phenomena and psychological explanations. During and immediately after this 1855 moment, understanding economics in terms of psychology may have become compelling because, simultaneously, psychology was talking about itself in economic terms. Psychological texts drew their conceptual grounds from the economic language and imagery with which they saturated their prose, and at the same time they argued for the psychological foundations of economic relations. Early psychology *already* modeled the psychological anchoring of economic figures by gratuitously employing economic tropes and financial images to define mental functioning and by quite curiously taking up questions about the essence of money and other financial instruments. This curiosity performs the symbiotic justification between psychology and economics: on the one hand, psychology underwrites its new knowledge with the language of economics; on the other, importing this language disposes psychologists to naturalize economic phenomena, betraying in the process of this ideological suture the unmoored and ungrounded topoi of finance.

By the middle of the nineteenth century public interest in the new science of psychology was widespread, and articles on psychology ran regularly in a variety of non-specialist publications.[70] The year 1855 saw the publication of two hugely influential, widely reviewed works generally heralded as the first modern psychology texts: Herbert Spencer's *The Principles of Psychology* and Alexander Bain's *The Senses and the Intellect*. Within these and other texts, the relentless and casual use of economic language is enough to make one wonder if the critique of finance as tropological inadvertently endorsed the use of financial language as tropes. Early psychology became an engine of the very hyperbolic proliferation of financial figures assessed by critics of fictitious capital. From "production," "expenditure," and "accumulation" to "surplus," "capital," and "the division of labor," economic language saturated psychological exposition, intoning "that law of economy which dominates all of mental life."[71] In their commitment to this law psychologists consecrated the construct of "inner economy" to encapsulate the object of their new science. Evoking affective investments, energetic gains and losses, and a tendency to equilibrium of pleasure and pain, this image appropriates "economy" as the essential structure of the psychological core.

For Spencer the consummate image of the "economy of mental energies" was indispensable for constituting his new science, for it enabled him to differentiate psychic from physical life.[72] Moreover, the metaphor of psychic economy provided him with the means to accomplish the great aim of all his synthetic philosophy, the construction of strong "parallelism between vital economy and social economy."[73] The attraction of this parallelism, evidently, is its reciprocal explanatory purchase: economic concepts explain mental functioning, and mental functioning explains economic concepts.[74] For Bain, who promised in *The Senses and the Intellect* to elucidate "the important points of economy," economic exchange was the fundamental referent behind "associationism," the process of conversion he thought organized all mental functioning. The mind is most elementally a forum of ceaseless exchange, and this primary faculty for substitution then gives rise to higher order abstraction.

Like the financial journalists who problematically turned to psychological investigation, the early psychologists compulsively developed economic elucidation. Strikingly, in both Bain and Spencer, as well as in successive psychological bestsellers such as George Henry Lewes's *Problems of Life and Mind,* the privileged exemplar of higher-order mental functioning is *money.* Money is the supreme abstraction, the exalted end-stage of natural cognition.[75] When the psychologist looks for proof of his model of the mind, he turns to economy, where, at the moment of financialization, it should be plainly evident that symbolic mediations reign. But even as these psychologists borrowed from economics to verify their claims about the mind, they also curiously registered that economic abstractions were themselves enigmas in need of grounding. Where money might be useful evidence that the mind works in abstract ways, derivative abstractions like credit and stock required mental truisms for proof of their import:

> Another example of an association displacing the original source and
> purpose of a feeling, is seen in connexion with the *forms* of business.
> Book-keeping, legal formalities, and technical procedure, are intended as
> aids to the transaction of business. In themselves nothing, they have great
> value in furthering our substantial ends; and we contract a sentiment to-
> wards them on that ground. As with money, however, this reflected interest
> sometimes detaches itself from the original ends; and we take a pleasure in
> maintaining formalities that time and change have reduced to an empty
> letter.

"In themselves nothing," the "empty letter" of fictitious financial instruments is inscribed as *something* when tethered to a universalized psychology. In the mercantile metaphor "we contract a sentiment towards them," we can see how the economic trope of emotional experience substantiates economic activity itself. From this metaleptic circuit of economic figures and psychological ground emerges a psychological theory with the aspiration to explain economics.

Political economists would soon incur a debt to psychology. As voluble as the year 1855 was for psychologists, it was also the year of explicit pronouncements on the role of the new science of mind in enriching the science of wealth. Political economists of this period, keen to denude their discipline of specific political connotations and to instead propound a science useful to a wide political spectrum, were perspicuous about the support psychology could offer to their enterprise.[76] In the preface to his 1855 *Natural Elements in Political Economy*, Richard Jennings makes numerous calls for further research into psychology in order to properly develop political economy, most emphatically declaring, "this branch of philosophy [Political Economy] cannot be thoroughly understood until the subordinate principles of psychology have been adequately investigated." Jennings distinctly outlines the mutual benefits from the collaboration of psychology and political economy: "Psychology, when brought to bear upon the problems of Political-Economy, must conduce largely to a right understanding of their character"; and reciprocally,

> whilst the advantages possessed by Political Economy, in the enduring continuity of its phenomena, in their certainty placed beyond the reach of cavil, and in their exact representation by numerical expressions, when imported into the study of Psychology, must furnish a more definite language for the representation of its principles.[77]

The notion of a natural psychological basis for economic abstraction thickened into a conceptual revolution in which what we might call a "desire theory of value" replaced the labor theory of value. Where once goods were thought valuable because of the labor expended by their producers, the new economics sourced value to the pleasure goods afforded their consumers. This paradigm shift is generally recognized as the marginal utility revolution, so named for the initial observation that there exists a margin at which ready availability of desirable commodities ultimately decreases the utility consumers find in them. But where that revolution is seen by Regenia Gagnier and others to be launched by William Stanley Jevons's 1871 *Theory of Political Economy,* the evolving idea of a continuity between psyche and economy that I have been tracing suggests that this revolution was less revolutionary and more the consolidation of psychologisms circulating from the late 1850s onward.[78]

A follower of Spencer and Bain, Jevons coined the disciplinary name change from "political economy" to "economics," substituting for an outmoded labor theory of value the "novel opinion, that value depends entirely upon pleasure."[79] Casting aside classical political economy as quickly as its cumbersome predicate, Jevons formulated "economics" as an ostensibly rigorous mathematical science with an unimpeachable empirical basis in universal psychology. The only problem for this science was the hurdle of converting psychic experiences into price-denominated values, a problem a *Punch* magazine essay of the same year evaluated: "the worst of Political Economy sums is that they have to be worked with men's interests, principles, passions, and pockets as factors, and these are very difficult counters to cipher with. You can't *prove* your sums, as we used to have to do at school."[80] John Stuart Mill had called this the "paradox" of "what ratio there can be between a quantity and a desire," so Jevons immediately tackled the question in his magnum opus, anticipating the likely objection that "the notions which we treat in this science are incapable of any measurement," only to flippantly reply that those objectors lack imagination: "I answer, in the first place, that nothing is less warranted in science than an uninquiring and unhoping spirit."[81] With this hand-slap for the unimaginative, Jevons proceeds:

> I hesitate to say that men will ever have the means of measuring directly the feelings of the human heart. A unit of pleasure or of pain is difficult even to conceive; but it is the amount of these feelings which is continually prompting us to buying and selling, borrowing and lending, laboring and resting, producing and consuming; and *it is from the quantitative effects of the feelings that we must estimate their comparative amounts* (italics original).[82]

Here metalepsis again: in the effects is the proof of the cause.

By the late century *Palgrave's Dictionary of Political Economy* permanently emblazoned this foundational function of "subordinate" psychological principles: "The economist must from the first to last realize that he is dealing with psychological phenomena, and must be guided throughout by psychological considerations."[83] Psychology lent a ground to economic relations; the idea of an economic psychology in particular moored the worrisomely abstract illogic of finance in the putatively concrete laws of subjectivity. If analysis of the metalepsis at the moment of financialization contextualizes the disappearance of the very idea of fictitious capital, it may also help deflate institutional economics' psychologism of capitalism. The novels to which I now turn shed exemplary light in this direction.

2. *Investor Ironies in* Great Expectations

This book began with a sentence from *Great Expectations,* a novel published in 1860, and now that we have established the "case of metaphysics" posed by realizing capital from the 1840s through the 1860s, we can do no better than return to that novel and to that sentence: "As we contemplated the fire, and as I thought what a difficult vision to realize Capital sometimes was, I put my hands into my pockets."[1] The rhythm of the sentence encloses the difficult metaphysical vision of realizing capital between two markedly simple physical images: the fire and the hands. Fire and hands, hearth and labor, these are the roots of the *oikos,* the grounds and bounds of economy—while the vision of capital is some other matter entirely. As the action progresses across this sentence, we also find a shift from "we" to "my," from the collaborative sharing of the hearth to the individual subject of possession. Moreover, the verbs subtly range from definite speculation to infinitive speculation ("contemplated . . . thought . . . to realize"), until foundering on that simplest of material actions, "put." The digressive progression through two comparative clauses before a final indicative clause further underscores that speculative/ active tension. Amid all these contrasts, the clause structure positions capital at the center of everything, linking fire and hands, ideal and material, ours and mine. At the center is a kind of unity of opposites, the becoming real of the fictitious.

As it tells a tale of social climbing and bad investments, of trading up and losing all, *Great Expectations* derives its energy from these contrasts between hearth and capital, community and selfishness, expectation and action—and it moves in a sway defined by their undoing. Most strikingly, the essential contrast at the heart of the novel, that between the character Pip and the narrator Pip, is, I will suggest in the following pages, ultimately undermined by the narrator's insufficient development. Though perpetually acclaimed as an account of redemption, *Great Expectations,* I contend, actually audits the irredeemable.[2] Our sentence describes a decisive scene before the hearth, a moment of contemplation and of pocketing that together conjugate Pip's self-proclaimed moral maturation, his reflection on his misdeeds, and his investment in Herbert's success. Yet the novel implicitly questions his claim, querying how acts of investment can possibly atone for investor mania. Its questioning is both cause and effect of its ironization of Pip. Reading for this irony in its linguistic, situational, and dramatic guises, I explore how it over-shadows the protagonist's reputed redemption and how it works to shade the constructs of self-development and self-capitalization that we have seen to organize much mid-century Victorian discourse about the role of the self in the financial economy.

Wrapping its head around the enigma of realizing capital in a manner fundamentally different from that of the financial journalism we have just considered, Dickens's fiction perspicaciously sustains awareness of fictitious capital and disdains the ideological project to found a natural capital in "the innermost life" (236). It represents the interiorizing gesture of putting hands into pockets as a response to the difficulties of realizing capital, but it cautions against that gesture all the same. Heeding this critical edge can hew new readings of some of the most persistent oddities in and of the text: Why is Pip's story told in the first person, and why does he tell it at all? Why are both the beginning and the ending dramatically unclear? Why is the narrative temporally out of joint? These enigmas of the text, its unfinished business—these are the crenulations of *Great Expectations'* financial form. It is through these aesthetic contours, rather than through any referential por-trayal of banking and trade, that its financial thinking unfolds. I argue that *Great Expectations* uses its first-person narration to investigate the logics of personhood in the culture of finance: the unreliable corporate person legally birthed in the late 1850s and the investor-subject, the psychic economy, con-structed contemporarily with Dickens's literary subjects.

Pocketing Irony

Although an industrial complex trains us to understand *Great Expectations* as the archetypal *Bildungsroman,* the novel systematically destabilizes the milestones of that growth.[3] To pick just the most important milestone, the friendship that Pip eventually builds with Herbert Pocket stands as a lone example among his relationships in its apparent kindness of spirit and provides Pip with the circumstances for the ultimate act of generosity he concords to his moral maturation. But the novel frantically uproots this milestone, employing a deceptively simple prop: pockets. In the sentence with which we began, before the hearth of their shared London apartment, in the good company of the aptly named Herbert Pocket, Pip puts his hands into his own pockets. Though a small gesture, it mimes what Pip will eventually claim as his one great deed: investing in Herbert's company, putting his hands into Herbert's pockets. Through this illustration it begins to become apparent that the very word "pocket" works overtime, an irrepressibly Dickensian portmanteau. On one shift, "pocket" acts every bit the overly determined name we recognize as a Dickens signature, stitching the character Herbert on the seam of the economic and the small. Pocket is a pocket-protagonist, a minor character whose subplot for economic and romantic advancement is pocketbooked within Pip's, and whose pockets are ultimately lined out of Pip's pockets. On another shift, the continuity sewn between Pip's pocket and Pocket recalls "investment" to its etymological origins: "to clothe, to envelop in a garment." Pip's gesture ("I put my hands in my pockets") profoundly literalizes *both* the plot in which he invests in "my dear Pocket" and the word "investment" itself: it revokes investment, that most elaborate of figurative activities, back to its vestigial literal roots. In this way "pocket" materializes de Manian "irony": "the sign points to something that differs from its literal meaning and has for its function the thematization of this difference."[4] "Pocket" differs from itself, signifying Pip's most intimate relationship and banal economic transactions; "investment" differs from itself, signifying the splitting of quotidian clothing from financial adventures, etymological origins from tropological destinies.

Throughout *Great Expectations* the rhetoric of the pocket weaves a garment of many folds, thematizing the difference between figural and literal meanings at every crease, pulling the threads that bind clothing and capital, the real and the fictitious. There are "pocket-handkerchiefs," "pocket-flasks," "pocket-money," and "pocket-books"; "holes in pockets," "emptied pockets," "hands in pockets," and "notes in pockets"; hypothetical pockets ("as if his pocket were full of secrets," "as if his pocket were a drawer"); and, most disturbingly, a corpse "so horribly disfigured that he was only recognizable by the content of his pockets." Marking the hard "pock" of "pocket," this latter image of lethal disfigurement alludes at once to the defiguring irony unfolded by "pocket" and to the malformations of Pip's *Bildung*.

By pointing to the seamy figures of the investor economy and thematizing the difference between the competing semes of "investment," the figural irony of the rhetoric of the pocket in turn accents the situational irony: Pip's deed recapitulates the act of secret investment originally igniting his expectations. In secretly investing in Herbert, Pip positions himself exactly in the shoes of his own anonymous benefactor, fortifying the very network of finance that occasioned his sin in the first place. Propagating further investments is a paltry restitution, one that unleashes an irony deepened by the way that Pip's act of investment maintains Herbert's illusions about the accumulation of capital. Though he first introduces himself to Pip as "A Capitalist, an Insurer of Ships," Pocket must quickly admit that his pockets are unfortunately empty, his mercantile insurance venture languishing in the purely prospective quarter: "I haven't begun insuring yet, I am looking about me . . . it doesn't pay me anything." Pip appraises the outlook with some chagrin, thinking, "it would be difficult to lay by much accumulative capital from such a source." Thence ensues Herbert's technical précis of the accumulation of capital:

> "But the thing is," said Herbert Pocket, "that you look about you. *That's* the grand thing. You are in a counting-house, you know, and you look about you. . . . Then the time comes, when you see your opening. And you go in, and you swoop upon it and you make your capital, and then there you are!" (185)

Tempting as it is to pity Herbert for believing in fortune's stork, he is surely in the company of fools for whom the futurity of finance capital signals nothing so much as practical magic. Indeed, as the infinitive in the sentence with which we began indicates, the difficulties here are general, besetting ambitious naïfs *and* their generous friends *and* every other player in the mid-Victorian economy as it underwent the process of financialization. This generality of "looking about you" is underscored by its repetition of Pip's own economic acumen. He is the protagonist of "expectations," the literally connoted prince of "looking about," an expert in the commerce that conducts itself almost exclusively by "looking":

> Mr. Pumblechook appeared to conduct his business by looking across the street at the saddler, who appeared to transact his business by keeping his eye on the coachmaker, who appeared to get on in life by putting his hands in his pockets and contemplating the baker, who in his turn folded his arms

and stared at the grocer, who stood at his door and yawned at the chemist. The watchmaker, always poring over a little desk with a magnifying-glass at his eye, and always inspected by a group of smock-frocks poring over him through the glass of his shop-window, seemed to be about the only person in the High Street whose trade engaged his attention.

Eyes darting, eyes poring: saddler, grocer, baker, and so forth, busy looking about. Appeared, appeared, appeared: eyes peering descry other eyes peering, the agora distorted into a speculative funhouse. In the epoch of financialization, when speculation surpasses industry and the virtual is rapidly realized, such a depiction of the pervasiveness of looking is hardly parodic.

Although Pip's sentimental education eventually sends him abroad, where he presumably learns to appreciate capital's links to foreign extraction, the lesson he imparts to Herbert pertains to domestic reserves.[5] Here is one level at which the novel activates and criticizes the psychic economy metaphor: Pip puts his hands in his pockets, reaching inward to substantialize what looking aboutward does not, and drawing on generous expansiveness in atonement for selfish contractions. "As we contemplated the fire, and as I thought what a difficult vision to realize Capital sometimes was, I put my hands into my pockets": the realization of capital is the withdrawal of previously hoarded affective resources. Though wiser on first blush than Herbert, Pip's deed supplants Herbert's laughable précis with an even stranger one: that affection will engender capital. Herbert's mistaken notions are exchanged for a no-less-problematic imaginary in which "pocket" signals the private sector where feeling grounds finance. The novel problematizes this imaginary in many ways, not the least of which is the direct contradiction between Pip's investment in Herbert and the sage wisdom of the famously bifurcated clerk John Wemmick. Wemmick, keeper of one of the novel's most memorable motifs, counsels, "My guiding star always is, 'Get hold of portable property.'" In addition to a brooch, many rings, and a pair of pigeons, "portable property" refers in the novel to wealth of a pocketable form: bank receipts, stock certificates, cash money, the universal bond.[6] No matter his trade, "every man's business is portable property," and it is likely his business what he does with it—with one crucial exception. "A man should never," Wemmick inveighs, "invest portable property in a friend." For Wemmick, investing in a friend is "less pleasurable and profitable" than "pitching your money into the Thames," and is a most efficient way to "get rid of the friend." The errant hero Pip flagrantly transgresses this prohibition, repeatedly citing his ultimately large investment in his friend Herbert Pocket as "the only good thing I had done" (416). The friction between Pip's self-proclaimed moral ennoblement and Wemmick's enduring instruction undermines Pip's supposed redemption, while also affording a radical irony that galvanizes a broader critique of investor relations.

One of the ways this contrast burgeons into critique is through its tacit extension to Magwitch, who makes the biggest investment of his life on the basis of his friendly feelings for Pip and who is led by those feelings to defy legal and financial rules, returning to London despite his sentence of transportation and paying for his trip with both his wealth and his life. Pip is Magwitch in his regeneration of secret investment; and Magwitch, who makes his reentry under the pseudonym "Provis"—the provider, the insurer, the foreseer—is Pip, looking forward to great expectations, while blind to facts. As Provis Magwitch is also Herbert writ large, "a capitalist, an insurer of ships" (*proviso* meaning also, in nautical usage, a hawser to steady a moored vessel), tragically ignorant of the proviso that return from transportation will forfeit his fortune; he is the one who giveth and the one who taketh away. Pip, Magwitch, and Herbert are consumed by opaque investment schemes and faulty financial logics, the most foundational of which is not the ruse of "looking about," but the bait-and-switch of affect for asset.

Putting his hands into his pockets and into his dear Pocket, Pip's paradigm (like Magwitch's) mimics the internal requisition to human resources implemented by the broad Victorian wisdom of the 1860s: thinkers in political economy, emergent psychology, thermodynamics, self-help, and household management were collectively intoning that the self was best understood as an economy. As we have seen in the previous chapter, these intonations worked to harmonize the more troubling notes of rapidly innovating financial capitalism, hailing a real ground of fictitious capital. The psychic economy notion promised that the financial economy unleashing abstract figures of the abstraction "value" was in fact anchored in the psychological subject; in *Great Expectations* Pip's anonymous investment issues that same promissory note. In exposing the pocks of this promise, the novel ironizes both its own protagonist and the mid-century matrix that realized capital through the construct of psychic economy.

Along with the figural irony of restitching "investment" to "vestment" and the situational irony that Pip's "one good deed" perpetuates Herbert's economic confusion and repeats the anonymous investment that drives the plot, the rhetoric of the pocket thus also intervenes in the models of interiority that secrete economics at the heart of the person. The novel's wholesale problematization of the person commences from its very first word. Unlike almost every other novel Dickens wrote, and against the grain of the mid-Victorian perfection of omniscience, *Great Expectations* finds its voice in the first person. Dickens made this choice very rarely: since *Bleak House* necessarily functions through split narration, *David Copperfield* is his only other properly subjectively narrated text, and *Great Expectations* tensely revisits it, for Dickens reread *Copperfield* just before writing *Great Expectations,* stressing that he feared "unconscious repetitions" of it.[7] But considering that Trollope and Eliot each wrote only one first-person project (and, at that, novellas), *two* novels might be a lot.[8] In this singularity that fears unconscious repetition, the choice of first person does heavy lifting. I propose that the novel formulates its critique of investor relations through, rather than despite, its unusual usage of personal narration in the age of social realism. The limitations of first person commonly authorize the scholarly tendency to subordinate *Great Expectations* to ostensibly more social and more complex multi-plotted third-person texts of the 1850s. Against this tendency, Alex Woloch perceives that *Great Expectations* "tells the story of a first-person narrator stuck in a third-person narrative world"—where "tells the story" denotes the novel's critical dramatization of, rather than unthinking absorption in, its own perspectival oddities.[9] *Great Expectations,* I submit, chooses the first person to work out problems of the person, including those tropes of personhood and personation provoked by the logics of financialization and emerging psychology.

From its very first sentence *Great Expectations* stumbles over the obstacles of the first person. It begins with the personal possessive pronoun "my," but proceeds to problematize the possibility of self-presentation, self-nomination: "My father's family name being Pirrip, and my Christian name Philip, my infant tongue could make of both names nothing longer or more explicit than Pip. So, I called myself Pip, and came to be called Pip" (3). We might expect a first-person narration to introduce its voice with the conventional "I am born" (as *David Copperfield* does) or "My name is," but this text spurs forward from a failure of name, an inarticulate stuttering contraction from Philip Pirrip to "Pip." The stutter of beginning here instantly materializes the difficulties of first-person narration. The next sentences explicitly link this failure of self-possession to confusions about the figurative power of linguistic inscription:

My first fancies regarding what they were like, were unreasonably derived from their tombstones. The shape of the letters on my father's, gave me an odd idea that he was a square, stout, dark man, with curly black hair. From the character and turn of the inscription "Also Georgianna Wife of the Above," I drew a childish conclusion that my mother was freckled and sickly (3).

If, as Peter Brooks has noted, this anxiety of origins sparks fears of unreliability, we might add that this elusive self is directly associated with the figurative dimension of language, with reading graphically and allegorically.[10] Making figures of the person in place of departed persons: this is the original untrustworthy act. Such suspicion magnetizes the immediate context of composition for this novel, when the very idea of "the person" was being disarticulated from accountability: The Limited Liability Acts of 1855–1856 gave birth to the corporate person as an alter ego bearing sole responsibility for corporate losses, while the individuals who comprised the corporation bore none. Corporate personhood ushered in an era of inexpensive investing and of formal liability for the abstract person that could foster the freedom of individual investors.[11] In their function of legal normalization, these acts might seem reassuringly stabilizing, but the abstraction they authored aroused what one Member of Parliament called "considerations which concern metaphysics," and extrapolated the fictitious financial figuration perceived as unstable.[12] Limited liability, some currents in the Victorian press bemoaned, amounted to a wholesale license for "unlimited lie-ability."[13] For the Victorians swept away in these whirling lies and metaphysical concerns, the very notion of "a person" might therefore contraindicate reliability.[14] We should thus read *Great Expectations* as a work that organizes itself amid questions about the conjured person, about the reliability of personal accounts, about the insufficiency of the proper noun and unspeakability of the proper name, about the wayward and alienable property of the self.

Time Out of Joint

Stumbling among gravestones, stuttering through names—such an indefinite beginning finds its complement in the novel's notoriously ambiguous ending. Exacerbating the uncertainty and questioning with which it commences, the novel ends with an obtuse negative construction that shades any romantic rapprochement between Pip and Estella: "I took her hand in mine, and we went out of the ruined place; and, as the morning mists had risen long ago when I first left the forge, so, the evening mists were rising now, and in all the broad expanse of tranquil light they showed to me, I saw the shadow of no parting from her" (484). When Dickens bowed to pressure to change the ending, in 1862, he retained the ambiguities: "I saw no shadow of another parting from her."[15] In the crush to interpret this ending as a chiefly romantic quandary, albeit one that engrosses readers because of their generic expectations, we lose sight of the way that this ending obscures the narrative origins even more profoundly than does the beginning. Whether or not Pip and Estella are apart or together from this day forward, a different, persistent question also subtends this non-ending: when does Pip tell his story? This narrative rises up from the mists in a graveyard and dissolves into the mists at a ruined place, drawing an account that cannot be reconciled and inaugurating a first person who cannot be held accountable.

The shaky beginning and uncertain ending bookend the novel's curiously disjointed temporality. Structured by flashback, going back to the past with respect to the present, *Great Expectations* gives us a narrator whose present is the future of its narratee; the narrator Pip is narrating because he has surpassed the character Pip. Narratology deems this type of narrative temporality "analepsis," "an anachrony going back to the past with respect to the present."[16] Analepsis in the first person deploys the temporal progression entailed in viewing the past from the point of view of the future as a metonym for moral growth: the narration comes from an older, wiser narrator reflecting on a younger, callower character, localizing the developmental impetus of narrative within the developing sensitivity of a character. "The self looks at itself from a certain distance"—so goes a Schlegelian definition of irony that might accompany this kind of narration.[17] As is to be expected from such a temporal structure, Pip peppers his story with exclamations ("Wretched boy!") or allusions to hard-won wisdom ("I knew nothing then") that chart the experiential, emotional, and temporal distance between himself qua narrator and himself qua character. Narrative distance and perspectival aggrandizement inscribe themselves in the graphic *Pip,* the majuscule P looking about over the small p.

But like the volleying anagram of p-i-p, this wisdom is tautological: "I know what I know," he states—but what does he know? And more importantly, when did he start knowing it? Kindling the question of what has happened in the lapse between the time of the action and the time of first-person reflective reporting, first-person past-tense narration lures the reader with the curve of shifting perspective, for the narrator knows *now* what he did not know *then,* and what we do not know *yet.* Just as a "crowd of speculations and anticipations" (286) encircles Pip's fantasies of his future, the narrative's analeptic temporality catalyzes our own state of great expectation, our eager anticipation of the point at which the action will finally catch up with the narration and the origin of the narrative will be clarified.[18]

Yet the narrative never returns to its own present: though Pip is emphatically exact about time throughout the course of his narration, chronicling the precise intervals of visits, the duration of events, the length of journeys, and the hours of the day, in the end the novel steadfastly refuses to fix its own time of enunciation, situating itself only as against "that time, which is far enough away now" (15). Pip mentions that he did not see Joe and Biddy "for eleven years," but the narrative does not situate itself relative to this interval, leaving it equally possible that he is narrating at the time of this reunion, or sometime after it, or very much later in life, in the manner of a deathbed confession. In general, analepses are measured by their "extent" (how much of the narration they cover) and by their "reach" (how much distance lies between the moment they cover and the present).[19] *Great Expectations* remarkably amplifies analepsis: in extent, there is never a present of narration at which the action being recounted has ceased; in reach, the moments covered by the narration have an unspecified distance from the present. I suggest that this total analepsis—the fact that the narration has no defined present from which the flashback may be differentiated—leaves us with a novel whose radically suspended temporality subverts anything as conclusive as redemption. Moreover, this unsettled account proves crucial to the novel's engagement with finance, especially the measure with which it is exactly coterminous: the 1860 legalization of futures contracts. In creating a past that does not come back to the future, the narration's strangely dangling analepsis countermands the relentless futurity of investment. The analepsis of *Great Expectations* contravenes the prolepsis of the Stock Exchange; the refusal of any definite time of enunciation, of any present at which the past meets the future, voids the very *chronos* of speculative expectation.

Great Expectations works in several ways to call attention to this temporal disjuncture. The problematic open-endedness is brought into bright light by the generally circular morphology of the plots—so many closed circles highlight the overarching one left open. For one thing, a repetitive loop propels Pip repeatedly back to Satis House, the house of sufficiency, satiation, and satisfaction.[20] Satis House sets both the origin of Pip's perspective upon himself that allows for narration and the final resting place of the narrative. As literalized in the lingering scene when he climbs the stairs of the house for the first time, the house instigates Pip's social ascendancy. Even his activities when he spends time there center on loops, pushing Miss Havisham's chair around the dining room in "the old slow circuit round about" (239). Life cycles that more broadly encircle these circuits are encoded in the name: "Satis, which is Greek, or Latin, or Hebrew, or all three—or all one to me—for enough" (56) draws a promise that the dissatisfaction it inspires will eventually come around, that what is excited will in some way be discharged, even if the final peace comes only in death. After all, this satiety of "Satis" needs merely one letter to be "stasis," laying this peace to rest at the home of stopped time and unconsummated desires, of stagnancy and suffering, of deteriorated hearts and desiccated bride cakes.

Like the recurrent returns to Satis House that emplot Pip's circular journeys, another loop encompasses Pip's plot, heightening the contrast between the novel's completed circles and the narration's incomplete temporality: Magwitch's paternity. The conventionally melodramatic question of a child's uncertain origins has a curiously condensed answer in this text. Pip's doubly occluded origins—as orphan and as beneficiary of anonymous investment—are excessively tripled by Estella's eccentric adoption. While Pip's parents cannot return from the dead, Estella's buried lineage can be uncovered in a revelation that also finally answers the enigma of Pip's patronage. Magwitch fathers Estella twice, as partner to Molly, the biological mother, and as partner in crime to Compeyson, with whom he makes Miss Havisham what she is, the adoptive mother. The peripatetic unveiling of Magwitch standing behind both Pip and Estella compresses two different types of origination into one character: he is Estella's biological father and Pip's beneficent one. Such condensation again effects a circularity of the story—both of the text's questions of origin have the same answer; both of the melodramatic revelations of origin are spoken by the same mouth. What is more, Magwitch's beneficent paternity duplicates the adoptive *pater familias* Pip has in Joe, not only because both men play fatherly roles toward this orphan, but because both men are forgers: Magwitch a swindler who forges contracts and banknotes, Joe a blacksmith who welds at "the Forge." Like the rhetoric of the pocket, Magwitch's redundant, redoubling circular paternity fires the novel's irony, converging the seminal and the financial, the corpus and the corporation. All links in the chain come around, except for the analepsis.

The Psychic Economy of Narrative Origins

Great Expectations encompasses many circular returns, even as it refuses to square the circle of its analeptic temporality. This absence of closure about the opening appears even more incongruous when we consider that the novel explicitly offers a theory of narrative origins, one that would motivate Pip's narrative even if not situating it in time. Proffered near the beginning of the novel, this theory explicitly engages the logics of psychic economy that we have seen circulating in Victorian thought. *Great Expectations* appeals to a notion of psychic economy to understand the production of fictions: because the psyche is predisposed to equilibrium, it must dispense surpluses; telling stories balances the budget. Pip's very first encounter with Estella and Miss Havisham leaves him "so humiliated, hurt, spurned, offended, angry, sorry" that he is desperate for release: "As I cried, I kicked the wall, and took a hard twist at my hair; so bitter were my feelings, and so sharp was the smart without name, that needed counteraction" (63). "Counteraction" was precisely the principle of affective "equilibrium" promulgated by the influential psychologist Alexander Bain in his 1859 *The Emotions and the Will:* "When a pain concurs with a pleasure, we find, as a matter of fact, that the one can neutralize the other . . . such also is the nature of a passionate stimulus . . . if we would neutralize it, we must provide some adequate counteractive."[21]

Perhaps because of the magnitude of his feeling, Pip only briefly finds this counteraction, saying "I got rid of my injured feelings for the time, by kicking them into the brewery wall, and twisting them out of my hair" (63). When he arrives back at the forge, that humble home newly alien to him, the feelings resurface. Asked about his adventures, Pip invents an outlandish tale to inflate the wonders of Satis House (though it remains a tad unclear just what about a half-mummified deserted bride in a deserted brewery requires embellishing with black velvet, enormous dogs, and veal cutlets). Admitting his fabulations later, Pip sources the story in his pain: "Then I told Joe that I felt very miserable . . . and that there had been a beautiful young lady at Miss Havisham's who was dreadfully proud, and that she had said that I was common, and that I knew I was common, and that I wished I was not common, and that the lies had come of it somehow, though I didn't know how" (70). Rather than apologize for lying to Joe, and rather than presenting their actual exchange, Pip reports a summary in which the rhetoric of psychic economy, of counteracting excitation and release, authorizes fictions full of hyperbolic detail and displaced desires.

If at a critical level this implies that the very idea of psychic economy lends itself to extreme tropological productions, it also provides, at a logical level, an explanation for Pip's macro-narrative (not just the lies, but the confession; not just the embedded story, but the frame). Pip spins yarns when he hurts. Such a *raison d'être* for Pip's overarching story helps us make sense of an anomaly in the narrative structure, two striking moments of apposition:

> That was a memorable day to me, for it made great changes in me. But it is the same with any life. Imagine one selected day struck out of it, and think how different its course would have been. Pause you who read this, and think for a moment of the long chain of iron or gold, of thorns or flowers, that would never have bound you, but for the formation of the first link on one memorable day (72).

> O dear good Joe, whom I was so ready to leave and so unthankful to, I see you again, with your muscular blacksmith's arm before your eyes, and your broad chest heaving, and your voice dying away. O dear good faithful tender Joe, I feel the loving tremble of your hand upon my arm, as solemnly this day as if it had been the rustle of an angel's wing! (141)

As the first indirect apposition pierces the fourth wall of the story and hails a *reader* rather than a listener, the second direct apposition to Joe seemingly appoints him as that reader. But then the question arises: why does Joe receive an apology in the *form* of narrative, but not *within* the narrative? Why might Joe be "you who read this," but never be he who hears it? It doesn't take much of a reading to observe that there is nowhere in the novel a scene of explicit apology to Joe—that Pip commands "strike me Joe, tell me of my ingratitude," but doesn't take ownership of it himself, that he allows Joe to smooth over the troubles, and that he never confesses the origin of his relationship with the convict. Associating storytelling with the idea of psychic economy represents the narrative as a whole as an act of counteraction, of atonement for the guilt of bad acts to attain equilibrium, but such associations also focus our eye on the remaining disequilibrium, the unspoken apologies to Joe.

A novel with an irresolute ending, a novel with an unclosed narration harkening from an unspecified future—these are problems overlooked when we canonize *Great Expectations* as a novel of redemption.They point to the incompleteness of Pip's development—to the folding of the narrator back into the character who cannot see himself. This incompletion, I have argued, goes some way to explaining the disjunctive analepsis—Pip's self-consciousness is partial, and therefore his narrative must also be partial. The irony forged around the blacksmith Joe exposes the plot's lack of reconciliation, reinforcing the lack of development conveyed by the temporal disconnect. Although reportedly matured, Pip remains in bad standing. His account is in the red.

Psychic Downsizing

The narrative and emotional imbalances made legible by the psychic economy image in the case of producing fictions come into even greater relief at crucial points when Pip uses the image to inventory his feelings.We have already noted that he offers no direct apology to Joe; instead, Pip tabulates his debts to Joe and Biddy, whom he calls "my creditors":"I shall never rest until I have worked for the money . . . and sent it to you . . . don't think that if I could repay it a thousand times over, I suppose I could cancel a farthing of the debt I owe you, or that I would do so if I could!" Like the credit plan that here betokens emotion, the few moments of regret that Pip voices only to himself are sadly impeached by the persistence of the logic that inspired the misdeeds in the first place, a compulsive investment scheme, always on to the next thing, the financialized self. And here we come to the novel's critical engagement with the metaphor of psychic economy. Pip's ongoing entanglement in the psychic economy metaphor undermines both his alleged growth and that metaphor itself as it unfolds in other contexts.

Trouble begins with Estella, the star-like object of desire always out of Pip's universe. In clearly admitting that he was "all the while knowing the madness of my heart to be so very mad and misplaced" (129), Pip makes no mistake about the confusion of economic and affective registers from which his love springs:"Truly it was impossible to dissociate her presence from all those wretched hankerings after money and gentility that had disturbed my boyhood . . . in short, it was impossible for me to separate her, in the past or in the present, from the innermost life of my life" (236). From the perspective of narratorial access to the character's psychic interior, Pip portrays his "innermost" intimate existence as a confusing collapse of romance and resentment. The story accords an independent force to this confusion by making it the sole source of Pip's love for Estella, since their actual interaction would doubtless fail to inspire such feelings. After all, the reader can hardly fail to remark that the lovely Estella never once falters into sweetness to Pip nor gives him excuse to imagine that she will soften, telling him frankly that such softening is impossible: "you must know that I have no heart. . . . I have no softness there, no—sympathy—sentiment—nonsense" (237). And just a bit later he can discern that "she held my heart in her hand because she willfully chose to do it, and not because it would have wrung any tenderness in her, to crush it and throw it away" (270). In the absence of an emotional rapport, Pip's feelings for Estella are minted entirely from her glittering surface, from the shame and stirrings of class ambition she ignites in him, and from the sheer force of manipulated repetition, like some kind of compulsory prayer to mold the believer: "Miss Havisham's words, 'Love her, love her, love her!' sounded in my ears. I adapted them for my own repetition, and said to my pillow, 'I love her, I love her, I love her!' hundreds of times" (243).

As she signifies Pip's confusion of finance and feeling, Estella characteristically enunciates the psychic economy metaphor in parsimonious terms. She herself admits she has "no heart," and she callously advises Pip on the rules of trade: "Since your change of fortune and prospects, you have changed your companions . . . necessarily . . . what was fit company for you once, would be quite unfit company for you now" (237). This directive integrates Pip's shame of Joe and brings new clarity to his prospectus for his company. To get with Estella, he must give up Joe; for the prospect of an uncertain future with a fickle female, he must roundly renounce the fires of the forge.

That profit-and-loss model, precisely the rubric that logically follows from representing the psyche as economic, organizes all three of Pip's moments of self-reproach about his conduct toward Joe. The first moment comes during Joe's acutely undesirable visit to Pip in London. Rather cold and impatient with Joe throughout the evening, Pip at last learns that Joe has actually come to deliver a message from Estella. "I felt my face fire up as I looked at Joe. I hope one remote cause of its firing may have been my consciousness that if I had known his errand, I should have given him more encouragement" (224). The narrator's show of modesty, his hoping for a shred of redeemable intention in the bad actions, remains predicated upon the conceit of using Joe as a means to an end: treating him better in order to more expediently access Estella. Treating Joe better for his own sake is simply not material.

Precisely this logic recurs in even balder form at the plot's climax, the second moment of reproach, when Pip discovers that his speculation about his benefactor was unfounded, and consequently that he has made a bad investment: "the sharpest and deepest pain of all—it was for the convict, guilty of I knew not what crimes . . . that I had deserted Joe" (323). Sharpest and deepest, yet still shallow: the unfortunate, unavoidable implication here is that *it would have been worth it* to desert Joe for Estella, but deserting him for Magwitch is a raw deal. Even from the purview of repentant hindsight, the narrator Pip still sees his affiliates through the very same economic formula that made Joe expendable in the first place. Thus the novel makes a very specific investigation of the consequences of this metaphor, contributing a literary critique of the ruling ideas under financialization: figuring the self as an economy rationalizes ethically dubious rationing of affective ties. Pip's persistent investor framework, his commitment to trading up, conspicuously entails the exclusivity of his affections. He simply cannot imagine loving Estella *and* loving Joe.

Pip's ruthless zero-sum logic regarding Joe is that much more charged for its contrast with Joe's own logic of reciprocity and generosity, for its likeness to Mrs. Joe's stinginess. Joe's values are most powerfully crystallized in his trademark form of speech, what Pip calls his "arguing circularly," his characteristic tautologies: "lies is lies," "your health is your health," "a gridiron is a gridiron," around the clock. Via these circuitous routes, the blacksmith Joe locates not only "the identity of things," but the self-referentiality of language; the irony smelting around him calls figurative language back to its figurative status. Joe's tautologies also betoken reciprocity in love of family and friends. Thus "the tenderness of Joe was [so] beautifully proportioned to my need" (466), and "If I had been easier with Joe, Joe would have been easier with me" (222), and so forth. The aneconomic generosity of Joe's gift love is illustrated by the stark contrast with the nasty Mrs. Gargery's garnishing of the young Pip's earnings to repay her for the burden of nurturing an orphan sibling:

> a money box was kept on the kitchen mantelshelf, into which it was publicly made known that all my earnings were dropped. I have an impression that they were to be contributed eventually towards the liquidation of the National Debt, but I know I had no hope of any personal participation in the treasure (43).

Explicitly aligned here with one of the most common investment vehicles, Mrs. Gargery brokers an emotional parsimony that appropriates monetary compensation.[22] She offers only "a hard and heavy hand" (8) and hard unloving declarations, like her first words in the novel: "(I) brought you up by hand . . . and why did I do it, I should like to know! . . . I don't! . . . I'd never do it again! I know that" (11). Mrs. Gargery is tireless in her reminders that Pip burdens her acutely, and she uses this burden to excuse siphoning his earnings.

By contrast, Joe operates outside the bounds of such mean economy: freely loving Pip, carefully nursing him back to health after the dramatic denouement (and despite their estrangement), and, most strikingly, paying off all of the debts Pip has accrued in expectation of his Expectations. It is the disavowed and unrectified asymmetry of this relationship to Joe that annuls most psychoanalytic readings of *Great Expectations,* which emphasize the disproportion of Pip's guilt.[23] Far from excessive, Pip's guilt is insufficient: never apologizing for abandoning Joe, never repaying Joe for his affection, Pip instead pays forward to Herbert. In this way Pip's declarations of character growth draft his moral redemption not within an arena of mutuality, reciprocity, or even the gift, but rather within the financial world of investment. While this irony should shift the way we think about the redemption trajectory of the novel, it also points to something unredeemable about trading up, forsaking the reciprocity of hearth emblematized in Joe's fires and tautologies for unsure bets on uncertain requiting. Even as an edified, self-aware narrator, Pip is ensnared in a regime that exceeds him, a cultural prism that compulsively banks on the rhetorical exchange between psyche and economy.

That prism also refracts the novel's starkest moment of self-reproach, when Pip has returned to his hometown to see Miss Havisham and is busy convincing himself that he shouldn't "inconvenience" Joe with a visit to him, as well:

> All other swindlers upon earth are nothing to the self-swindlers, and with such pretences did I cheat myself. Surely a curious thing. That I should innocently take a bad half-crown of somebody else's manufacture, is reasonable enough; but that I should knowingly reckon the spurious coin of my own make, as good money! An obliging stranger, under pretence of compactly folding up bank-notes for security's sake, abstracts the notes and gives me nutshells; but what is his sleight of hand to mine, when I fold up my own nutshells and pass them on myself as notes! (225)

Surely a curious thing. While this language is ostensibly delivered by narrator-Pip as against character-Pip's frauds, the narrator's import of economic metaphors to define self-relations upholds the character's misrepresentations: narrator and character share the same rhetorical commingling of psyche and economy that has caused trouble in the first place. Through the awkward anacoluthonic syntax of the recriminations and the arrhythmia of the exclamations ("but that I should knowingly reckon the spurious coin of my own make, as good money!"), the novel bristles around this intersection of economic language and personal interiority. Everything from "manufacture" to "abstraction," from "security" to "pretence," from self-deceit to self-delusion, folds into cheating, swindling, counterfeiting. Through all these repetitions of fraught motifs of investment—doing the deed of investing in Herbert, sacrificing the substantive goods of the present for the elusive fruits of the future, tendering economic metaphors as self-recrimination—Pip's putative moral development dramatically depreciates. He is deplorable as a person wholly produced by the psychic economy model of subjectivity.

A Bank of Some Sort

These patent repetitions of the psychic economy metaphor become the means by which *Great Expectations* ironizes Pip's *Bildung*. Proliferating, ungrounded economic figures, figures promiscuous in their powers of conjuring, overdetermine Pip's intimate relations, metaphorizing the "innermost life of my life." *Great Expectations* reveals the logic that united financialization and psychic economy—the logic of economic tropes destabilizing and misdirecting relations of hearth and heart. The ultimate revelation of this troping of the self comes in a stunning moment of literalization. Pip and Herbert engage in an organizational bookkeeping they call "looking into our affairs," through which they collocate their debts, transcribing scraps of paper into an official ledger. It is worth quoting at length:

> We spent as much money as we could, and got as little for it as people
> could make up their minds to give us. We were always more or less miserable, and most of our acquaintances were in the same condition. There
> was a gay fiction among us that we were constantly enjoying ourselves,
> and a skeleton truth that we never did . . . the sound of our pens going
> refreshed us exceedingly, insomuch that I sometimes found it difficult to
> distinguish between this edifying business proceeding and actually paying
> the money . . . we always ran into new debt immediately, to the full extent
> of the margin, and sometimes, in the sense of freedom and solvency it

imparted, got pretty far into another margin. But there was a calm, a rest, a virtuous hush, consequent on these examinations of our affairs that gave me, for the time, an admirable opinion of myself. Soothed by my exertions, my method, and Herbert's compliments, I would sit with his symmetrical bundle and my own on the table before me among the stationary, and feel like a bank of some sort, rather than a private individual (276).

Now, one of the striking things about this sequence is that what would probably be the stressful activity of reconciling accounts that are "getting on badly" is instead experienced as relaxing, inducing a release whose power is flaunted by its repetition: "a calm, a rest, a virtuous hush." The brunt of this counterintuitive effect would seem to further uphold the psychic economy thesis: emotional life is subject above all else to a principle of oscillation—from stress to calm, from misery to refreshment, from freedom to rest. However, dallying too much with this notion rather precipitously gives rise to category errors in self-perception. Exulting in the rhetoric of psychic economy can make "private individuals" mistake themselves for financial institutions and financial institutions mistake themselves for private individuals.

Besides being a fallacious construction, the bank of the self is, as the accounting scene shows, financially insolvent. The bankruptcy of psychic economy is further confirmed by the repetition of Herbert's erroneous formula of capital in terms that chart his diurnal emotional vacillations:

he looked about him with a desponding eye at breakfast-time; that he began to look about him more hopefully about mid-day; that he drooped when he came in to dinner; that he seemed to descry Capital in the distance rather clearly, after dinner; that he all but realized Capital towards midnight; and that at about two o'clock in the morning he became so deeply despondent again as to talk of buying a rifle and going to America, with a general purpose of compelling buffaloes to make his fortune (273).

In these associations of cyclical affect with poor understanding of finance, the novel embarks on a critique of the imperfect homology between the psyche and the economy.

If the irony in and around the person who is the product of exorbitantly circulating economic figures negates the redemption trajectory and intimates that the person is not what he seems, this is perhaps because *Great Expectations* finally portrays not a personal character, but an institution of the person—as Pip accords, "I felt like a bank of some sort, rather than a private individual." Here where the private individual dissolves into a bank, where the first person becomes the corporate person, where the psyche gilds as an economy, the irony of Pip's first-person tale realizes in the linguistic sense— performs, formalizes—the facades of personation countenanced by finance.

As the irony of *Great Expectations* smolders before us, it locally undermines Pip's *Bildung,* and it continually undoes the forms of the person—selfish and intimate, private and corporate—that order our world. It is this profound, complete irony (narrative, temporal, situational, figural) that crystallizes the novel's financial thinking: "what connection can there be" between unaccountable persons and proliferating economic figures, between a past that does not come back to the future and a network of fantastic expectation that subsumes all substantive relations of the heart and the hearth? The prosopopoeia of the corporate person, the propulsive velocity of financial poiesis— these are, to recall the lament of the *Morning Chronicle,* the "fictions in which we move, live, and have our financial being," the fictions that comprise the regime of the fictitious.[24] The time out of joint, the rhetoric of the pocket, the irony forged around the blacksmith Joe—these are the means through which *Great Expectations* ironizes not only Pip's development, but also the figures we still live by—the means through which it unmasks the prosopopoeia of the corporate person, arrests the metaleptic momentum of financial poiesis, and stresses the paradoxes of realizing fictitious capital. This irony accrues to close readers. Those who are *busy*—verifying the novel's correlation to technological advances in blacksmithing or train travel, to spice trade ledgers or the advertisements that appeared with the serial—can easily miss it. And what a cold, wrinkled shame to miss that irony, the heat of its pressing on the financial metaphors that corrugate our world.

3. *The Economic Problem of Sympathy*

Parabasis and Interest in *Middlemarch*

Mr. Casaubon had imagined that his long studious bachelorhood had stored up for him a compound interest of enjoyment, and that large drafts on his affections would not fail to be honoured; for we all of us, grave or light, get our thoughts entangled in metaphors, and act fatally on the strength of them.

Thoughts entangled in metaphors. Of all the indelible adages in *Middlemarch,* that paragon of nineteenth-century novels, this one may be the most cherished. Critics love its reverence for the powers of literary language, its awe before metaphor's fatalities. For this book the lure of this line comes not from its generality, but its specificity, the precise example it furnishes of perilously entangling metaphors: psychic economy, the conflation of financial instruments and affective states. Casaubon imagines that his transactions with the world will repay his psychic savings with pleasurable returns—that his affections will appear to others as creditable windfalls. In taking the rhetorical exchange of intimacy and economy as the archetype of a dangerous metaphor, *Middlemarch* (1871) directly inveighs against the psychic economy construct that we have seen to coordinate Victorian political-economic discourse after the mid 1850s. I argue in the following pages that concern about this construct animates both the romance plot of the novel, in which the excessively passionate heroine moderates her redistributive convictions to pursue true love, and the novel's distinctive narrative mode, in which an excessively meddlesome narrator's mediation of the affections between characters and readers results in conspicuous formal disruption.

Economy chez Eliot

If the works of Eliot factor none too frequently into studies of literature and finance, they nonetheless rank highly among critics focused on psychology and moral philosophy.[1] Indeed, of late in Victorianist circles, the very name "George Eliot" is synonymous with "sympathy," the very idea of her novelistic practice evoking ethical experimentation. In these thoughtful accounts Adam Smith's model of sympathy stands unsurpassed as a formulation of the fundamentally *aesthetic* structure of affective exchange: in order to feel with others, we must imagine ourselves in their place, crafting a scene, painting a picture, or penning a narrative that enables us to substitute ourselves for the intended object of our sympathy.[2] Tabling for later a discussion of the ideological limitations of Smith's formula, let us simply note by way of beginning that Eliot herself identified an additional, rather different source of inspiration, one who points to sympathy's inextricable connections not to aesthetics, but to economics: Thomas Carlyle. In his 1843 *Past and Present*, Carlyle decried the reduction of "all the engagements of man" to the "cash-nexus," and he charged the Victorians to create alternative media for "the relation of human beings":

> We call it a Society; and go about professing openly the totalest separation, isolation. Our life is not a mutual helpfulness; but rather, cloaked under due laws-of-war, named "fair-competition" and so forth, it is a mutual hostility. We have profoundly forgotten everywhere that Cash-payment is not the sole relation of human beings; we think, nothing doubting, that it absolves and liquidates all the engagements of man.[3]

Though Friedrich Engels thought the world could do with fewer novels and more Carlylean indignation, Eliot's 1855 review of *Past and Present* cited it as a catalyst for her turn to the novel genre:

> The most effective educator aims less at perfecting specific acquirements than at producing that mental condition which renders acquirements easy; does not seek to make his pupils moral by enjoying particular courses of action, but by bringing into activity the feelings and sympathies that must issue in noble action. . . . The influence of such a writer is dynamic. He does not teach men how to use sword and musket, but he inspires their souls and sends a strong will into their muscles. He does not, perhaps, enrich your stock of data . . . but he strikes you, undeceives you, animates you.[4]

Animated with the Carlylean vitality so appreciable here in her vigorous verbs and perpetual present tense, Eliot would soon after this review compose both "The Natural History of German Life," a manifesto for her realism, and *The Sad Fortunes of Amos Barton,* her first fiction. In both of these texts and thereafter, Eliot endeavored to keep pace with Carlyle as a "dynamic" and "effective educator" defined by a twofold effect: "bringing into activity the feelings and sympathies that must issue in noble action." Her renowned strategy involved crafting a realist aesthetic whose careful attention to the experience of socially diverse fictional characters could inspire feeling with and therefore "noble action" on behalf of real people.[5] In oft-quoted maxims like "if art does not enlarge men's sympathies, it does nothing morally"; or "the greatest benefit we owe the artist is the extension of our sympathies"; or "art is the nearest thing to life; it is a mode of amplifying experience and extending our contact with our fellow-men beyond the bounds of our personal lot," Eliot venerated sympathy as the *raison d'être* of her aesthetic.[6]

Although many scholarly accounts have explored how Eliot's sympathetic aesthetic designs sympathy itself as an aesthetic practice, the Carlylean catalyst reveals that Eliotian sympathy was also pivotally situated with respect to an alternative axiologic: the economic. Like Carlyle, Eliot wanted sympathy to be economically operative: the "noble action" engendered by the sympathetic aesthetic was meant to remedy unsympathetic economic associations; fellow-feeling would inspire charity for those left behind by the rising tide of industrial capitalism and tame the alienation and isolation unleashed by profiteering and greed among those who prospered. Over the interval between Carlyle's decrial of the cash-nexus in the 1830s and Eliot's major works in the 1860s and 1870s, the economic dimension of sympathy became all the more pointed as the Victorians took *laissez-faire* to new extremes, perfecting that nexus in which cash exceeds its deplored role as medium of relation between human beings and, in the words of Marx, "enters into private relations with itself."[7] Financialization might even be best defined as the promotion of money's "private relations with itself," abstracting the economy from the basic needful "engagements of man" and in the process redefining "economy" as a constitutively tropological sphere. With the birth of the corporate person, the booming volume of investment, and the development of instruments like futures contracts, the cash-nexus became an intensely structured network of metaphoric and metaleptic mediations further complicating "the relation of human beings." In articulating sympathy with the economic in addition to the aesthetic, Eliot therefore engaged a rapidly changing complex of values in which "economy" was more and more figuratively inflected. Her notion that sympathetic affect can be economically efficacious illuminates the prehistory of compassionate conservatism, impugning sympathy as the paramount bourgeois bargain: one who deeply feels common humanity can call himself ethical and thereby absolve himself of political responsibility to restructure economic inequality. More immediately, however, Eliot's project to think sympathy and economy together torques the very figure of sympathy itself. Invested with economic importance and investigated with economic language, Eliotian sympathy itself starts to appear as an economy. Sympathy figures as an economy of attention and affection—a distribution of psychological resources—subject to laws of scarcity and clamoring for regulation. This appearance is of a piece with the broader Victorian logic of rationalized affect and equilibriate desires that "psychic economy" denominates.

Whether distilled in single words like the quantifiers in all the maxims quoted above ("enlarge," "extend," "amplify") or dispersed throughout the entire rhetorical system of a novel like *Middlemarch,* this figure of the economy of sympathy primarily represents, as it did for Adam Smith, a presumed scarcity of resources.[8] The problem of sympathy's limited supply and inequitable apportionment surfaces everywhere from *Adam Bede*'s early prospectus for benefitting "more or less ugly, stupid, inconsistent people" to *Daniel Deronda*'s later program for consolidating a "too diffuse sympathy."[9] Although recent readers find in sympathy's limits evidence that Eliot feared violating the alterity of the other with too much assimilative sympathy, the scarcity connotations of her imagery posit a subject who has only so much to give.[10] Constrained from the inside out, sympathy threatens less the swallowing of the other than the bursting of the self, with consequences that Eliot explicitly deems fatal.

In this light Eliot's sympathy often reveals connections to the broader Victorian psychic economy constellation. But like Dickens and Trollope, Eliot in no way naively adopted the truisms propounded by psychology and political economy. Her engagements with sympathy as an economy are profoundly complicated by the standards she scrupulously elaborated at the start of her novelistic career, which directly conflict with simple scarcity principles. In "The Natural History of German Life" she opined, "We want to be taught to feel, not for the heroic artisan or the sentimental peasant, but for the peasant in all his coarse apathy, and the artisan in all his suspicious selfishness."[11] Sympathy, it would seem, becomes an ethical category precisely to the extent that it enjoins us to transcend our proclivities for the exceptional—heroic, sentimental, lovely. Sympathy worthy of its name reaches out toward the thoroughly unsympathetic, resisting its instinctual dispensation and exceeding any economy of feeling. Moreover, sympathy must always oppose "the vulgarity of exclusiveness," exceeding partiality and striving for generous inclusion.[12] Given this redistributive expansiveness of the ethical as such, the limited distribution implied by the economy image grants immunity against ethical imperatives. Victorian psychology and political economy became infatuated with the economy metaphor of mental and affective functioning, but Eliot's philosophy of sympathy primed her to render the costs of that figure more transparent: the assertion that the subject can only tolerate limited quantities of excitation and affection would seem to naturalize the contingent constriction of social ties that Carlyle and Eliot decried in the cash-nexus.[13]

Thus, while the economy of sympathy figure usefully distills the scarcity that prompts Eliot's ethical plea, it soon thwarts those ethics in advance. Nowhere is this contradiction more acutely construed than in *Middlemarch,* a text remarkable for the economic rhetoric employed by the narrator to deliberate sympathy and for the narrator's anxious tone. Reading that anxiety as a symptom of that rhetoric, the novel can be seen mapping the attractions and dangers of the metaphor of the economy of sympathy. Along the way the novel works in both thematic and narrative registers to evade the ethical pitfalls in the economy model of sympathy by refiguring "economy" itself. Where it initially evokes the concrete scarcity of sympathy that troubles Eliot, economy later comes to signify metaphoric excesses projecting ever outward. This refiguring, I maintain, parallels both financialization's reorganization of the dynamics of "economy" and the rise of the rhetoric of psychic economy. Under financialization, economic production and transactions moved away from finite material goods and toward abstract representations of value like derivatives, untethering "economy" from connotations of closure and constriction, adjoining it instead onto images of open expansion. At the same time, as this book analyzed in Chapter 1, prose thinkers in a variety of traditions were constructing the continuity between psychology and economics emblematized by psychic economy.

By transforming the economy of sympathy from a scenario of scarcity to a refraction of finance, *Middlemarch* performs the developments in the consolidation of financial capitalism with which it is contemporaneous in both penning and setting. An indispensable stimulus for financialization was the

1833 Bank of England Charter Act, which both authorized the Bank to print paper money and repealed bans on usury, normalizing the money-begotten-by-money that previous epochs from Aristotle to Defoe had deemed "monstrous birth."[14] Set in the 1830s in the run-up to the Charter Act, *Middlemarch* is consumed with questions of usurious and non-usurious gifts, loans, and debts, and the legal formalization of interest dynamically materializes in the text's thought about sympathy. This happens in three ways. First, the figure of the economy of sympathy shifts over the course of the book, initially connoting a scarcity of goods, but eventually connoting an expansive financial horizon. Second, in making this shift, the narrator recodes "sympathy" as "interest," evoking the polysemy of personal and pecuniary shares in the same project. Third, and most strikingly, these developments in the sympathetic economy are elaborated by the formal disruptions to which I earlier alluded, strange moments in which the text is conspicuously self-reflexive. These moments formalize the self-reflexive pattern of financial "interest," money generating more of itself. As these recurrent, extra-diegetic moments break the frame of the narrative, they reverberate with ironic energy, accentuating the metaphoric contrivance of the sympathetic economy.

In the first part of this chapter I focus on these impressive narrative structures in *Middlemarch*, suggesting that their amalgamation of financial form and affective content encapsulates the novel's vexed connections between sympathy and economy. I propose to call these structures by the Greek term "parabasis" (meaning "to step beside") because they are distinctive in their extra-diegetic stance: they are moments in which the narrator steps beside the text to talk about the allocation of sympathy within it. Parabasis may thus be thought of as a subset or particular case of the class of metalepsis as defined by Genette—the transgressive code-switching between levels of discourse. Parabasis is also the stroke whose "permanent" repetition comprises irony as defined by Friedrich Schlegel and appropriated by de Man.[15] *Middlemarch*'s recurrent and dramatic parabases, I argue, frenetically ironize the very idea of an economy of sympathy and thus of psychic economy more generally.

Middlemarch's parabases are regulative insofar as they intervene in and codify an economic distribution of interest, but they are also excessive, because they are self-reflexive dispositions that stand beside the narrative to call attention to narrative ethics. They are therefore unusual for their inversion of this novel's normal narrative economy, in which a tightly woven web encompasses problematic excesses of various kinds (Dorothea's ardency and her wealth, Will's aestheticism, Casaubon's jealousy, Rosamund's greed, Lydgate's profligacy, Fred's debt, Bulstrode's deceit). Furthermore, they are notable for their difference from the more generic intrusions for which Eliot's narrators are both commended and reviled. The difference lies in the degree to which their self-reflexivity performs and intensifies their content: the reflexive narrative about narrative mobilizes the reflexive contour of "interest" through which money accumulates itself. I read this extraordinary dimension of the narrative form as a measure of the complexity of *Middlemarch's* economic thinking. In their content, the parabases advocate sympathetic interest; in their form they perform financial interest; and in their effect of irony they disclose the inconsistency of a sympathy that ostensibly ethically opposes economized relations, even as it draws its form from them.

In the chapter's second portion I attend to another aspect of this irony, contending that the novel attributes this ethical inconsistency to capitalist modernity, principally by emplotting an opposition between the ardent ethics and "fanaticism of sympathy" of the philanthropist Dorothea Brooke and the normative wisdom of Adam Smith. Dorothea initially envisions sympathy as the ways and means of an alternative resource allotment, but is compelled over the course of the novel to moderate her "fanaticism," learn to "understand political economy," and accede to the economized sympathy it calls "interest."[16] As the novel draws to a close, Dorothea's concession to this economy of sympathy brings the compensatory pleasures of romantic love. In a complementary fashion, the parabastic narrator engineers a deal for its own distribution of sympathy that allows the novel to arrive at a consoling conclusion. Yet both of these deals crackle with disquiet, evincing the novel's ongoing trepidation and ambivalence about both of the economies of sympathy it explores. By calling attention to the aestheticized quality of its thematic and formal compensations, *Middlemarch* moves to theorize sympathy as the "moral currency" of the realist novel and the affective correlative of financial capitalism.[17]

Parabasis and Dangerous Metaphors

In Chapter 1 I explored the metaleptic sliding by which the image of psychic economy came to organize much Victorian psychological and political-economic thought after the mid 1850s. Eliot's most proximate intellectual circle was deeply engrossed in such thought. The psychological writings and literary criticism of her consort, George Henry Lewes, and their mutual friend, Herbert Spencer, regularly employed the language of "economy" in discussing both literary form and ethical affect, establishing an important touchstone for Eliot's representation of psychic economy. Lewes deemed what we now call realism "Economy of Art" and composed his "Principles for Success in Literature" with a first principle of "the Law of Economy."[18] "Economy" was the basis from which all other aesthetic principles were derived and referred predominantly to a strategic equilibrium between an author's language and a reader's comprehension: "Economy dictates that the meaning should be presented in a form which claims the least possible attention to itself as form, unless when that form is part of the writer's object, and when the simple thought is less important than the manner of presenting it."[19] The purpose of this inconspicuous form is to enable the most efficient readerly assimilation:

> It is the writer's art so to arrange words that they shall suffer the least possible retardation from the inevitable friction of the reader's mind. The analogy of a machine is perfect. In both cases the object is to secure the maximum of disposable force, by diminishing the amount absorbed in the working.[20]

When a writer lacks this art, a reader "wastes, on interpretation of the symbols, force which might have been concentrated on meditation of the propositions."[21]

We have already reviewed Herbert Spencer's crucial role in promoting economic images of psychic dynamics. Lewes's *Principles* markedly reproduce Spencer's earlier treatise, "The Philosophy of Style," which emphatically insisted that the economy of art was warranted by "the economy of mental sensibilities":

> Language is the vehicle of thought, we may say that in all cases the friction and inertia of the vehicle deduct from its efficiency; and that in composition, the chief thing to be done, is, to reduce the friction and inertia to the smallest amounts. Let us then inquire whether economy of the recipient's attention is not the secret of effect, alike in the right choice and collocation of words, in the best arrangement of clauses in a sentence, in the proper order of its principal and subordinate propositions, in the judicious use of simile, metaphor, and other figures of speech, and even in the rhythmical sequence of syllables.[22]

The economy of literature is framed by the "economy of attention," which Spencer took as the inexorable fact that "a reader or listener has at each moment but a limited amount of mental power available."[23] As the "cause" of good literary style, the economy of attention is also the cause of the corollary economy of emotion, for Spencer classes emotions as simply more complex forms of thought, constructing a parallelism between the "economy of mental energies" and the "economy of mental sensibilities."[24] The "generalization" that a law of excitation and release, expansion and contraction governs the energetic economy is "equally true" of the sentimental economy.[25] Literary form must therefore respond to an economy of scarcity of mental energy and sentiment.

When Spencer praised the assured effect of Eliot's prose ("I can scarcely imagine any one reading it without having their sympathies widened and their better resolves strengthened"), he might therefore just as well have praised her obeisance to the law of economy.[26] Though glad for his approval, Eliot could not quite square her sympathetic mores with the equation between literary economy and affective economy, and would object to Spencer's causal connection between the economy of sentiment and the economy of literary form. She was well acquainted with the economy of narrative as both a material necessity and a stylistic merit, but her elemental premise that literature could widen our sympathies directly contradicts any mean economy of sentiment. If sympathies are rigidly economized, what can be the point of writing novels? More pressing, since "our good depends upon the quality and breadth of our emotion," how can the sympathy economy coincide with an ethical subject?[27]

It is this tension over the interaction of narrative economy and sympathetic economy that sparks the parabases in *Middlemarch,* which contemplate narrative practice in economic language. In one such moment the narrator contrasts the profligate digressions of bygone novelists with his own consideration for costs:

> But Fielding lived when the days were longer (for time, like money, is measured by our needs), when summer afternoons were spacious, and the clock ticked slowly in the winter evenings. We belated historians must not linger after his example; . . . I at least have so much to do in unraveling certain human lots, and seeing how they were woven and interwoven, that all the light I can command must be concentrated on this particular web, and not dispersed over that tempting range of relevancies called the universe (132).

"This particular web" is woven with expediency and efficiency, containing digressions and conserving time and money. Despite all the humor in this critique of the affable Fielding, there hovers an urgency and imperative that avouch something more grave: all those wincing qualifications ("I *at least*," "*certain* human lots," "*this particular* web") and overreaching requirements ("time," "money," "needs," "must not linger," "so much to do," "all the light I can command," "must be concentrated") augur an anxious reluctance about the constraints the passage intended to justify. More than just a reprimand to the less disciplined Henry Fielding, these qualifications bear the earmarks of the immanent limitations of working with scarce resources. Time, money, light, concentration—all are measured by need, and demand seems to outpace supply.

Even with this inscription of the economy of narrative form, *Middlemarch* pursues different insights about its correlation to the economy of sympathetic sentiment. Lingering at length over Caleb Garth, for example, the narrator, not otherwise functioning as a character in the action, acknowledges that this award of specificity and time stems from her acquaintance with and love of Caleb, neither of which the reader shares:

> He took the paper and lowered his spectacles, measured the space at his command, reached his pen and examined it, dipped it in the ink and examined it again, then pushed the paper a little way from him, lifted up his spectacles again, showed a deepened depression in the outer angle of his bushy eyebrows, which gave his face a peculiar mildness (pardon these details for once—you would have learned to love them if you had known Caleb Garth), and said in a comfortable tone— (219).

With the interruptive force constitutive of parabasis, conspicuous self-consciousness erupts here: the direct address to the reader, the graphic paratext of parenthesis, and the repetition of the action of the passage ("measure(ing) the space at his command") in the narrative self-measurement (the plea for pardon). All this pointed fervor trembles around the unstable equation between narrative space and sympathetic affection—for the conditional "you would have learned to love them if you had known Caleb" not only folds affection into acquaintance; it also intimates that "love" is means enough to widen this particular web. In this moment, at least, the economy of sentiment is not the cause of the economy of narrative form; quite the contrary: it is the means of exceeding the textual economy. The novelist who devised her art to promote such sentiment could not entirely align with Lewes and Spencer on this question of the economy of feeling. While there is no guarantee that holdings in the narrative economy will mature into sentimental dividends (and hence so many moments of narrative injunctions like "think no unfair evil of her, pray" or "the faults will not, I hope, be a reason for the withdrawal of your interest in him"), to presuppose an economy of sympathy would be to defeat in advance the purpose of fiction (268, 159). Eliot's sympathetic imperative instead leads her to quite the opposite conclusion as Lewes and Spencer: the economy of narrative form catalyzes an economy of sympathy.

This departure from Lewes, Spencer, and the predominant discursive frame of psychic economy piques *Middlemarch*—especially its formally distinctive parabases. Not far into the novel's first book, the narrative assumes its first oddly self-reflexive stance. Readers have just been introduced to the dilettantish Will Ladislaw, but the narrator inveighs against passing "a too hasty judgment," advising, "Among all forms of mistake, prophecy is the most gratuitous" (77). Lest one be duped by this very caution into committing another mistake (exempting from judgment only special characters), the narration takes a remarkable turn—the paragraph breaks and markedly shifts to the present tense and the first person: "But at present this caution against a too hasty judgment interests me more in relation to Mr. Casaubon" (77). Up to this early point the narrator has entertained less than charitable appraisals of Casaubon (most amusingly, "he has got no red blood in his body . . . somebody put a drop under the microscope, and it was all semicolons and parentheses . . . he dreams of footnotes" [65]). Retracting these foregone devaluations of Casaubon's soul, the following parabasis equally scolds the readers, whose sympathies have too hastily gone awry, and the narrator, whose narrative has too capriciously promoted its protagonists. Stepping beside his own preceding narration and the collective judgments he has elicited, the speaker of this retraction singles himself out by using the first-person-singular voice for the first time in the novel ("at present this caution interests me"). And as this voice reverberates under the smart of its correction, it redoubles into a first-person plural:

> Suppose we turn from outside estimates of a man, to wonder, with keener interest, what is the report of his own consciousness about his doings or capacity: with what hindrances he is carrying on his daily labours; what fading of hopes, or what deeper fixity of self-delusion the years are marking off within him; and with what spirit he wrestles against universal pressure, which will one day be too heavy for him, and bring his heart to its final pause. Doubtless his lot is important in his own eyes; and the chief reason

that we think he asks too large a place in our consideration must be our
want of room for him (78).

As the narrator aligns himself with the reader by using the first-person-
plural pronoun, he closes the gap between narrative form and readerly interest: they conjoin as the same economy, which reigns over the rhythm of this
passage itself. Like the pulse of expenditure and withdrawal that Neil Hertz
gauges in Eliot's journals and letters, a movement of expansion and contraction hums within this novel: the meter taps out an economy of narrative
feeling.[28] At first the shift from "outside estimates" in toward Casaubon's
"own consciousness" discovers there the possibility of "universal pressure."
Already in the next sentence, however, this expansive turn to a suppositional
universalism of the heart contracts, abutting the economy that has exiled
Casaubon from our affections: "our want of room for him." That economy is
at once textual and affective, a scarcity of narrative room and readerly sympathy merged under the common "our." The polysemic "want" is further
indication of the equivocation: do we lack room, or are we unwilling to give
it? These are the poles of the ethical antagonism inherent to the economy
model of sympathy: is the limit to sympathy our inability to feel, or our un-
willingness? Would not any true ethics demand that both limits be equally
trespassed?

   This trespassing enormity of the ethical continuously violates the narrative economy, provoking the excesses of self-reflexive parabasis. The most
monumental parabasis quite vividly tears apart the very syntax of ordinary
narrative progression:

> One morning, some weeks after her arrival at Lowick, Dorothea—but why
> always Dorothea? Was her point of view the only possible one with regard
> to this marriage? I protest against all our interest, all our effort at under-
> standing being given to the young skins that look blooming in spite of
> trouble; for those too will get faded, and will know the older and more
> eating griefs which we are helping to neglect. . . . Mr. Casaubon had an
> intense consciousness within him, and was spiritually a-hungered like the
> rest of us. . . . For my part I am very sorry for him (261).

The anxious anacoluthon here—the grammatical incompletion, the graphic
interjection of the dash—frenetically bespeaks the strain of the ethical imperative for abundance. One would think it behooving an ethical code that
it is difficult to fulfill, but here narrative is rendered literally disjointed, im-

possible. For, as the proprietary tenor of "for my part" rings clear, a narrative whose narrator was ethically edified in keeping her part to herself would progress no further than a narrative whose every sentence was broken midstream by its own ethical protest against too much focus on any given character. While it may be a legitimate constraint of nineteenth-century fictional form that focalization tends toward the individuated and successive, rather than the collective and sustained, Eliot here again finds an exclusive "point of view" to cause the exclusivity of "all our interest."

Like the parabasis with which I began, there is an acute apprehension in this momentous eruption about the inequity of Casaubon's share—ugly, unsympathetic, self-aggrandizing Casaubon. Taken in concert, these moments intone both an admission of what Alex Woloch would consider "asymmetrical distribution of attention" and an ethical intervention against that asymmetry.[29] The breadth of that ethics, I have been maintaining, drives these strange narrative structures. Even though the parabases are often motivated by solicitude for those dispossessed in the economy of sympathy, it must be noted that they also arouse unease about the fortunes of that economy's heir apparent, the heroine. During one of the most painful periods of disillusionment for Dorothea, when "all this vast wreck of ambitious ideals . . . jarred her as with an electric shock," the narrator is compelled to oddly reduce Dorothea's intense emotion to "not . . . anything very exceptional" (181), and to proceed with low expectations for readerly sympathy:

> nor can I suppose that when Mrs. Casaubon is discovered in a fit of weeping six weeks after her wedding, the situation will be regarded as tragic. Some discouragement, some faintness of heart at the new real future which replaces the imaginary, is not unusual, and we do not expect people to be deeply moved by what is not unusual (182).

It is a somewhat contrived treatment of the heroine's extreme suffering, and I would submit that the contrivance symptomatizes the narrator's confusion about whether indulging the heroine necessarily means depriving other characters. So charged are the stakes that observing the probable lack of readerly sympathy—even for the heroine, even at the acme of her troubles— paves the way for the ultimate formulation of the inexorable economy of sympathy:

> That element of tragedy which lies in the very fact of frequency, has not yet wrought itself into the coarse emotion of mankind; and perhaps our

frames could hardly bear much of it. If we had a keen vision and feeling of all ordinary human life, it would be like hearing the grass grow and the squirrel's heart beat, and we should die of that roar which lies on the other side of silence (182).

One of the novel's most commonly beatified adages, this diagnosis of Attention Surfeit Disorder consecrates a scarcity of sympathy—a scarcity that equally disadvantages unsympathetic "semicolons and parentheses" and preeminently sympathetic protagonists. Even if the narrative can afford more sympathy toward its heroine than toward her obstructive nemesis, both will eventually founder in the economy of sympathy.

The solemnity and foreboding of this passage betoken the severity of the ethical deadlock the novel reaches. While cautious not to presuppose the fatal metaphor of psychic economy confidently bandied about by the broader Victorian discourses of finance, psychology, and even literary criticism, the narrator nonetheless recounts a limit to sympathy whose violation is equally fatal. What I would like to propose now is that the very form in which this deadlock is broached—the irony of parabasis—brilliantly provides a way out: parabasis models extension via self-reflection. When the "economy" in "psychic economy" evokes a system of exchanging one durable good for another, the distribution of sympathy can only be finite. But when, as under financialization, "economy" means the exchange of metaphors for themselves, the self-reflexivity of capital begetting capital facilitates infinitely expansive circulation. Just as finance boomed in the period between the novel's setting and its penning, Eliot's sympathetic economy undergoes a comparable structural adjustment: the sympathy that cannot be literally extended is reformulated into an interest that can be metaphorically so. The solution to narrative economy, and therefore sympathetic economy, is metaphor:

> Since there never was a true story which could not be told in parables where you might put a monkey for a margrave, and vice versa—whatever has been or is to be narrated by me about low people, may be ennobled by being considered a parable.... Thus while I tell the truth about loobies, my reader's imagination need not be entirely excluded from an occupation with lords; and the petty sums which any bankrupt of high standing would be sorry to retire upon, may be lifted to the level of high commercial transactions by the inexpensive addition of proportional ciphers (320).

Here Eliot's own "economy of art" emerges as the forum in which petty sums pass into high commercial transactions on the security of metaphor, "proportional ciphers." Significantly, this method of ennobling limited narratives by imaginatively investing outward buys *Middlemarch* a certain ethical breathing room, but it also reverses realism's reputed privileging of metonymy over metaphor.[30] Rather than driving toward particularity, promoting an exchange of types for individuals (as Gyorgy Lukacs and Catherine Gallagher have argued), Eliot here trades "loobies for lords."[31] With such an exchange of types for other types, the aesthetic and ethical principles of Eliot's realism cohere around metaphor. As this coherence is explicated through patently financial language, Eliot reformulates the ethical promise of her realism by borrowing the metaphorical premise of the financializing economy. Metaphor becomes the means, in the words of Gillian Beer, of "reaching constantly at something that is near it, at qualities which elude or strain, or poignantly are debarred to us."[32] For "want of room," for the debarring fatal "roar," neither the realist novel nor the sympathetic subject can represent or feel for everyone. But through metaphoric exchange the novel can broker transactions that propel outward, and the "reader's imagination need not be entirely excluded" from making substitutions that exceed these bounds. Through this brokerage the economy of narrative form can once again cause an economy of sympathy, with the difference that both economies are opened away from scarcity by the propulsions of metaphor.

In consecrating these emanations *Middlemarch* passes its own Bank Charter Act, tuning its philosophy of sympathy to the chorus of Parliament Members, journalists, and bankers who supported that 1833 law. As was clear in the Parliamentary debates and media coverage around the act, unrestricted interest is the necessary precondition and medium of a financial economy in which money buys and sells itself in a diverse variety of self-reflexive instruments devised to issue returns—an economy, in other words, of fictitious capital. "The repeal of Usury laws," proclaimed the *Morning Chronicle* on the day after the act's introduction, will "increase circulation and augment fictitious capital."[33] Constellated as interest, sympathy is reformulated from an economy of goods governed by scarcity and lack to an economy of finance licensed by interest and governed by ceaseless exchange. "Interest" is the affective dispensation of fictitious capital. The utmost tribute to this redemptive diffusion is the immortal final words that enable the book at last to rest in peace:

But the effect of her being on those around her was incalculably diffusive:
for the growing good of the world is partly dependent on unhistoric acts;
and that things are not so ill with you and me as they might have been,
is half owing to the number who lived faithfully a hidden life, and rest in
unvisited tombs (785).

"Incalculably diffusive" applies both to Dorothea's effect and to the effect of *Middlemarch* itself. The surplus sibilance ("re*s*t in unvi*s*ited tomb*s*")
of the novel's final words vibrates beyond the closed economy of the text
and any closed economy of sympathy. As all those "s" syllables swirl around
the second person in a future indefinite, but always apace with the present
tense of "rest," that celebrated Carlylean pulse "strikes you, undeceives you,
animates you."

With these financial flows *Middlemarch*'s figurative move from scarcity to
emanation displaces, rather than resolves, the contradiction between expansive sympathy and narrow economy. In place of the critical socioeconomic
program Carlyle outlined for sympathy, Eliot here amalgamates sympathy
and finance. We have seen how a scarcity economy of sympathy is problematic in that it installs an exculpatory limit to ethical obligations. But
the financial economy of sympathy is even more so, for it dissipates any
opposition between economic relations and sympathetic ethics by creating an "analogous relation between the moral tendencies of men and the
social conditions they have inherited"—for, in other words, calibrating "the
social affections" to the scales of advancing financial capitalism.[34] No longer
emboldening ethical critiques of the "mutual hostility" of *laissez-faire,* as in
its early conceit, the sympathy performed in the late *Middlemarch* is formally
consistent with financialization and its attendant alienations.

But *Middlemarch* is not without dismay over its appropriation of the financial topology of metaphor. Composed in the early 1870s at a point in
financialization by which both investment mania and chronic crises were
lived reality, and looking back to one origin of all that turmoil in the early
1830s, the novel's long view of finance and its many subplots of financial
distress manage the necessary risk that an interest economy busts as often
as it booms. While reconstituting sympathy as interest and reconceiving the
scarcity economy of feeling as a financial economy of feeling, *Middlemarch*
also murmurs about risk and loss. Through this inquietude the novel's realism critically ruminates on the tropes encompassing finance and intimate
affiliation.[35] Ironizing the coincidence between the philosophy of sympathy

and the formalization of finance, the novel exposes the collusion between normative wisdom of the psychological self and emergent economic activities: the economy of sympathy realizes fictitious capital. Crucial gestures in the novel delineate this exposure. The plot surrounding the unsavory banker Nicholas Bulstrode is only the most obvious. Guilty of deceit, diversion of funds, and perhaps even negligent homicide, Bulstrode gives the banking industry a bad name and the episodes in which he appears a tense air. "Bulstrode seems the most unsympathetic fellow" in the entire novel (658), and when his crimes must be confessed to his wife, tremendous effort is required to set aside her shame and "espouse his sorrow" (707). While Mrs. Bulstrode can silence her reproaches, she cannot verbalize her sympathy:

> Open-minded as she was, she nevertheless shrank from the words which would have expressed their mutual consciousness, as she would have shrunk from flakes of fire. She could not say, "How much is only slander and false suspicion?" and he did not say, "I am innocent" (708).

Quite tellingly here, there is no simple marriage between sympathy and finance.

I will return to other such gestures later, but for now let us turn to the most emphatic. All the while that it has been improvising a financial metaphor, the narrative has from the outset explicitly delineated the danger of financial metaphors. The precise warning, our epigraph, comes just after the very first parabasis:

> Mr. Casaubon had imagined that his long studious bachelorhood had stored up for him a compound interest of enjoyment, and that large drafts on his affections would not fail to be honoured; for we all of us, grave or light, get our thoughts entangled in metaphors, and act fatally on the strength of them (79).

Of all the sentences in *Middlemarch,* this is probably the favorite of literary critics—but only in its truncated form: habitually, the phrase before the semicolon is left unquoted.[36] Such truncation unfortunately occludes the precision of the meta-literary pronouncement here. Metaphors in general may entangle us, but the particular archetype of such entangling, the ur-metaphor, is the conflation of financial interest and emotional affection. Psychic economy is *the* paradigmatic dangerous metaphor.

On the strength of this construct, one might act fatally. As was the case in *Great Expectations,* these bad acts include rationalizing away our ethical obligations (if sympathy is a precious resource, not everyone deserves our stores), and codifying precepts about psychology that naturalize a historically specific socioeconomic structure. When the novel proposes the substitution of loobies for lords, offering metaphor as an outsourcing solution to the problem of scarcity and reorienting sympathy as interest, it conflates sympathy itself with the very cash-nexus that Eliot and Carlyle conceived sympathy to redress.

The danger of this metaphor is only exacerbated by its prevalence: not peculiar to Casaubon, the economy of sympathy is a figure in which "we all of us" are implicated. In point of fact, economic figures for affect tellingly consumed Eliot herself in letters from the time of writing *Middlemarch*. "I never before felt so keenly the wealth one possesses in every being to whose mind and body it is possible to minister comfort through love and care," she wrote in a letter of December 10, 1869 to Harriet Beecher Stowe.[37] Just a few months later this "wealth" is amassing: "For learning to love any one is like an increase of property—it increases care, and brings many new fears lest precious things should come to harm. I find myself often thinking of you with that sort of proprietor's anxiety."[38] Both of these letters commit Casaubon's error, casually presuming such language's suitability for intimate correspondence.

But where Eliot herself vacillates on the metaphor, debating with Spencer and Lewes while nonetheless un-self-consciously inscribing it in her letters, the novel sustains a more critical contemplation, starting with its self-conscious implication of the narrative in the fatal actions against which it cautions. Indeed, one need only reread the parabasis with which I began to confirm this epidemic: the exhortation to a "keener interest" that initiated the foray into Casaubon's thoughts practically trips over these conjunctures. We all of us get entangled in metaphors, and recognizing this pervasiveness is the necessary first step to unmaking them.

The Political Economy of Sympathy

The extent to which the novel is preoccupied with means-testing the psychic economy metaphor can be seen in the plot's repetition of what we have just explored as the narrative's dilemma. As the parabases achieve a tenuous ethics by reformulating economized sympathy into the propulsions of "interest," a corresponding denouement transpires in the plot, which follows the philanthropist Dorothea Brooke as she moderates her "ardent sympathy" to more greatly reflect political economy. My analysis focuses on the economic tensions in the dominant plot of Dorothea's *Bildung* and her courtship with Will, but I take this major plot as exemplary rather than exceptional, for many of the minor plots also revolve around such tensions.[39] The major plot recapitulates the narrative's formal dilemma: Dorothea's misgivings about resource distribution echo those of the narrator's about sympathetic distribution, and the compromise she makes to mitigate these concerns rehearses the parabastic embrace of financial exchange.

While in the parabases it is the polyvalence of "interest" that often intones the novel's articulation of sympathy and economy, in the romance plot the same conjunction is accomplished through the minor, yet essential "character" of Adam Smith. Both in name and in idea, Smith appears in the pages of *Middlemarch* as a philosopher both of capitalism and of sympathy. Though it is not generally received as such, Smith's *The Theory of Moral Sentiments* seems to have functioned as a strong precedent for the praxis of sympathy in *Middlemarch,* and there are a number of judicious references to *The Wealth of Nations* in the novel.[40]

In *The Theory of Moral Sentiments* Smith's depiction of sympathy as metaphoric is practically philological: his famous definition of sympathy as an imaginative activity to "carry us beyond our own person" by "changing places in fancy" with another deploys a transliteration of the Greek "metaphor": "carrying beyond."[41] What is so noteworthy about his conception (and what marks Smith's break from earlier theorists of sympathy) is the total refusal that sympathy could operate as spontaneous affinity for an other, and instead the insistence that sympathy is always a self-motivated exchange tendered by metaphor.[42] Sympathy in Smith is never feeling for an other in her own right; it is always feeling "what we ourselves should feel in the like situation"—there is no such thing as feeling for the other, only self-interested projection.[43] *The Theory of Moral Sentiments* apprehends this scarcity economy of sympathy as a product of nature: "Nature, it seems, when she loaded us with our own sorrows, thought that they were enough, and therefore did not command us to take any further share in those of others."[44] To exceed these insuperable bounds, sympathy can only operate metaphorically. Both the scarcity economy of feeling and the metaphoric exchange that extend that economy are Smithian constructs *Middlemarch* appropriates at the level of narrative form through the parabases that at once avow the scarcity of sympathy and affirm the potential of metaphor to overcome material limitations.

In just this visage as theorist of the economized sympathy that grounds capitalism, Smith also makes a cameo within the plot as Dorothea's ethical and political antagonist, serving to foreground the conflict between Dorothea's uneconomized ardent sympathy and the discourse of political economy. "Ardent" is the preferred descriptor of Dorothea, who is "alive to anything that gave her an opportunity for active sympathy" (191), and who is throughout the novel busy "trying to get light as to the best way of spending money" to help others (756). In the first few pages of the novel, when she debates with the more learned male characters, Dorothea pronounces of philanthropy with characteristic zeal: "It is better to spend money in finding out how men can make the most of the land which supports them all, than in keeping dogs and horses only to gallop over it. It is not a sin to make yourself poor in performing experiments for the good of all" (16). Mr. Brooke roundly dismisses her sentiment: "Young ladies don't understand political economy, you know. . . . I remember when we were all reading Adam Smith. *There* is a book now" (16).

Exactly what Dorothea does not understand takes some maneuvering to establish. For she certainly grasps economic injustice all too well, channeling "all her desire to make her life greatly effective" into "schemes" for redistribution, and opining "we deserve to be beaten out of our beautiful houses—all of us who let tenants live in such sties as we see around us" (29). To motivate an opposition between this ethical economic knowledge and political economy, the novel might easily rely on extant ethical critiques of what Carlyle termed "the dismal science." With more nuance, however, it orchestrates a clash between the ardency of Dorothea's generosity—the "gift" branded in her name *dorothea*—and the scarcity restraints reified by the dismal discourse of economics.

When Dorothea kindles another version of the same debate about "the good of all," this tension comes into stark relief. The scene is her first substantive interaction with Will during a visit to an art museum on her honeymoon in Rome:

> "I fear you are a heretic about art generally. How is that? I should have expected you to be very sensitive to the beautiful everywhere."
>
> "I suppose I am dull about many things," said Dorothea, simply. "I should like to make life beautiful—I mean everybody's life. And then all this im-

mense expense of art, that seems somehow to lie outside life and make it no better for the world, pains one. It spoils my enjoyment of anything when I am made to think that most people are shut out from it."

"I call that the fanaticism of sympathy," said Will, impetuously. "If you carried it out you ought to be miserable in your own goodness, and turn evil that you might have no advantage over others. The best piety is to enjoy—when you can. And enjoyment radiates. It is of no use to try and take care of all the world; that is being taken care of when you feel delight—in art or in anything else" (205).

There are great Kantian overtones of beauty and the *sensus communis* here, and a strict Kantian sense of "fanaticism" as the supercession of limits. Even more remarkable than this philosophical resonance is the aesthetic debate's overt economic valence: Dorothea's "fanaticism of sympathy," an expansive concern for "everyone," economically opposes Will's "radiat(ing)" individual "delight." Because art is inaccessible, it does not do enough in the world; because it is bounded and finite, it will always "shut out" "most people." When Dorothea sees "the beautiful everywhere" she perceives this vulgar exclusivity. Her commitment to collective enjoyment logically complements her sensitivity to mass suffering, "all the troubles of all people on the face of the earth" (730). By contrast with this aneconomy, Will counters with a more moderate localized "piety" of "enjoyment" that "radiates," an idea deeply evocative of Smith's infamous figure of the "invisible hand," with which, "by pursuing his own interest (every individual) frequently promotes that of the society more effectually than when he really intends to promote it."[45] Indeed, Will's disquisition on the fanaticism of sympathy makes the very same Smithian point in even stronger terms: "It is of no use to try and take care of all the world; that is being taken care of when you feel delight—in art or in anything else."

The divergence in aesthetic judgments between Will and Dorothea involves not so much a difference in taste as this economic conflict between lateral equitable expansion and trickle-down radiation: while Dorothea would socialize access to art, Will would disseminate aesthetic enjoyment. Curtailing her fanatical sympathy and becoming a young lady who does "understand political economy" are therefore two sides of the same coin, and with this coin Dorothea buys into the economy in which sympathy cannot be literally extended/expended—it can only be metaphorically circulated through substitutions, monkeys for margraves, one figure for another, along the metaleptic chain.

Refiguring the causal association between Dorothea's ardent sympathy and her ignorance of political economy, this lover's quarrel between expansion and radiation accordingly instantiates the dissolution of extensive sympathy into emanating interest that I have asserted plagues the narrative form itself. Sharing these conflicts, the plot and the narrative ultimately share a solution. Just as the narrative settles on the framework of interest to inflate its sympathetic economy, the plot espouses the framework of "radiating delight"—for Dorothea eventually marries Will, a final choice that has scandalized every reader from the first reviews in 1871 to recent issues of *English Literary History*.[46] While these readers are usually quite frank about their simple dislike of Will and therefore tend to confine their analysis to the characterological level, the novel as a whole seems less bothered by his personal shortcomings than by the fact that he comes at such a high price, both fiscally and ethically.

Will's dear value is set by Casaubon. Dorothea's original marriage offered her an irresistible opportunity "to be of some use," both as a secretary for Casaubon's *Key to All Mythologies* and as a philanthropist backed by his funds. When "The Dead Hand" of Casaubon's will mandates that Dorothea forfeit her fortune if she marries her Will, it adumbrates a chasm between love of man (philanthropy) and love of one man (monogamy).[47] Dorothea faces a choice between lovingly pursuing "the good of all" and pursuing her singular beloved, between resisting market logic and consummating the principle of the Invisible Hand by obeying the mandate of the Dead Hand. The belabored, uncertain, and climactic choice of Will represents the great act amid this masterful catalog of "unhistoric acts": Dorothea simply loves him, and so she opts for this private pleasure, economizing her fanatical sympathy and downsizing her redistributive program. With her pick Dorothea also confirms the great ethical decision of the parabases, the construction of a radiating economy of sympathy. Far from an error marring *Middlemarch,* as it is so commonly perceived, the marriage to Will might therefore be reappraised as the novel's careful emplotment of its acute formal dilemma.

Indeed, the marriage is further legitimated by the text's meticulous certification that, though the price is high, Dorothea completely comprehends price: the romantic climax of her decision is bookended with references to political economy that highlight her learning. Having up until this late point capitulated to Casaubon's codicil, Dorothea is at work "in the library before her particular little heap of books on political economy" (756). Will enters the scene to take his final leave in what the text portends as the last word on their unactualized love. He is fortuitously derailed by the dramatic eruption of a bolt of lightning, after which he seizes Dorothea's hand with "a spasmodic movement" (761). She exclaims, "Oh I cannot bear it—my heart will break," and casts off her troublesome fortune:"I don't mind about poverty—I hate my wealth," choosing Will over the will of the dead hand (761). The by no means euphoric closing words of the chapter seal their vows: "We could live quite well. . . . I want so little—no new clothes—and I will learn what everything costs" (762). Choosing Will means withdrawing from philanthropy, which also means overcoming ignorance of political economy to "learn what everything costs." Moreover, to return to the dilemma about sympathy, this knowledge redefines sympathetic and loving communions to be "spasmodic" rather than ardent. In the hard-won union between Dorothea and Will, *Middlemarch* therefore does more than repeat Smith—it evolves the notorious missing link between the two major moments of his thought, the sympathetic *Theory of Moral Sentiments* and the self-interested *Wealth of Nations*.[48] Through Dorothea's romantic preference and the narrator's realist techniques, the novel illuminates that financialization grounds itself on the streamlined subjectivity of the psychic economy.

The spasmodic, radiating, political economy–sanctioned merger of Will and Dorothea certainly hushes her economic critiques and stoppers her philanthropic restitution. But the novel calls attention to the artifice of this compromise—with the lightning bolt's overwrought evocation of the pathos of nature simulating the lovers' passion, with the setting of the lovers first prolonged conversation in an art museum, and with their distressingly understated bliss. Like the Bulstrode plot, these gestures reiterate the keenest ironic zest in the text, the unshakable angst of parabasis itself. In both the plot and the narrative, these hyper-aestheticized gestures illustrate that, while abandoning the ethical mandate for expansive sympathy in favor of the prevailing radiating interest may well enable Dorothea to actualize personal happiness and the narrative to close the book on further exploits monkey or margrave, this development is itself aestheticized and dangerous, made possible by "get[ting] our thoughts entangled in metaphors and act[ing] fatally on the strength of them."

Through the melodramatic frisson of this conspicuous aestheticization the novel becomes less an instrument and more an illustration of the entangling of sympathy and economy. Via irony, in other words, *Middlemarch* indicts modernity's sympathy-economy figure as a metaphor upon whose strength we might act fatally. Though the narrator and Dorothea both quell their distress about inequitable distribution by incorporating the radiations of the financial economy, the text as a whole tarries over the tropology of this bargain. Its irony rustles: "we deserve to be beaten out of our beautiful houses—all of us" who accede to arrangements of dispossession because we have "but a limited amount of mental power available" to feel for others. To borrow just one of the novel's many resounding final phrases, the "incalculably diffusive" legacy of *Middlemarch* may well be this commitment to think those metaphors of relation from the bourgeoning financial economy of the Victorian era that continue to advance the triumphant neoliberalism of our own.

4. "Money Expects Money"

Satiric Credit in *The Way We Live Now*

> The novelists who are considered to be anti-sensational are gener-
> ally called realistic. I am realistic. . . . It is not sufficient that there be a
> meaning which may be hammered out of the sentence, but that the
> language should be so pellucid that the meaning should be rendered
> without an effort to the reader;—and not only some proposition of
> meaning, but the very sense, no more and no less, which the writer
> has intended to put into his words. What Macaulay says should be
> remembered by all writers: "How little the all-important art of mak-
> ing meaning pellucid is studied now!" The language used should be
> as ready and as efficient a conductor of the mind of the writer to the
> mind of the reader as is the electric spark which passes from one bat-
> tery to another battery.
>
> —Anthony Trollope, "On Novels and the Art of Writing Them,"
> in *An Autobiography*

For over 150 years the aggressively pruned realism of Anthony Trollope's
mechanically manufactured forty-seven novels has been appraised as almost clinical in the "stringent," "photographic," and "copious" manner of its
"anatomization."[1] None have been more definitive than Henry James: "Trollope, from the first, went in, as they say, for having as little form as possible."[2]
Whether the bottom line of such appraisals is amused or damning, Trollope's readers from his own century up through ours have broadly shared
this account of his deficit of form. In "On Novels and the Art of Writing
Them" and elsewhere, Trollope himself would seem to have authorized this
consensus, anticipating the reviews of his craft as a "strikingly transparent"
"absolutely literal, not metaphoric" "lack of rhetoric" with his own theory

of realism as "pellucid language"—language devoid of its inherent semantic equivocality.[3]

Realism, as Trollope stringently distinguished it from sensationalism, manumits unequivocal meanings. Nothing could be plainer here than Trollope's endorsement of Lewes's "economy of art": realism precisely adequates "means to ends, with no aid from extraneous or superfluous elements."[4] In the pellucid enterprise, the work of writing realistic novels comes to be regulated by demands for what is "sufficient," by precise quantifications ("the very sense, no more and no less"), and by an "efficient" relation between minds, while the ground of meaning becomes in turn this carefully calibrated, equilibriate relationality. Nothing could be plainer—and yet this plain text has a subtext: just as for Lewes "economy" itself is a trope, Trollope's instruction for writers in the mechanics of reference conspicuously recruits the flashy simile of "the electric spark" to most pellucidly designate pellucidity.

In its very formulation, then, Trollope's theory of unequivocal language equivocates. Beyond this figural irony there is another dimension, too, of this equivocation—a kind of situational irony: he penned his theory of pellucidity soon after writing what is undoubtedly his least pellucid text. Trollope's most elaborate satire, the financial roman-a-clef *The Way We Live Now*, foments all the usual opacities of satire: what, precisely, does the satirist deplore, and why doesn't he just tell us what to do about it? As satire *The Way We Live Now* problematizes pellucidity. And I propose that this problem is constitutive for this novel: where the metaphors in Trollope's definition of realism symptomatize an inevitable slippage from the literal to the figurative, *The Way We Live Now* interprets this irony. Composed and set immediately after the great financial crisis of 1873, a stage in financialization by which regular crises were widely expected even as the volume of and tools for investment continued to expand, *The Way We Live Now* objects to the hyperbolic proliferation of figures that we have seen the Victorians to decry as "fictitious capital." But, just like the discussion of pellucidity that is its counterpart, that novel is arguably defined by the dynamic subsumption of the literal by the figurative. Satire, in all its excess and indirection, is after all a far cry from pellucidity—and way too close to the formal technology of fictitious capital itself. Trollope contracts a dilemma in *The Way We Live Now*: the distorted bloating of satire is formally collusive with the distended hyperbole of finance. I argue in this chapter that this dilemma explains the novel's curious modal mixture: though it is widely heralded as the most "vitriolic satire" dared to be dashed off in the earnest Victorian age, a "massive social indictment" with unrelenting ire, in its final quarter, I maintain, *The Way We Live Now* patently abandons satire.[5] It is this modal crisis, not the satire per se, I will contend, that secures the novel's incisive critique of finance. Through this modal crisis the novel registers financial crisis: the implosion of its system of hyperbolic figuration performs the inevitable breakdown of fictitious capital. In its representations of finance and in its formal engagement with the figurative topologies of credit, *The Way We Live Now* thus formalizes the analysis of fictitious capital that circulated in Victorian discourse until the 1860s. At the same time it also vividly captures the psychologistic turn that we have seen to supplant that analysis. In the process of exhibiting the figurative proliferation of finance, the novel dramatizes the propulsive extrapolation of economic imagery and economic prisms to intimate arenas, depicting the psychic economy matrix as a product of the hyper-extended figurative economy. The novel ultimately discloses both the structural instability of credit and the artifice of the psychic economy idea conjured to answer this instability.

Literary Surplus

Trollope's *An Autobiography* devotes considerable attention to *The Way We Live Now*, indicating its unique place in his massive oeuvre. Curiously enough this attention consists of recapitulating, at length, the objects of the satire, as though they had not been clear in the text itself. Satire can be obdurately opaque, and this worrying of the satire is inextricably linked to concerns about satire as a procedure—one that Trollope evidently found distastefully harsh. He had complained in a letter written while *The Way We Live Now* was under construction that "there is an injustice in satire which always offends me, and robs the work of my perfect sympathy," and the *Autobiography* makes these complaints more explicit, painting the satirist as a sadist who exceeds the vices he deplores:

> And as I ventured to take the whip of the satirist into my hand, I went beyond the iniquities of the great speculator who robs everybody, and made an onslaught also on other vices,—on the intrigues of girls who want to get married, on the luxury of young men who prefer to remain single, and on the puffing propensities of authors who desire to cheat the public into buying their volumes.[6]

Through the grammatical ambivalence "I went beyond" we can trace a bizarre association between the work of the satirist, he who circulates distortions in pursuit of truth, and "the great speculator," he who circulates distortions in pursuit of wealth. "I went beyond" implies not simply that the novelist's incisive vision broadly encompasses a social panorama of suspicious speculators *and* girls on the make *and* incorrigible bachelors *and* cheating authors—not only this, but also that the novelist's practice *surpasses* "the iniquities of the great speculator who robs everybody." Trollope the author goes beyond the speculator, perpetrating his robberies not with mere words, but with that most potent weapon of excess, "the whip of the satirist." Striking a different note than earlier practitioners like Alexander Pope, who exalted in the armament of satire ("O sacred Weapon!"), Trollope laments the impulsive force of satiric violence: "Who, when the lash of objurgation is in his hand can so moderate his arm as never to strike harder than justice would require? The spirit which produces the satire is honest enough, but the very desire which moves the sage to do his work energetically makes him dishonest."[7] The satirist is complicit with the excesses he ostensibly deplores; the satirist of dishonesty is especially ensnared by the hypocrisy of his own excessive, dishonest form. With these concerns about excesses we can begin to see just how fraught are the connections between satire and the financial and literary excesses under satirization in *The Way We Live Now*.

Indeed, *The Way We Live Now* weighs in as the longest novel by one of the most prolific writers in one of the most voluble periods in literary history, ambivalently belying its critique of profligate authorship through its very verbosity. Even after finishing it Trollope continued to associate the novel with the problem of fulsome literary production, an association made rather literally by the opening of the final chapter of *An Autobiography*, in which the inspiration to write about novelists, profligacy, and dishonesty is tacitly attributed to the grunt work of hauling books. Upon moving to a new residence in Montagu Square in 1873, the "first work in settling" was to unpack and organize a library of no less than five thousand books. Directly after this description, and directly after organizing the library, *An Autobiography* explains that Trollope began *The Way We Live Now*:

> to the writing of which I was instigated by what I conceived to be the commercial profligacy of the age. Whether the world does or does not become more wicked as years go on is a question which probably has disturbed the minds of thinkers since the world began to think. That men have

become less cruel, less violent, less selfish, less brutal, there is no doubt; but have they become less honest? If so, can a world, retrograding from day to day in honesty, be considered to be in a state of progress? (353–34)

Given the narrative sequence, it is hard not to ascribe Trollope's concern with "the commercial profligacy of the age" to his firsthand experience of "how great is the labor of moving and arranging a few thousand volumes" (353). It's a rather tempting picture to imagine Trollope, surrounded by five thousand dusty tomes in want of cataloguing, projecting his predicament onto the profligate novelists of the day. But if we resist this temptation toward psychobiography, a surprising association emerges. Specious literary production, coldly calculating courtships, and financial investment—these share a logic for Trollope, the logic we have seen in Dickens and Eliot, of overextending economistic prisms through the extrapolation of economic figures. Tracking a "new era in literature, a new order of things," the satire takes aim at the market for publishing lowbrow trade fiction, at a rank sea of unmarriageable fish,—and, above all, at the structuring force of the voracious vortex of finance. In that vortex in which the economy becomes figurative, figures of economy infiltrate other arenas of life; prisms of economy over-determine other axes of relation. If *The Way We Live Now* issues from Trollope's sense of promiscuous, dishonest economic relations, it is also the case that it exposes a particular formal dynamic of those relations: the hyperextension of economic figures. In this, Trollope's novel shares the broader Victorian critique of fictitious capital that we have traced earlier; but while the prose texts we have studied dissolve that critique into psychologism, his novel, like those of Dickens and Eliot, ironizes that recursive embrace of affect or the psyche as ground.

The Absent Center and Nowness on the Move

One of the primary distinctions of *The Way We Live Now* is its instantaneous presentism. The first object of this satire, we might say, is the "now." Through its present tense, first-person-plural pronoun, and temporal deixis the title forcefully presses upon us its immediacy: "we" are all, actively, complicitly, at this moment, living in the unsavory manner about to be disclosed. Beyond the title, the explicit setting of the novel at the exact time of its composition attests to the absorbing context of the 1873 financial crisis while simultaneously activating the narrative problem of temporal immanence, of writing to the moment and breathlessly keeping pace.[8] But even if the present cannot be unendingly inhabited in the time of reading when the mode of writing is retrospective narration, the present can be fully distinguished from the past with which it has broken. As Paul Delany notes, "*The Way We Live Now* is an elegiac novel, a lament for the passing away of the old prestige order where identity depends on one's rank, lineage, and connection with the land."[9] The bygone order, personified in the novel by the hopelessly outdated Squire Roger Carbury, is an order of the identity of things, the rootedness of land, and the honesty of words evidently guaranteed by the solidly referential situation of real estate. Trollope's notes for the novel inventory all these properties: "Roger Carbury of Carbury Hall in Norfolk. 38. Straightforward. About 2000 pounds a year—ready money. Very good."[10] Here we see the constellation of plain speech, virtue, land, and hard cash. But "the spirit of honesty that was always strong within him" is what makes Roger old, just as his landed rank is what makes him outmoded.[11] Contemporary readers found him "tiresome" and "an overbearing prig," his characterological and sociological nobility unappealing in equal measure.[12] Early in the novel his own sister frames the nowness of the financial world as one in which real estate is not only not the primary source of wealth, but an encumbrance for wealth: "If a moderate estate in land be left to a man now, there arises the question whether he is not damaged unless an income also be left to him wherewith to keep up the estate. Land is a luxury, and of all luxuries is the most costly" (45). Gone are the days of land and honesty; here are the ways of finance and lies. Constant contrasts are drawn between "real money" and credit money, even as any consequences of this contrast are ancient, forgotten history:

> "Fellows used to pay their gambling debts," said Sir Felix, who was still in funds, and who still held a considerable assortment of IOUs.
> "They don't now—unless they like it. How did a fellow manage before, if he hadn't got it?"
> "He went smash," said Sir Felix, "and disappeared and was never heard of anymore. It was just the same as if he had been found cheating. I believe a fellow might cheat now and nobody would say anything" (174).

Then, there were consequences. Now, there are none. Unpaid debts and unpunished insolvents, unsecured paper and ungrounded credit: the satire rather plainly renders the networks of fictitious capital that comprised Trollope's "now."

The action in *The Way We Live Now* swirls around the absent center of Augustus Melmotte, an *arrivante* financier of uncertain origins who is presently very big in London. In the novel's frontispiece an illustration shows Melmotte standing proudly, one hand in his pocket and one hand extended, his head tilted in thought, with the simple caption, "Mr. Melmotte speculates." After the fashion of David Morier Evans's 1864 essay collection, *Speculative Notes and Notes on Speculation, Ideal and Real,* the joke derives its humor from condensing the polysemy of the verb "to speculate": the tilted head evokes contemplation; the hands evoke circulation from pocket outward and expectation of return inward; while the caption conjectures about Melmotte's thinking.[13] From this first representation onward, the novel levies its gaze at the semantic promiscuity of "speculation," which signifies vision, contemplation, and meta-investment, expecting profit from share fluctuations that are independent of underlying asset value.

Just as the frontispiece invites the reader to collude in the speculative enterprise, conjecturing about the great man, the text arouses all sorts of fantasies about him before he appears. Melmotte's introduction into the text is wending and deferred, mediated by fantasies and speculation about his daughter, herself not yet introduced, either:

> Now there was another young lady, to whom the reader shall be introduced in time, whom Sir Felix was instigated to pursue with unremitting diligence. Her wealth was not defined, as had been the $40,000 of her predecessor, but was known to be very much greater than that. It was, indeed, generally supposed to be fathomless, bottomless, endless. It was said that in regard to money for ordinary expenditure, money for houses, servants, horse, jewels, and the like, one sum was the same as another to the father of this young lady. He had great concerns;—concerns so great that they payment of ten or twenty thousand pounds upon any trifle was the same thing to him (21).

The unnamed man at the center of it all is, like his wealth, "not defined," and the layering of passive constructions of what "was known" and "was said" and "was generally supposed" encodes the ambiguities of agency and opacity that do define him. These mediations are repeated in the passage leading up to his actual introduction into the text, when the budget and guest list for an ostentatious ball are "talked about," "expressed," and "declared" for two pages, until "it became known at the last moment," "though how this had been achieved nobody quite understood," that incredible amounts had been spent, that royalty would be in attendance, and that "the giver of the ball might before long be the master of considerable parliamentary interest" (30). Still yet he remains unidentified, until finally a declarative introduction is made: "The giver of the ball was Augustus Melmotte, Esq., the father of the girl whom Sir Felix Carbury desired to marry."

But no sooner is this long-awaited declaration of the novel's absent center made than its declarative force dissipates under competing accounts of his character. Sometimes a Frenchman, sometimes a Jew, certainly a hero, and perhaps a criminal, "as the great man was praised, so also was he abused" in an eddy of contrasts:

> It was at any rate an established fact that Mr. Melmotte had made his wealth in France. He no doubt had had enormous dealings in other countries, as to which stories were told which must surely have been exaggerated. It was said that he had made a railway across Russia, that he provisioned the Southern army in the American civil war, that he had supplied Austria with arms, and had at one time bought up all the iron in England. He could make or mar any company by buying or selling stock, and could make money dear or cheap as he pleased. All this was said of him in his praise—but it was also said that he was regarded in Paris as the most gigantic swindler that had ever lived; that he had made the city too hot to hold him; that he had endeavored to establish himself in Vienna, but had been warned away by the police; and that he had at length found that British freedom would alone allow him to enjoy, without persecution, the fruits of his industry (31).

Reminiscent of the famous oscillating opening passage of *A Tale of Two Cities,* extreme contrasts here provide an unstable introduction to our anti-hero. He was the best of guys, he was the worst of guys—and this volatile appraisal of Melmotte recapitulates the variable values of the complex credit instruments of which his business is made. Facts matter little, speculative representations matter immensely. The equivocality is crucial here: Melmotte himself is not the object of the satire—he is not exaggerated or distorted; rather the proliferation of ungrounded representations takes center stage. In such a climate any final analysis of Melmotte's creditability is undecidable, but that is the nature of credit itself (undecidable in advance). Like the fictitious capital that begets its own new real, "Mr Melmotte was indeed so great a reality, such a fact in the commercial world of London, that it was no longer possible . . . to refuse to believe" (74). The presumption of fact that becomes its own rationale—what Marx called "the leap" of credit—proves the irrelevance of Melmotte's creditability to his centrality. He is "the strong rock, the impregnable tower of commerce, the very navel of the commercial enterprise of the world"—a consolidated cipher of finance as such.

Melmotte's undecidable creditability bespeaks his association with a system of value that is not absolute, but relative. The newness and nowness of Melmotte are his facility with credit, his industrious installation of a "regime" under which credit transactions supersede "real" transactions in which something (land, goods) is bought with something else ("actual money"): "As for many years past we have exchanged paper instead of actual money for our commodities, so now it seemed that, under the new Melmotte regime, an exchange of words was to suffice." Though the decreasing materiality in this chain of successive displacements from "commodities" to "actual money" to "paper" to "words" *should* function here as a satiric exaggeration of the immateriality of value in the new financial economy, though the situation is one in which "the words had no reference at all," it in fact divulges the alarmingly minimal difference between "words" and "fictitious capital" (72). The fictitious capital of the "shares" of Melmotte & Co. presents the flourishing financial capitalism of the mid-Victorian era and not some satiric exaggeration thereof. Indeed, one contemporary review lamented that the novel felt too much like being at work in The City: "everybody is always striving for money by every device except work, thinking of money, talking of money, till sordidness appears the mainspring of every character, and the reader is as tired as he would be if he waited too long in a dirty anteroom in a City office."[14]

The words that are to suffice for value in the Melmotte economy include his own name: "in the City Mr. Melmotte's name was worth any money" (33). But Augustus Melmotte's very name already denominates the fragility of this "worth": no sooner has the inspiring reverence of his august first name ensured his credibility than the dishonest clang of "mal-mot" sullies it. The man whose "name was worth any money" and who can inspire financial activity "simply on his word" treads this eponymous tightrope. Words suffice, the name suffices, and soon just exhalation suffices: "money was the very breath of Melmotte's nostrils, and therefore his breath was taken for money" (268). The exaggerated metonymy of "breath taken for money" should convey that Melmotte's case is extreme, but it merely broaches the prosopopoeia actually operative in Victorian financial culture: the accordance of personhood to joint stock companies that effectively literalized "corporation" into "corpus." The would-be satiric tender of breath taken for money merely reiterates the real legal standing of the corporation in the real Victorian financial economy. Passed in 1855 and 1856, the Parliamentary acts licensing the incorporation of limited liability partnerships into a single corporate subject effectively de-personalized the individual members of a company, transubstantiating them into the corporate person. Trollope here anticipates another satire, published soon after *The Way We Live Now*: Laurence Oliphant's *Autobiography of a Joint Stock Company* (1876). Observing "of whom the Co. was composed no one knew" (71), Trollope's satiric narrator articulates the cultural indignation at the insubstantiality of the amalgamated corporate person through emphasizing the body-economic that secretes corporate dealings:

> Melmotte was not only the head, but the body also, and the feet of it all. The shares seemed to be all in Melmotte's pocket, so that he could dis-tribute them as he would and it seemed also that when distributed and sold, and when bought again and sold again, they came back to Melmotte's pocket. Men were contented to buy their shares and pay their money, sim-ply on Melmotte's word (268).

"Simply on Melmotte's word" should again be our indication that there's no there there. But this would-be exaggeration of the exchange of words ulti-mately occasions some of the novel's most direct insights into the financial economy, once again bringing the satire into alarming proximity with the "oppressively real" value of words.

If, as Dickens's *Household Words* instructed, it was possible to "raise a ficti-tious capital at the commencement of your business by the stroke of a pen," the "exchange of words" Trollope designs to exaggerate this possibility folds back upon itself as simple documentation.[15] The world of fictitious capital— the world in which, as David Morier Evans noted, "the speculative mania of such a fantastic kind, that the very names of the 'Bubble companies' . . . look like a sarcasm upon speculation in general"—cannot be exaggerated by the world of fiction; it can only be registered.[16] We find this registration in the murky, circumlocutionary, and mumbo-jumbo-lala quality of the actual financial transactions depicted in the satire. The world is flat: tautology is the new physics, metalepsis the reigning trope. "Where's the money to come from?" one hopelessly helpless corporate board member asks another, who only returns the question: "Money to come from, sire? Where do you sup-pose the money comes from in all these undertakings? If we can float the shares, the money'll come in quick enough" (69). The question is answered with itself; money comes from where it will come from.

Like this "Who's on First?" routine, tautologies and paradoxes supera-bound in the novel, propounding the critique of finance as the illicit genesis of something from nothing. A Melmotte Companies board meeting, in the chapter simply entitled, "The Board Room," assembles the "directors of the company," who enjoy the profits of the business but "do not in truth know anything about it," for a bit of corporate theater (285). Once the meeting "was now commenced as usual," one member attempts to read aloud recent records, "stumbling over every other word, and going through the perfor-mance so badly that had there been anything to understand no one would have understood it" (282). Lack of understanding is never an obstacle, and the meeting progresses mostly informally, with small conversations around the floor and no official business, except for "flipping bits of paper across the table," so many symbols of floating shares and unanchored words.

One hollow gesture is made by "the great head of it all": "'Gentlemen,' said Mr. Melmotte, 'it may perhaps be as well if I take this occasion of saying a few words to you about the affairs of the company.' Then, instead of going on with his statement, he sat down again, and began to turn over sundry vo-luminous papers very slowly" (283). For twenty minutes the board members amuse themselves "flipping their paper pellets backwards and forwards" until finally Melmotte pronounces:

> If I know anything of the world, I know something of commercial affairs. I am able to tell you that we are prospering. I do not know that greater prosperity has ever been achieved in a shorter time by a commercial company. . . . I am able to inform you that in affairs of this nature, great discretion is necessary. On behalf of the shareholders whose large interests are in our hands, I think it expedient that any general statement should be postponed (284).

The ambivalent constructions ("I do not know"), the highly conditional certainty ("If I know anything"), and the sheer assertion without the trouble of facts ("we are prospering") evince the satire's effect of negation, while the long-awaited statement that turns out to recommend postponement captures the futurity and deferral of finance. Only one board member sees through the smoke and mirrors, protesting that directors "ought to know what is being done. We ought to know where the shares really are. I for one do not even know what scrip has been issued" (285). Without missing a beat, Melmotte retorts, "You've bought and sold enough to know something about it" and leaves his chair "so as to show that the business of the board was closed for that day without any possibility of reopening it." Conclusively, emphatically, end of story: in the effects become proof of their cause—there are shares, there must be a there there. In this way *The Way We Live Now* illustrates the metalepsis we have seen Marx and other Victorian financial thinkers locate at the heart of finance.

Metaleptic formulations constantly recur in the novel. Just as Melmotte declares "we are prospering" and the company marches on thereafter, sheer assertion seems in general to wield the power to make the money "come in quick enough"—assertions become imperatives; effects become proof of their cause:

> There is money going. There must be money where there is all this buying and selling of shares. Where does your uncle get the money with which he is living like a prince at San Francisco? Where does Fisker get the money with which he is speculating in New York? Where does Melmotte get the money which makes him the richest man in the world? (321)

With these images of the metaleptic sway of finance, *The Way We Live Now* depicts "a tower of strength . . . built upon the sands," an economy "standing on ground which might be blown from under . . . at any moment" (74, 172). This is the economy of credit, "dealings in unsecured paper" through which men "pay nothing" for everything, "even get (their) hair cut on credit," and write down debts as "just paper" (79, 23, 193). What is more, according to the novel, the ungroundedness of finance is an open secret; what matters is not whether men believe in the credit system, but that they all participate in it, even though they avow its defaults—what matters is that they disavow. For *The Way We Live Now* the material illusion of fictitious capital is that it grows stronger as more people come to know its weakness; that the more men "understand how delicate a thing is credit," the more they participate in credit transactions (566). "When a man's frauds have been enormous, there is a certain safety in their diversity and proportions," and when an economy's base is fraudulent, strength stems from its actors' willful ignorance (472).

Capturing this quicksand of finance, the novel contrives a syntax of swishing, slippery movement:

> He had been put in the way of raising two or three hundred pounds on
> the security of shares which were to be allotted to him but of which in the

flesh he had as yet seen nothing. Wonderful are the ways of trade! If one can only get the tip of one's little finger into the right pie, what noble morsels, what rich esculents, will stick to it as it is extracted! (78)

Raising hundreds of pounds now on the basis of unsecured nothings promised in the future—this is the metaphysical swerve by now familiar to us. The swerve materializes in the striking sibilance of this passage—the surplus of "s" phonemes—the excess of "esculents," the ambiguity of the sticking, the hissing swerve of "s" and "x" in the chain "morsels . . . esculents . . . stick . . . as it is extracted" (an effect repeated elsewhere, as when Melmotte is referred to as a "surfeited sponge of speculation")—which simulates the sticking it apprehends as the accretion of wealth from out of the speculative vortex of inflation and deflation.

In effecting this slippery sibilant ground, the novel presents verbal speculation as both narrative tone and plot arc. Whistles onomatopoeize what the novel calls "the system of puffing," the hissing and whispers of speculative murmurs that set swindles aswirl. Gossip is in fact given overweening force in the novel by the way in which it constitutes the plot and defines the narrator's tone. Shifts from dialogue to diegesis are often accomplished by way of incredulous or affirmative repetitions that form verses of gossip. Apropos a remark from Mr. Alf, "She's a nice little girl enough . . . but how is she, poor thing, to talk to royal blood?" the narrator chimes in "Poor thing indeed!" (39). At other moments, the narrator's gossipy exclamations more directly hail the reader: "Was there ever treachery like this!" (163). But most dramatically, the narrative circulates unattributed speech. In a hilarious inflation of Jane Austen's formidable first line, "It is a truth universally acknowledged," in *The Way We Live Now* practically every chapter begins "it was known," "it had been confidently asserted," "it was rumored," "there is a general opinion," or "it was very generally said," creating hundreds of pages of diegesis that are dizzyingly unattributed. The resulting gossipy speculations that define the narrative equally define the action of the plot.[17]

Huffing and Puffing and Blowing the House Down

Melmotte repeatedly theorizes "that peculiar susceptibility of great mercantile speculations," cautioning that the precarity of the financial system issues from "gentlemen who don't know the nature of credit, how strong it is,—as the air,—to buoy you up; how slight it is,—as a mere vapour." This vaporous strength is difficult to fully grasp, and men less wise than Melmotte "don't understand how delicate a thing is credit." "How delicate a thing is credit" formulates the novel's essential critical point about rampant and intertwined financial and social speculation. Indeed, *The Way We Live Now* represents the delicacy of credit and volatility of finance as a compounding of finance's own tropological system (its exchange of words) by the information about it that circulates in the form of rumor—ungrounded words. "Speculation" triply names this delicacy, for speculative instruments like futures contracts circulate figures as value; speculative statements both propel and obstruct that circulation, and "speculation," in the semantic promiscuity activated from the frontispiece onward, effectuates this material efficacy of words.

Where words are omnipotent, as our anti-hero Melmotte states very clearly, "it isn't what I've lost that will crush me, but what men will say that I've lost" (621). It is absolutely crucial to the novel's account of finance that ultimately what crushes Melmotte is neither swindling, nor bad investment, nor the failure of the company he floats, but the collapse of his reputation, the deflation of his word. In the financial economy, words work as the "material illusions" Marx grasped with the concept of "fictitious capital." It follows logically that they have material effects, a point both Trollope and the financial journalist Walter Bagehot penned in the same year:

> Incipient panic amounts to a kind of vague conversation: is A.B. as good as he used to be? Has not C.D. lost money? And a thousand such questions. A hundred people are talked about, and a thousand think—"Am I talked about, or am I not?" "Is my credit as good as it used to be, or is it less?" And every day, as a panic grows, this floating suspicion becomes both more intense and more diffused. . . . No doubt all precautions may, in the end, be unavailing . . . banks which hold the reserve may last a little longer than the others; but if apprehension pass a certain bound, they must perish too.[18]

Even earlier, in reporting on the financial crisis of 1847, David Morier Evans employed personification to capture this agency of speculation: "Rumor, in the mean time, had insidiously pointed her finger at several houses, which, she avouched, would be unable to resist the strong current of the crisis."[19] Trollope's satire therefore operates in the same discursive register as financial journalism: it achieves a "realistic" picture of the world of fictitious capital. That this documentary effect comes through, rather than despite, the hyperbolic distortions mandated by the technology of satire should prompt us to view the question of the novel's mode in relation to the paradoxes of realizing capital.

Today's readers, whether scholarly or lay, have no qualms about celebrating *The Way We Live Now* as the most vitriolic satire of the Victorian age. Indeed, in December 2008, at the height of the global financial crisis and the nadir of the fraud of Bernard Madoff Investment Securities LLC, the *New York Times* had occasion to report, "Even the name is sort of Dickensian: Made-Off. So perfect . . . Merdle, Melmotte, Madoff—it sounds like a literary hedge-fund." The perfection audited here is the magnetic collision of the made world and the novelistic world, the coincidence of literary invention and fraudulent finance. But while this perfection underwrites the *New York Times's* erudite joke, it poses a problem for the satirist: when reality itself is hyperbolically absurd, is it desirable or even possible to further hyperbolize? The literary anatomist Northrop Frye opines, "satire . . . breaks down when its content is too oppressively real to permit the maintaining of the fantastic or hypothetical tone."[20] In the appositions I have been making between the critique of fictitious capital and the satire of finance, it has perhaps become clear that *The Way We Live Now* is "too oppressively real"—that its own system of hyperbole realizes, graphically performs, and realistically renders the uncanny reality of fictitious capital. In point of fact, for many of Trollope's contemporary readers, the novel was all too real:

> Mr. Trollope's novels are not only among the enjoyments of life, they are also among its instructors; for no modern novelist, and perhaps no novelist of any time, has depicted with such scrupulous fidelity to the truth the actual facts of society, the phases of our national and social life which almost inevitably escape the historian, and which are rarely caught even by the tourist or the essayist. There is nothing false about *The Way We Live Now.*[21]

The Way We Live Now tells no lies, exaggerates no dynamics; it operates with "scrupulous fidelity." Other reviews, such as one from the *Spectator* earlier cited, which laments that reading this novel is like spending a day at work in London's financial center, echo this sense that the novel offered "only too faithful a portraiture" of present-day affairs.[22]

This tension within the reception of the novel is already formalized in the novel itself. As the novel's hyperbolic exaggerations continuously produce realistic accounts of Victorian financial capitalism, its satire begins to break down. Hyperbole is the technology of satire; but the heaping on of figurative language is also an object of this satire. *The Way We Live Now,* like Victorian financial journalism, depicts finance as the proliferation of "the representative of the representative of the representative" and as "poetry," imaginative making, doing things with words. Far from hyperbolic exaggeration that achieves critique, the satire becomes a mere presentation of hyperbolic reality—it becomes, in other words, realism that realizes the impossibility of satirizing credit. The modal crisis also thereby registers the credit crisis: it is impossible to indefinitely sustain the circulation of ungrounded symbolic mediations.

In Frye's theory of literary modes satire is a subset of irony, a "militant" irony that "demands at least a token fantasy, a content which the reader recognizes as grotesque."[23] Should this element of the grotesque disappear, should the content become "too oppressively real," the satire dissolves into a more general irony "consistent with complete realism of content." I would suggest that when the crisis of satire in *The Way We Live Now* occasions such a modal switch, the resultant irony destabilizes the very stuff of realism: in its recursive motion inward from a satire operating at the level of appearance to a more conventional realism focused on interiority, the novel critically depicts the quest for an intimate ground of ungrounded financial proliferation. As that turn toward intimacy belies its own desperation, the frenetic pace of the novel's non-satiric portion itself ironizes the movement of grounding the economy in affect that we have deemed "realizing capital"—making capital real by correlating it to affect. The modal conversion begins as a radical turn inward, the gesture of putting hands into pockets with which I began this book. After this inward turn a kind of delirium of intimacy takes over, and the final quarter of the book hysterically pursues understanding, reconciliation, and marriages. In all this tonal affectation, the final portion of the novel insistently undermines the supposed contrast between fictitious financial speculation and real intimate relation that drives the Victorian psychic economy matrix.

To the first point: the moment at which the satire begins to implode is, perhaps fittingly, the climax of the plot. In the vacuum of speculations about speculations, Melmotte discerns that "it was known everywhere that there was to be a general ruin of all the Melmotte affairs," and his assessment climactically activates the passive tense of that ruin: "at that moment the most utterly wretched man in London . . . was able to deliver himself from the indignities and penalties . . . by a dose of prussic acid" (642). As the text moves to the rare territory of suicide in the Victorian novel, it requires a radically different kind of narration than the satire that has preceded it.[24] Exaggerations and caricatures give way to compassionate characterization and lengthy focalization; the whip of the satirist lies lax under the lilt of free indirect discourse, in an unprecedented (in this text) interiority that unfolds uninterrupted over three pages, constituting a totally remarkable plunge from the superficial level of hyperbole and shallowness in all its senses. In this lengthy interior discourse the narrator compresses Melmotte's emotional and mental history into an anaphora of pluperfect expressions:

> He had always lived with the consciousness that such a burden was on him and might crush him at any time. He had known that he had to run these risks. He had told himself a thousand times that when the dangers came, dangers alone should never cow him. He had always endeavored to go as near that wind as he could, to avoid the heavy hand of the criminal law of whatever country he inhabited. He had studied the criminal laws, so that he might be sure in his reckonings; but he had always felt that he might be carried by circumstances into deeper waters than he intended to enter. (470–71)

Five sentences in a row commence with what Melmotte *had* known and thought and learned and felt and done, catching the narrative up to his perspective in the past with compact rigor, pressing to compensate for having deprived Melmotte of sympathetic focalization for almost five hundred pages.

As soon as this compression takes effect, the narrator offers a simile to elevate our "bloated swindler, the vile city ruffian" (184) to the pillar of newly sympathetic heroism:

> As the soldier who leads a forlorn hope, or as the diver who goes down for pearls, or as the searcher for wealth on fever-breeding coasts, knows that as his gains may be great, so are his perils, Melmotte had been aware that in his life, as it opened itself out to him, he might come to terrible destruction. He had not always thought, or even hoped, that he would be as he was now, so exalted as to be allowed to entertain the very biggest ones of the earth; but the greatness had grown upon him—and so had the danger. (471)

The stutter of the simile—its indecision and imprecision—registers the strain of bridging the chasm of satiric disdain for Melmotte, which has dominated the narrative to this point, and of crossing into sympathy. At the climax of this passage the narrative self-evaluation of its satiric distortion of its "own character" manifests in Melmotte's new self-reflection: "Perhaps never in his life had he studied his own character and his own conduct more accurately, or made sterner resolves, than he did as he stood there smiling, bowing, and acting without impropriety the part of host to an emperor" (471). Studying his own character, Melmotte comes in a few lines to the same conclusion as the narrator of the forsaken satire: "Men should know at any rate that he had a heart within his bosom" (472). From this point onward the novel strives to efficiently inform men of what they "should know," and the formal technique of satire dissolves into a more reciprocal and compassionate narration.

The inquest after Melmotte's death provides an opportunity for the narrator to continue to attend to this interiority, and in so doing to achieve a moral distance more substantiated than satiric. At the inquest, "there was a very strong feeling against Melmotte," resulting in a ruling that he was sane at the time of his suicide. The narrator carefully contests the ruling:

> But it may be imagined, I think, that during that night he may have become as mad as any other wretch, have been driven as far beyond his powers of endurance as any other poor creature who ever at any time felt himself constrained to go. . . . He had assured himself long ago—he had assured himself indeed not very long ago—that he would brave it all like a man. But we none of us know what load we can bear, and what would break our backs. Melmotte's back had been so utterly crushed that I almost think that he was mad enough to have justified a verdict of temporary insanity. (673)

The final judgment of Melmotte cannot be left as unsympathetic, not only because the crime of suicide would ominously condemn him to "the cross roads, or whatever scornful grave may be allowed to those who have killed themselves with their wits about them . . . carried away to the cross roads—or elsewhere" (672–73), but also because such condemnations to hell dismantle the possibility for ongoing mutual meaningful relation: the meeting of the minds again in heaven. Within this same space of extending a certain sympathy to Melmotte, the narrator also reminds the readers that they are likely intimately familiar with the circumstances of both Melmotte and the narrator, for "we none of us know what load we can bear." Across these moments, then, the satire is traded for a more interiorizing narration that attempts to neutralize the alienating effects of the whip of the satirist. In the aftermath of the suicide and the burst bubble, matters of the heart occupy the narrator, who busily presides over the romantic resolutions of the novel's many love triangles—and these are resolutions of mutual "sharing," of promise-keeping and felicitous speech-acting (marriages) that are all strictly opposed to the logic and rhetoric of "floating shares." This choreography of recourse, this embrace of the psychological as more substantive than the financial, models the dynamic that I find in Victorian thought: the logically nongrounded structures of finance come to appear as reconcilable on the grounds of psychological nature.

Marriage Mania

This brings us to the second point about the modal conversion, for this grounding gesture is soon ironized by the events and images in the remaining quarter of the novel. The satire comes to an abrupt halt—the hyperbole dissipates, the censure lessens, the surface deepens—but a more subtle irony takes its place. Melmotte, after all, exits the action by his own hand, and though that prompts the narrator to construct a different paradigm for narrative relay, this paradigm can only train its sights on a dead man for so long. All those other noxiously living characters clamor for resolution of their own. One obstacle to suddenly treating these characters more affectionately is that they have been presented as unsavory products of the fusion of finance and psychology, little psychic economies obsessively pursuing their frisky business. Depicting the everyday lives of investors as over-inflected with economic figures and frameworks, the novel's insights into the logic of finance become insights into the culture of finance. The speculative metaphysics of realizing capital organize and galvanize what the novel repeatedly calls "the business of life": the intimate transactions of friendship, kinship, love, and marriage. In this way the novel dramatizes that distribution of economic language to affective, relational, and psychological experience that defines financial psychologism. It presents a world become grotesque in its economism, its figuring of everything through an economic prism.

   Both before and after the implosion of the satire, interpersonal relations and interior dynamics are presented in economic language, or as economically over-determined. The marriage market topos of the nineteenth century is rendered absurd by Sir Felix's brazenly economic pursuit of a bride: "For the girl herself he cared not the least. . . . He regarded her simply as the means by which a portion of Mr. Melmotte's wealth might be conveyed to his uses" (138). Marie may be "simply the means" of wealth accumulation, but she is no naïve victim, plotting an equal partnership "venture" in which both she and Sir Felix will profit: "Her proposition, put into plain English, amounted to this:'take me and marry me without my father's consent—and then you and I together can rob my father of the money which, for his own purposes, he has settled upon me'" (227). The novel is at pains to high-light the audacity of this proposition: first the note from Marie that makes this proposal explicit is enclosed, then Sir Felix's reactions are detailed for a paragraph, and then finally the narrator curiously reiterates a third time, in "plain English." Though Felix has met his match in Marie, his uncertainty about her father leaves him repeatedly auditing his romantic chances: "If a man plays and loses, he can play again and perhaps win; but when a fellow goes in for an heiress, and gets the wife without the money, he feels a little hampered, you know" (178).

Amid all this gaming, Felix's mother, Lady Carbury, cares little for her son's honesty or fortitude of character, but "the prospect of his fortune and splendour was sufficient to elate her into a very heaven of beautiful dreams" (148). When Sir Felix purports to give relationship advice and moral guid-ance to his sister's suitor, Paul Montague, his obvious deficits in this arena re-quire him to muster authority by puffing himself up: "Sir Felix still blustered, and made what capital he could out of his position as a brother" (535). As the analogy to capital makes clear, like the system of puffery that drives the financial markets, he can sheerly assert his authority; the macro-economic practices have schooled him in how to conduct himself intimately. Felix has no heart, no proper sentiment, whether on behalf of his sister and mother or toward his multiple romantic interests; the novel characterizes his lack of a conscience as a result of his economized affections and his economic tem-porality: "It seemed he lacked sufficient imagination to realize future misery though the futurity to be considered was divided from the present but by a single month, a single week—but by a single night" (20). Felix lives in the present, keeping the future at bay, deferring his confrontation with it just as financial instruments precipitate in the present what will have been a future whose moment of reckoning may be deferred indefinitely.

And these economistic intimacies are not confined to the Carburys. Am-bitious, social-climbing Georgianna Longestaffe diagnoses another dimen-sion of nowness: "Who thinks about love these days? I don't know anyone who loves anyone else" (728). Grimly appraising the state of romance today, she also forges an explicit equation between male privilege, autonomous desire, and lines of credit: "a man is so different. You can go just where you please, and do what you like. And if you're short of money, people will give you credit. And you can live by yourself, and all that sort of thing" (198). Lord Nidderdale issues the boldest cry for full financial disclosure on the initial public offering of marriageable girls:

> "I don't think a woman of forty with only a life interest would be a good speculation. Of course I'll think of it if you press it."
>   The old man growled again.
>   "You see, sir, I've been so much in earnest about this girl that I haven't thought of inquiring about any one else. There always is some one up with a lot of money. It's a pity there shouldn't be a regular statement published with the amount of money, and what is expected in return. It'd save a deal of trouble" (654).

Lord Nidderdale's distorted angst outlines the semantic instability of "speculation" and identifies the convergent risks of financial and mental speculation, of not knowing in advance what one is in for, matrimonially or financially. His wish for "a regular statement" is as much a wish to extricate himself from this polysemic confusion as it is for a profitable marriage. His bald wishes only naturally stem from his father's attitudes:

> In such a family as his, when such results have been achieved, it is generally understood that matters shall be put right by an heiress. It has become an institution, like primogeniture, and is almost as serviceable for maintaining the proper order of things. Rank squanders money; trade makes it—and then trade purchases rank by re-gilding its splendor. The arrangement, as it affects the aristocracy generally, is well understood and was quite approved of by the old marquis—so that he had found himself to be justified in eating up the property, which his son's future marriage would renew as a matter of course (435).

Beyond these frank discussions of marriage as "purchasing rank" and "regilding," the movement of the plot establishes an isomorphism of romance and finance. The very same technology of speculation that brings about the financial crisis first causes and then solves the romantic crisis. Rumor and gossip, ungrounded floating speech, furnish the resolution of the main romance plot by clarifying the love quadrangle between Hetta Carbury, Paul Montague, Roger Carbury, and Mrs. Hurtle. Originally involved with Mrs. Hurtle, Paul has developed a great love for Hetta, and though "in all his aspiration, and in all his fears, he was true to Hetta" (173), "nevertheless, had Hetta known everything" she would have doubted his trueness and "endeavored to dismiss him from her heart" (173). By the grace of rumor, Hetta does eventually learn everything. Sir Felix first says, "I suppose you'd be surprised to hear that Master Paul is engaged" (514); and the narrator then tracks the chorus line of confidences and rumors:

> Very much of the story Felix had learned from Ruby. Ruby had of course learned that Paul was engaged to Mrs. Hurtle. Mrs. Hurtle had at once declared the fact to Mrs. Pipkin, and Mrs. Pipkin had been proud of the position of her lodger. Ruby had herself seen Paul Montague at the house, and had known that he had taken Mrs. Hurtle to Lowestoffe. And it had also become known to the two women, the aunt and her niece, that Mrs. Hurtle had seen Roger Carbury on the sands at Lowestoffe. Thus the whole story with most of its details—not quite with all—had come round to Lady Carbury's ears (515).

The movement in the passage's syntax from short, simple sentences with clear subjects to more compound sentences with imprecise verbs and indefinite actions inscribes the obscuring of the truth through the machinations of assumptions and boasts, and yet this circulation is ultimately successful in bringing Hetta and Paul together. Hetta, after all, appeals to Paul himself, excessively iterating the oral circulations: "a strange report has come round to me. . . . I have been told. . . . It was from my brother I first heard it . . . so I ask you. Of course I can write about nothing else till I have heard about this" (580). Embroiled in rumor, Hetta asks not for the truth from Paul, but to hear more, perpetuating rumor. Since the narrative has included multiple speculative accounts of Paul's actions, it omits the final reckoning between the couple: "then he did tell his story, with a repetition of which the reader need not be detained" (582). The novel's ultimate romantic climax must be abridged to dramatically arrest the circulation of rumor at the threshold of truth, yet this abridging ironically consigns the readers to ongoing speculation about the lovers' hush. Just when the narrative wants most fervently to have accomplished a decisive ground of "speculation," it deposits us anew in an echo chamber of ungrounded circulation.

Romantic uncertainty apprehended through the language of financial speculation is extremized by the novel's astronomical proliferation of love triangles. Hetta could be with Paul or Roger; Paul could be with Hetta or Winifred; Felix could be with Ruby or Marie; Marie could be with Felix or Nidderdale; Ruby could be with Felix or John; Georgiana could be with Breghert or Batherbolt; while Lady Carbury could be with Broune or remain purposefully alone. From this excessive array of romantic potentials the final pages of the novel feverishly pursue a maximum number of marriages, as if satirizing the very generic conventions of closure in Victorian novels. In the end, Hetta marries Paul; Georgianna, Mr. Batherbolt; Marie, Mr. Fisker; Lady Carbury, Mr. Broune; and Ruby, John; while Roger and Felix remain bachelors. This comedic flurry of marriages furnishes the means by which the novel is "formally reconciled" (717), as John is to Ruby, because the marriages, as quintessential performative speech acts, consummate the performative topos of finance.

In the nuptial bubble that forges more perfect unions between so many characters during the final manic chapters of the book, the novel represents the transaction we have seen between ideas about finance and ideas about psychology: ungrounded capital is made real by a hypostatized nature of desire. That is, in finding its closure in so many marriages, many of which are true affective partnerships, while others are true business partnerships, the novel depicts a movement from financial volatility to affective stability, from straits to settlements. What makes the novel's movement a revelation of this cultural matrix, rather than merely an enunciation of it, are the many ironies that propel the final section of the text. Perhaps most apparent is the preposterous number of marriages that drive the final hundred pages; but more granularly, the final quarter of the novel obsessively calls attention to the semantic ambivalence of the very signifiers "share" and "credit" by saturating its depictions of interiority and intimacy in economic language. Thus Lord Nidderdale finds himself in a situation "requiring more intelligence than he gave himself credit for" (544), Georgianna "had always given herself credit for high spirits" (599), John Crumb "was not prone to give himself undue credit" (611), Lady Carbury "gave Marie little credit either for affection or generosity" (633), the marquis "did not give his son much credit for either diligence or for ingenuity" (653), and so on *ad absurdum*. In parallel fashion, the "shares all afloat" are no longer the endless "bits of paper" that derivatively represent financial value, but become the portioning of alliance and favor: Roger says "share my toils" (552), Breghert says "share with me the discomfort" (609), the narrator says of John Crumb that "he never attributed to Ruby her share of the evils that had befallen him" (612), and of Dolly that he might "share with his father the honor" (673), and so on and so on. This logic is consummated in the poignant disentangling of the triangle between Hetta, Roger, and Paul, when Roger has at last resigned himself both to doing without Hetta and to making nice with Paul. It is the penultimate page of this lengthy novel, and the hopelessly outmoded Roger has at long last become modern, representing his inner life, to himself and others, in financial terms:

> There goes the last of my anger.... I hold my property as steward for those who are to come after me, and ... the satisfaction of my stewardship will be infinitely increased if I find that those for whom I act share the interest which I shall take in the matter. It is the only payment which you and he can make me for my trouble (766).

In each of these and many other instances, the texture of the novel's discourse ironizes financial language, reminding us that the ungrounded figures that float throughout the financial economy not only over-determine intimate relations, but also over-signify them. We live now in a way that is puffed with fictitious capital, but also in a way made artificial by the hyper-extension of economic metaphors to personal relations. The metaphor of "psychic economy" encapsulates such overreaching, even as it founds our own "now."

In 1880 the *Nation* called Trollope "the last of the realists."[25] Trollope stands as the last novelist in the three-decade swath of high Victorian realism I study here. More important than chronology, what makes *The Way We Live Now* definitive for this book is its pellucid presentation of the collusion between the propulsive figurations of fictitious capital and economic metaphors of desiring relations. Other Victorian discourses, we have seen, resolve the artifice of capital into the naturalness of economized desire. In his novel, Trollope, like Dickens and Eliot, could not have directly foreseen the legacy of psychic economy that defines our present; nonetheless, its title harkens not only to the strange time of the "now," but also to the bonded sociality of the "we." This collective subject is none other than we millennial Victorians, denizens of a world of finance built in the nineteenth century and still buttressed by the metaphoric grounds of psychic economy.

5. *London, Nineteenth Century, Capital of Realism*

On Marx's Victorian Novel

> Of course we have all read, and all do read, Capital. . . . But some day it is essential to read *Capital* to the letter, to read the text itself.
>
> —Althusser and Balibar, *Reading Capital*

> Marx has not yet been received. The subtitle of this address could thus have been: "Marx, das Unheimliche." Marx remains an immigrant chez nous, a glorious, sacred, accursed, but still a clandestine immigrant, as he was all his life. He belongs to a time of disjunction, to that "time out of joint" in which he is inaugurated, laboriously, painfully, tragically, a new thinking of borders, a new experience of the house, the home, and the economy. Between earth and sky. One should not rush to make of the clandestine immigrant an illegal alien or, what always risks coming down to the same thing, to domesticate him. To neutralize him through naturalization. To assimilate him so as to stop frightening oneself with him. He is not part of the family, but one should not send him back, once again, him too, to the border.
>
> —Derrida, *Specters of Marx*

Marx is not part of the family, but one should not send him back. There is of late no more popular way to trivialize and exoticize Karl Marx than to dismiss his insuperable masterpiece of critical political economy as "a Victorian melodrama or a gothic novel . . . a picaresque odyssey through the realms of higher nonsense . . . a shaggy-dog story."[1] The intent of such claims is clearly to send him back, to bury Marx definitively in the nineteenth century, shrouded in a contempt as great for Victorian novels as for his own achievements. In Chapter 1 I argued that Marx's Victorianism is nothing to laugh at: he found the powerful idea of "fictitious capital" circulating in the press that he avidly consumed. In this chapter, as I discuss other linkages between Marx and the Victorian intellectual context, I will suggest that, far from composing Marx's eulogy, the analogy between his work and that of the Victorian realists may be the condition of his immortality. *Capital* may be, as one sneering biographer avers, "best understood as a Victorian novel," but in that case a different register of its meaning-making must open up from reading it that way; reading Marx's novel must enrich rather than impoverish our understanding of the Marxian edifice.

Two inversions propel this chapter. I have been arguing that Victorian literary realism can levy an incisive critique of financial metalepsis. I will now argue, through the looking glass, that an incisive critique of financial metalepsis may work as Victorian literary realism. Moreover, I have been exploring the troubling capacity of the construct of psychic economy to displace the structural understanding of capital's ungroundedness. I will now argue, on the other side, that Marx's structural understanding of capital's ungroundedness substantiates an alternative construct of psychic economy, one focused on the "drive" (*Trieb*) of the capitalist system. Where, for the psychologists, political economists, and financial journalists we have encountered, psychic economy names the essentially capitalist disposition of the subject, drive in Marx's theory names the essential subjectivity activated by capitalism. Marx articulates a version of the psychic economy metaphor in which the psychological subject in question is not *homo economicus,* but capital itself. If there is any heuristic value for the construct of psychic economy to be redeemed after the historicization of it this book outlines, it would stem not from the naturalization of capitalism as an emanation of the universal psyche, but from naming capital's self-universalization as subject. Where these two inversions meet, I ultimately claim that Marx's formulations of psychic economy are owing to his appropriation of the aesthetic of Victorian realism: for Marx, capital functions like a novelistic protagonist.

For this reading I ask hospitality for Marx the immigrant in Victorian London—Marx the minor Victorian, Marx the Victorian novelist. Only such a welcome may facilitate the type of encounter Derrida recommends: to deneutralize through denaturalization, to become intimate with "Marx, *das Unheimliche.*" Reading *Capital* as Victorian literary realism opens onto the dynamism of its insights into financial metalepsis and thus continues our project of reprising realism—unsettling the prevailing assumptions about the realist novel as a mirror of economic relations; affirming realism as an economically astute mode of thinking.

Marx in Soho

To welcome Marx the Minor Victorian, to read him among his novelist neighbors, casts new light on his inassimilable life and may therefore honor the inassimilable in his thought. Jew among Catholics, German in exile, invalid in Algeria, philosopher in poverty, renter in arrears, the perennially dislocated Marx was unhomely at home in London for thirty-four years. Denied British naturalization late in life, he nonetheless rests for eternity in Highgate Cemetery. To throw him in with the Victorian novelists is to limn this unnatural fate, to highlight what must be recast in order to be reread. Reading *Capital* as a Victorian novel pursues those insights that were themselves (and perhaps remain) inassimilable within the discourse of critical political economy. These insights precisely pertain to that which remains inassimilable in capitalism, what remains resistant to accounting: its ability to substitute effects for causes, to posit its own metaphysical preconditions. Neither flippant eulogy nor idealist elegy, such a reading might rather index Marx's command of manifold strategies for thinking—historically *and* transcendentally, scientifically *and* aesthetically, politically *and* poetically.

At home nowhere, at home everywhere, Marx took refuge in London in 1849. The first order of business was attaining a reader's ticket to the British Library Reading Room. On a daily basis thereafter he joined Thomas Carlyle, William Thackeray, Charles Dickens, and John Ruskin, furiously at work reading and writing. After osmoting all extant back issues of the *Economist* (which began printing in 1843), he quickly absorbed the local literary talent, voraciously consuming volumes of Shakespeare, Milton, Defoe, and Dickens.[2] Like Dickens and Ruskin, he was also up to his elbows in Blue Books, drawing information, references, stories, and ideas from these governmental reports on everything from sanitation to factory conditions to prostitution.[3]

As their rapture with the Blue Books suggests, for Marx and his companion intellectuals the context of London constituted the core of his work. Just as there could be no Dickens without London, there could be no Marx without the advanced bustling commerce of The City. As he put it in *Capital:*

No period of modern society is so favourable for the study of capitalist accumulation as the period of the last 20 years. It is as if this period had found Fortunatus' purse. But of all countries, England again furnishes the classical examples, because it holds the foremost place in the world market, because capitalist production here alone is completely developed.[4]

Appraising their development, inhabiting their milieu, drawing upon their sources, partaking of their canon, Marx also explicitly aligned himself with Victorian novelists by identifying his work as fundamentally aesthetic and, at that, whole: "whatever shortcomings they may have, the advantage of my writings is that they are an artistic whole, and this can only be achieved through my practice of never having things printed until I have them in front of me *in their entirety*" (emphasis original).[5] Along with the carbuncles and pressing debtors, these convictions about creative integrity help explain his infinite difficulty in finalizing *Capital* for publication. In point of fact, just before finally surrendering the manuscript in February 1867, Marx gave Engels a copy of Honoré de Balzac's story "The Unknown Masterpiece."[6] In the story a painter obsessively and painstakingly reworks a single canvas for over a decade, daubing and shading and blending in pursuit of "such depth" that it fathoms reality, an "atmosphere so true that you can not distinguish it from the air that surrounds us." In the tragic denouement, the artist proclaims his stylistic triumph: "Where is Art? Art has vanished, it is invisible!" But an outside perspective reveals the state of the canvas: "I see nothing. . . . I can see nothing there but confused masses of color and a multitude of fantastical lines that make a dead wall of paint."[7] The burning ambition for vanishing mediation, for art so real it is invisible, melts its medium, pooling in an inscrutable, proto-Impressionistic muddle. As a preface to the "artistic whole" of *Capital,* "The Unknown Masterpiece" bespeaks Marx's methodological predicament. While constructing a whole was imperative, cultivating an adequate aesthetic felt nigh impossible. Indeed it was to this predicament, and remarkably *not* to ideological antagonism, that Marx appealed in explaining the negative reviews of *Capital.* "The mealy-mouthed babblers of German vulgar economics fell foul of the style of my book," he wrote, proceeding to note that in falling foul they also fell short of a complete stylistic scrutiny: "No one can feel the literary shortcomings of *Capital* more strongly than I myself."[8] Conversely, Marx took great pride in the aesthetic appreciation from the London press, which celebrated his "unusual liveliness," and found that "the presentation of the subject invests the driest economic questions with a certain peculiar charm."

"Peculiar charm" and "unusual liveliness" perfectly capture the product of Marx's early career. Long before he aspired to the critique of political economy, the young Marx fluently pursued charming stylizations, conducting numerous "Early Literary Experiments," including love poems, "Wild Songs," and a "Book of Verse." And indeed, rather like enacting a kind of phylogeny of that ontogenetic generic experimentation that culminates in the novel as such, his experiments ultimately amounted to *Scorpion and Felix: A Humoristic Novel* (1837). Marx's novel is a *Tristram Shandy*-ish pursuit of deferred origins, told self-reflexively in the present tense by a first-person narrator. There are three principal characters, Felix, Scorpion, and Merten, and the plot encompasses their attempts to trace their own genealogical, philological, biological, and literary origins. The novel's bellowed fireside chat clearly ironizes the hot air of philosophy, and it seems at times to juxtapose ideas purely for the ring of cacophonous nonsense. Yet its strategy of provocative contrast and inversion enables rather than defuses its critical philosophical themes. Here, for instance, is the reported remonstrance of the character Merten, that he, and not Scorpion, is indeed the hero of the story: "He had a sh-sh-shadow as good as anybody else's and even better . . . and besides he loved the right of primogeniture and possessed a wash closet."[9] What do shadows, primogeniture, and indoor plumbing have in common, and how do they amount to a hero's qualifications? In the next chapter, the first-person narrator devotes himself to this conundrum of associations:

> I sat deep in thought, laid aside Locke, Fichte, and Kant, and gave myself up to profound reflection to discover what a wash closet would have to do with the right of primogeniture, and suddenly it came to me like a flash (*Blitz*), and in a melodious succession of thought upon thought my gaze (*Blick*) was illuminated (*verklärt*) and a radiant form (*Lichtsgestaltung*) appeared before my eyes. The right of primogeniture is the wash-closet of the aristocracy, for a wash-closet only exists for the purpose of washing. But washing bleaches, and thus lends (*leiht*) a pale sheen to that which is washed. So also does the right of primogeniture silver (*versilbert*) the eldest son of the house, it thus lends him a pale silvery sheen, while on the other members it stamps the pale romantic sheen of penury.[10]

Laying "aside Locke, Fichte, and Kant" (though not, it seems worth noting, Hegel), this text that insists on its status as something other than philosophy arrives at a historical-materialist insight into the connection between inheritance rights and indoor plumbing. The wash closet is a spring of polishing ablution; primogeniture polishes the first-born with silver, stamps the other brothers with poverty, launders the money of the aristocracy. They shadow one another; the site of sanitation provides a concrete material instance of the opaque and diffuse process of arbitrary resource distribution. Primogeniture and the wash closet are two different forms of appearance of the socio-material matrix in the shadows. As an *ur*-text in his oeuvre, then, *Scorpion and Felix: A Humoristic Novel* reveals not how far Marx eventually came, but how consistently he pursued logico-formal connections behind the veil of the visible, how thoroughly he tracked different forms of appearance of the real within ontologically positive reality. Across his career he thus evinced the fundamental impulse of literary realism: to defamiliarize reality.

After finishing *Scorpion and Felix,* Marx sustained a traumatic realization that it failed the bar of his aesthetic ideals. In a letter to his father, he confided, "Suddenly, as if by a magic touch—oh, the touch was at first a shattering blow—I caught sight of the distant realm of true poetry like a distant fairy palace, and all my creations crumbled into nothing."[11] Palpable here in the melodramatic excesses of the letter that preserve the creations the letter ostensibly negates, the distant realm of true poetry persists as an alluring destination.

Literary Surplus

One way to map the circuitous journey onward toward that distant realm, to excavate Marx's ruined literary ambitions, to receive Marx as a Victorian novelist, would be to enumerate those features of the late work *Capital* that demand literary reading. This is the path most taken, the way trod alike by artists (the Communist lithographer Hugo Gellert produced a book-length illustration of *Capital;* the director Sergei Eisenstein planned a film version) and by critics tackling the oddity of talking commodities, the sensationalism of dripping vampires, or the density of literary allusions.[12] Let us travel some way down this path before choosing another.

To the extant catalogue of excessive literary features we might add several more. The author of *Capital* continuously crafts that surplus of detail which Roland Barthes deemed "the reality effect"—for instance:

Bread adulterated with alum, soap, pearl ashes, chalk, Derbyshire stone-dust, and suchlike agreeable, nourishing, and wholesome ingredients . . . man had to eat daily in his bread a certain quantity of human perspiration mixed with the discharge of abscesses, cobwebs, dead black-beetles, and putrid German yeast, without counting alum, sand, and other agreeable mineral ingredients (278).[13]

We could additionally remark a comparable ambition between the realist novel's social inclusiveness and *Capital's* organizing principle of social difference as the *sine qua non* for exchange:

The exchange of products springs up at the points where different families, tribes, or communities come into contact; for at the dawn of civilization it is not private individuals but families, tribes, etc. that meet on an independent footing. Different communities find different means of production and different means of subsistence in their natural environment. Hence their modes of production and living, as well as their products, are different. It is this spontaneously developed difference which, when different communities come into contact, calls forth the mutual exchange of products and the consequent gradual conversion of those products into commodities. Exchange does not create the differences between spheres of production but it does bring the different spheres into a relation, thus converting them into more or less interdependent branches of the collective production of a whole society (472).

Like the Victorian realist novel, *Capital* balances this social expansiveness with psychological interiority. This is a discourse of *both* history and individuality, *both* materiality and consciousness, seeking "the fundamental cause of the misery of the people in modern times" (921). For instance:

In proportion as capital accumulates, the lot of the laborer must grow worse . . . the law . . . establishes an accumulation of misery, corresponding with the accumulation of capital. Accumulation of wealth at one pole is, therefore, at the same time the accumulation of misery, agony of toil slavery, ignorance, brutality, mental degradation at the opposite pole (799).

Similarly, we could continue to extend this list of similarities: like *Middlemarch* or *The Last Chronicle of Barset, Capital* subtly weaves its themes, deftly integrates its multiple plots, tightly regulates its symbols, masterfully conducts its voices, and continuously calls attention to the shifts in perspective that structure its narration. Like the Victorian melodramas with which it is derisively classed, *Capital* is animated by abyssal questions of origin.[14] Like the triple-deckers of English realism, it endeavors to describe the world in order to change it.[15] For *Capital* as for the novel genre, disjunctures in perspective and a plurality of voices are constitutive. Characters are spoken of, but also speak for themselves, with clunky self-consciousness attending these shifts in speaking:

> The capitalist therefore takes his stand. . . . Suddenly, however, there arises the voice of the worker, which had previously been stifled in the sound and fury of the production process: "The commodity I have sold you differs from the ordinary crowd of commodities in that its use creates value, a greater value than it costs. That is why you bought it . . . you and I know on the market only one law" (342).

Still yet, we could observe that the tension between particular commodity and universal equivalent that spurs capitalism is formalized in the tension between particular character and universal type that rouses realism.[16] All these features could be more comprehensively audited, confirming and advertising the book's "unusual liveliness."

Archiving authorial intent, auditing literary elements—these methods would amount to "contextual" and "paratextual" approaches to reading *Capital* novelistically. But such an inventory of literary elements appeals just as much to Marx's detractors as to those who would read him more supplely. We can learn nothing new about Marx's critique by counting up metaphors, unless the opposition between literature and critique is sublated. In the vein of the readings we have offered of other novels, it ought to be possible to begin our encounter with *Capital* otherwise—to begin from the conceit that there is such a thing as aesthetic thinking, a conceptual agency of literary form.[17] Commencing from the premise that *Capital* thinks aesthetically opens on to the ways in which the text constellates its ideas rhythmically in the tempo of the narrative and poetically in the circulation of tropes. The ultimate argument for reading *Capital* as a novel is neither contextual (Marx the Londoner, Marx the erstwhile novelist) nor paratextual (some taxonomy of anomaly in Marx's language and/or of political economic iteration in Victorian novels). The ultimate argument is textual: as a whole some of the text's most pressing insights find their most intense formulation performatively. *Capital* means what it means not simply through denotative reference, but through the connotative, associative, artful ways the language *works*. More specifically, the lasting ideas it bequeaths to us—about the drive of capitalism and the "case of metaphysics" it poses—are illuminated rhetorically through the trope of personification and the ironic verve of metalepsis.

Reading *Capital* as a Victorian novel, I will now suggest, should foremost mean reading for the ways that its insights materialize narratively, figuratively, and aesthetically, in addition to referentially or instantiatively.[18] It should mean posing that Dickensian question "What connexion can there be?" between the multiple plots, multi-linked chains of images, and multiplications of perspective that all, by virtue of their boundedness within one textual whole, engage the same underlying object.[19] Such a reading is therefore repelled by contemptuous analogies between *Capital* and Victorian novels, compelled by the Victorian novel's exemplary aesthetic thinking and impelled by the essential imperative to read again what has already been read, to defamiliarize the Marxian oeuvre.

Capital Personified

To begin, again. Let us consider the striking prevalence of two tropes in *Capital*: personification, the representation of an abstraction as a person, and metalepsis, the substitution of one figure for another with which it is closely related, such as effect for cause. The special importance of these two tropes shone through already in our discussion of the Victorian matrix of "psychic economy": financial journalists and other prose writers, in their attack on fictitious capital and exposés of the poetry of banking, essentially defined finance as a metaleptic series of "a representative of a representative of a representative"; eventually metaleptic reasoning by financial journalists reporting on constant crises transposed cause and effect, with psychological upheaval coming to be perceived as the source, rather than the consequence, of financial instability; personification of capitalism is entailed by the hypostasized continuity between psychology and economy, in which psychology is essentially economic and economics are fundamentally psychological. As we shall see in Marx's *Capital,* personification and metalepsis and the concert between them intone the concept of drive, a cornerstone whose singular bearing in the Marxian edifice has lately been registered by Kojin Karatani and Slavoj Žižek.[20] Any meaningful Marxian account of psychic economy—that is to say, of continuity between economy and subjectivity—centers on drive. Reading *Capital* novelistically—figuratively—allows us to encounter "drive" on its own circuitous and elusive terms.

Where the formulations we have seen elsewhere in the Victorian context effectively naturalize capitalism by imputing an economic structure to
human subjectivity, Marx imputes a quasi-subjective status to capital in order to underscore the strangeness of the capitalist metaphysic. The trope of
personification performs this strangeness. In the Preface to the first edition,
Marx fastidiously calls attention to his trope, instructing that a certain figural
awareness should govern reading of the text:

> To prevent possible misunderstandings, let me say this. I do not by any
> means depict the capitalist and the landowner in rosy colors. But individuals
> are dealt with here only in so far as they are the personifications of eco-
> nomic categories, the bearers of particular class relations and interests. My
> standpoint, from which the development of the economic formation of so-
> ciety is viewed as a process of natural history, can less than any other make
> the individual responsible for relations whose creature he remains, socially
> speaking, however much he may subjectively raise himself above them.[21]

To prevent possible misunderstandings, it must be understood that personification operates at the textual level because it operates at the social one:
within the text of *Capital* individuals are dealt with as personifications because within the historical reality of capital individuals are personifications
of social relations, even though they mistake personhood as their exemp-
tion from social determination. A trope, a way of dealing with individuals,
personification figuratively organizes the social world. "Psychic economy,"
figuring economic forces as soulful stirrings, and the corporate person, the
abstraction at the heart of financial investment, are only the most glaring
instances of a trope machine that confounds all forms of personation. It
is easy to see that misunderstandings might be quick to arise from these
multifaceted personifications, textual, social, and ideological. Marx's prefatory self-consciousness about these facets sounds a warning that the use of
personification within the text must be carefully scrutinized.

In the fashion of literary thinking, analyzing personification proceeds
most powerfully by performing personification, putting its powers to work.
In *Capital* personification emerges as an object of analysis when it is de-
ployed as a tool of analysis. Having declared from the outset the necessity to
commence with the commodity form, the narrative has inductively traced
the form from its "simple, isolated" status to its complex and relational status,
the "relative form of value." To illuminate the relationship at the core of the
relative form, the simple isolated commodity becomes personified, sum-

moned through a speech act ("let us take Coat and Linen," [132]). Coat and Linen, brought into relation with one another, are brought into personification by the text. Commodity exchange presumes that both commodities are expressions of value, but the text takes pains to mark that these expressions are heterogeneous to each other, that "these qualitatively equated commodities do not play the same part" (*spielen nicht dieselbe Rolle*) (141). Playing these differing roles, the commodities begin to stand as the agents of active verbs and become self-conscious:

> In the production of the coat, human labor power, in the shape of tailoring, has in actual fact been expended. Human labor has therefore been accumulated in the coat. From this point of view the coat is a bearer of value, although this property never shows through, even when the coat is at its most threadbare. In its value relation with the linen, the coat counts only under this aspect, counts therefore as embodied value (*verkörperter Wert*), as the body of value (*Wertkörper*). Despite its buttoned up (*zugeknöpften*) appearance, the linen recognizes (*erkannt*) in it a splendid kindred soul, the soul of value (*die stammverwandte schöne Wertseele*) (143).

In one stroke, as the result of the relation of commodities and of relaying the relation of commodities, Coat and Linen attain souls to go with their bodies. Even more striking, within that stroke, sexual innuendo animates the body and the soul. The linen (*die Leinwand*), a feminine subject in German, comports herself coquettishly, both "buttoned up" and "reserved" (literal denotation and figurative connotation of "*zugeknöpften*"), even as she is also buttoned into, incorporating the body of, the coat (*der Rock*), masculine subject in German. Her cognitive agency of "recognition" is carnal knowledge; and in general lustiness and promiscuity define the commodity: "a born leveler and cynic, it is always ready to exchange not only soul, but body, with each and every other commodity, be it more repulsive than Maritornes herself" (179).[22] Here personification endows the mysterious relationship between commodities with intellectual, physical, and sexual complexity, alluding to the transformative power of valorization: when valorization is the goal of relation, transformations of body and soul, mind and matter ensue. Furthering the innuendo, Marx names this transformation "going the way of all flesh," a "metamorphosis" of engaging with other bodies in bodily transformation, corporeal intercourse, value incorporation (207). Personification as a conspicuously brandished endowment of the commodity body with a soul figuratively records and performs the phenomenological and corporeal transformations precipitated by exchange. When value is conjured as spiritual abstraction that authorizes exchange, the spirit transforms material bodies; the trope of personification discloses this spiritualization of the commodity body.

It is this oddity of transformation, this mystery of metamorphosis, that constitutes these persons with bodies and souls as "very strange thing(s), abounding in metaphysical subtleties and theological niceties" (163). Indeed, already before the chapter on fetishism, in which commodities notoriously think for themselves (the table "evolves out of its wooden brain grotesque ideas, far more wonderful than if it were to begin dancing of its own free will" [163]), the figure of personification has entailed that commodities speak for themselves:

> We see then, that everything our analysis of the value of commodities previously told us is repeated by the linen itself, as soon as it enters into association with another commodity, the coat. Only it reveals its thoughts in a language with which it alone is familiar, the language of commodities (*in den ihr allein geläufigen Sprache, der Waresprache*) (143).

Wonderful to say, commodities speak their own language. And indeed, many of the most careful readers of *Capital* wonder at this oddity.[23] For our purposes let us simply remark that the strangeness is less *that* the commodities speak (after all, we have been prepared by the trope of personification to expect nothing less) than *what* they speak: a language with which they alone are familiar, a language to all others unfamiliar. The strangeness of commodity language thwarts any easy mapping of the language of commodities onto language in general, just as elsewhere, as we saw in Chapter 1, Marx has indicated that money must not be analogized to language in general, but to unfamiliar language, strange language:

> To compare money with language is not less erroneous. Language does not transform ideas, so that the peculiarity of ideas is dissolved and their social character runs alongside them as separate entity, like prices alongside commodities. Ideas which have first to be translated out of their mother tongue into a foreign tongue in order to circulate, in order to become exchangeable, offer a somewhat better analogy; the analogy is then not with language, but with its foreignness (*fremdheit*).[24]

With his emphasis on estrangement, Marx demonstrates that the introduction of a monetary economy does more than enhance or facilitate human intercourse; it works to transubstantiate goods and defamiliarize the means of that intercourse, to precipitate its becoming foreign. The language of commodities is the name of this strange language. Within *Capital* the trope of personification puts strange language into the mouths of strange subjects, performing that very defamiliarization of who speaks, who counts as a who, and what is spoken in capitalism. The strangeness of personified objects in the text recapitulates the strangeness that the regime of value wreaks upon the human world.

The text's strongest formulation of the radically defamiliarizing agency of capitalism is its proliferation of unfamiliar agents. Personification of things within the discourse of *Capital* presents the personification of things within capitalism—that is, the fetishism of commodities. But in addition to this type of personification, there remains another, to which Marx's Preface calls attention: the personification of persons. Not only objects, but also subjects find themselves refigured and distorted capital personifies persons, so *Capital* personifies persons; the individuals whom bourgeois economics would take as economic agents are treated in the text as personifications of the "social relations whose creature (they) remain." First and foremost of these categories is capital itself, and thus seldom is there a reference to "the capitalist" without the qualifying clause "i.e., capital personified."[25]

When persons are personified, they are made in the image and likeness of the *ur*-person, Capital. Capital is the subject in this world; all other actors are figures, masks, faces, prosopopoieaic personifications of the subject. This is the primacy of Capital already emblazoned in the title *Capital,* the place nineteenth-century novels most often reserve for the subject: Capital is the subject of *Capital,* as David Copperfield and Jane Eyre and Daniel Deronda are the subjects of *David Copperfield, Jane Eyre,* and *Daniel Deronda.* According this subject position to Capital, capitalizing the trope of personification in this way, enthrones Capital as the protagonist of modernity—and, more importantly, illuminates that the workings of capitalism are described by this subjectification and embodiment of an abstraction. Not unlike Hegel's movement of spirit, *Capital* is the story of Capital's becoming-subject, of the relentless self-constitution, the "valorization of value" that propels this mode of production.[26] The artifice of the trope of personification calls attention to the artifice and instability of this subject, to the fissures and crises in its course of becoming, in its adventure of *Bildung.*

Strange animation and soulful endowment, effected by the trope of personification, represent within the language of *Capital* the maneuvers of self-making that comprise the object of its critique. Marx's language charges those maneuvers with uncanny frisson by extremizing them in images of Capital as a self-making monster. This cluster of figures includes of course the notorious vampire images and the climactic conclusion on primitive accumulation and illicit origins: "capital comes dripping from head to toe, from every pore, with blood and dirt" (926). At the apex of this imagery lurks the autochthon, the self-generating value that can perform its own valorization process, an "animated monster that begins to work," Marx quotes Goethe: "'as if its body were by love possessed'" (302). Though it is unclear what love's got to do with it, Goethe's poetry clarifies something else. "As if its body were by love possessed" (*als hätt' es Lieb' im Leibe*): the interior transposition of vowels ("*Liebe*" into "*Leibe*") and the double elision of vowels ("*hätte es* into *hätt'es* and *Liebe im* into *Lieb'im*) syllabically perform the lurching and leaping of autochthonous self-generation. Faustian allusions reverberate as the relentless process of becoming-subject begets self-scission, when persons beget persons bipolarly divided from themselves:

> But original sin is everywhere. With the development of the capitalist mode of production, with the growth of accumulation and wealth, the capitalist ceases to be merely the incarnation of capital. He begins to feel a human warmth towards his own Adam, and his education gradually enables him to smile at his former enthusiasm for asceticism, as an old fashioned miser's prejudice. While the capitalist of the classical type brands individual consumption as a sin against function, as abstinence from accumulation, the modernized capitalist is capable of viewing accumulation as renunciation of pleasure. "The two souls alas do dwell within his breast, the one is ever parting from the other." . . . There develops within the breast of the capitalist a Faustian conflict between the passion for accumulation and the desire for enjoyment (740–41).

Divided against himself in a devilish fashion, the person of Capital writhes torn between competing imperatives of accumulation and enjoyment. Presenting these two souls in one breast uses the trope of personification to capture a dissociation that, precisely as a threat to decompose Capital, gives it its indispensable charisma.

This excessive dimension of the subject of capital is called "drive," a notion introduced as the culmination of personification: "As a capitalist, he is only capital personified. His soul is the soul of capital. But capital has one sole driving force, the drive to valorize itself" (342). The innermost soul of

Capital is drive, the force of self-infinitizing, subjectifying, repetitive motion. To almost every instance of personification, the text conjoins imagery of drive, and through this imagery *Capital* represents the core of capital even as it does not present this core in linear analysis. Rather than referring to the central importance of personification, the text performs it.

Such is a fitting effect for the dynamic of drive: the text grazes it, glances it, grasps it in its very elusiveness. Drive's eruptive recurrence enacts the propulsive structure it names. The "soul" of the person, the "animation" of Capital, the most elemental structure of the subject, drive figures the momentum of capital, its autotelic "circulation (that) is an end in itself, for the valorization of value takes place only within this constantly renewed movement. The movement of capital is therefore limitless" (253). Half a century later, Freud's psychoanalysis would come to theorize drive as a universal circuitous motion ultimately indifferent to any object or aim other than the repetitive motion itself; here already, Marx's image of drive points to the same topos, the objective "end in itself" that is "limitless" "constantly renewed movement." "Drive" is woven into the text of *Capital,* threaded through important compound nouns like *Triebwerk* (engine) or *Betrieb* (operation). And when it appears as an uncompounded noun, when it stands simply as *Trieb,* it is always accompanied by distinctive attributes: it is absolute (*absolute*), blind (*blinden*), immanent (*immanente*), and measureless (*maßlos*). Again and again these adjectives recur, their very repetition underscoring the repetitive, immutable, immeasurable propulsion of Capital's drive. Drive in its blindness, in its immanence, in its absoluteness, in its infinity, bespeaks a force terrifyingly indifferent to the subjects it animates.

Drive is the inner nature of those who are themselves personifications, the soulless soul of the automaton, the essential skeleton of the artificial person. Without grasping drive, the text has failed, for "a scientific analysis . . . is possible only if we can grasp the inner nature (*innere Natur*) of capital, just as the apparent motions of the heavenly bodies are intelligible only to someone who is acquainted with their real motions, which are not perceptible to the senses" (*wirkliche, aber sinnlich nicht wahrnehmbare Bewegung*) (433).[27] Where a trope-less discourse could only present "apparent motions," the trope of personification grasps this "real motion" of "inner nature." Imperceptible to the naked eye, unpresentable in instantiative language, the essential matter can be registered only figuratively.

The essential import of "drive" is indexed by the fact that it is precisely apropos "drive" that the vexed concept of "accumulation" first appears in the text. Accumulation, this entwining hints, is unthinkable without the idea of drive. "Drive" names the eerie consanguinity between the advanced capitalist and his primitive antagonist, the miser. The sentence reads, "the hoarding drive is boundless in nature" (*Der Trieb der Schatzbildung ist von Natur maßlos*), and it comes in the first subsection of the chapter on money, itself entitled "Hoarding" (*Schatzbildung*). Now, this is a strange word, not at all the most obvious signifier of "hoarding" (i.e., *horten, häufen,* or *anhäufen*), and Marx appears to have coined it.[28] As a compound noun it evidently signifies "the development and creation of treasure," but as an obscure compound it calls attention to the union of *Schatz* and *Bildung,* of treasure and growth, education, maturation—and further, to the substantification of *Bildung* from *Bild,* images, figures. We are dealing with here no unified process of accumulation, but a strangely changeable, affectively charged loving of imaging—of treasuring development, creation, shaping, and, indeed, aestheticization.

Engaging an obscure compound to figure the love of figuration, Marx doubly codes his concept of drive with aesthetic consequence. His image performatively condenses measureless motion and the motion of measurelessness, motion without end and the movement of exceeding measure, of growing, becoming, taking on new forms. With this condensation the measurelessness of drive is compounded by its proliferation of images. What attracts the image lover to money is money's aesthetic capacity, twice over: "that it is the universal representative" (*allgemeiner Repräsentant*) and that it is "made out of gold and silver" (*von Gold und Silberwaren*) (230–31). Each of these two capacities ignites different dimensions of the love of imaging; the first case Marx calls "the unmediated form of treasure" (*unmittelbaren Form des Schatzes*) and the second case "the aesthetic form" (*ästhetische Form*) (230–31).

Here, between the general, unmediated potential imaging and the aesthetic, mediated actual imaging, we find again the "two souls in one breast," the tension that galvanizes Capital: "this contradiction between the quantitative limitation and the qualitative lack of limitation of money keeps driving (*triebt*) the hoarder back to his Sisyphean task: accumulation" (231).[29] Accumulation is the object of drive, which must be distinguished from its aim: the object around which drive circulates is distinct from the circulation itself that is drive's aim.[30] Aim is irreducible to object; circulation is irreducible to accumulation, just as, on another plane, capital is irreducible to capitalists. The drive of capital is the drive to accumulate, but as drive it is finally indifferent to accumulation. It is, rather, maximally affixed to the movement of circulation. Drive has no object, no telos; it has only its own momentum: blind, immanent, absolute, infinite.

Marx's thoughts about drive formulate the intersection of subjectivity and capitalism in a different idiom, and for a different purpose, than the construct of "psychic economy" with which his project is coeval. Instead of an appeal to human nature to ground capital, he demonstrates that part of capital's roving, ungrounded power is its subsumption of the very idea of subjectivity: not only do persons become things, but monstrous systems become persons, assuming the agency of world-making. Dickens, Eliot, and Trollope have illustrated the moral shortcomings of subjects who economize themselves, forging poor relationships, downsizing valuable connections, dissolving ethical obligations. With his exploration of personification Marx helps us to see that these impoverished relations commissioned by the very idea of psychic economy are merely symptoms of that distorted order of production that estranges all intimates. The psychic economy metaphor, in the nineteenth century and in our own, is arguably nothing other than the personification of capital. *Capital*'s illumination of personification as an axis around which this political economic order revolves not only performs this argument aesthetically; it also prompts a revalorization of psychic economy by way of, as it happens, metalepsis. Marx reverses the slippage of cause and effect: where Victorian science fabricates psychic economy as a product only to precipitously conceive it as raw material, the aesthetic thinking of *Capital* restores effects to their rightful place, conceiving cause in capitalism as the system itself.

Worldly Metalepsis

The notion of drive consummates the succession of images generated by personification. The dynamism of this imagery finds its narrative analogue in the rhythmic shifts of the narrative that perform metalepsis, the suspension of one figure by another, the succession of figurative substitutions. *Capital* effects this metaleptic rhythm in its narrative through its succession of paradoxes and what it calls "double results" and dual forms of appearance, and through its perpetual motion of lifting the veil, starting anew the analysis from a different point of view.[31] It is, in other words, in the texture of the textual movement that we find a stunning engagement with the text's subject, a galvanized model of the metaleptic movement of capital itself.

In commencing his analysis with the commodity form, Marx approaches the world of appearances with a precisely levied gaze: his interest is in form and in the elemental formal unit. Within the first two sentences he affects a movement from general to particular, from appearance to form of appearance—but his story does not proceed in a strictly particularizing, miniaturizing, or interiorizing way, and it is the pattern by which this motion is arrested to which we should attend. Rather than illuminating everything, the investigative perspective engenders new mysteries: at the end of Section 1, the commodity is revealed to have a dual character as use-value and exchange value; at the end of Section 2, labor is revealed to have a dual character, as concrete and abstract; at the beginning of Section 3, having identified these dualities, the perspective shifts back to the form of appearance, wherein the dualities "lay hidden" (139). Within this form lies hidden the vertigo of equivalence, the way in which the act of making an equivalence sublates opposites, at once uniting across difference and preserving their differences: "use value becomes the form of appearance of its opposite, value" and likewise "concrete human labor becomes the form of appearance of its opposite, abstract human labor" (150). The narrative momentum of advances and retreats, assertions and digressions, itself performs this fishtailing reversibility of equivalence.

Thinking equivalence commands such a performance of oscillation because equivalence is logically nongrounded. Marx encounters this "real impossibility" of exchange by introducing another voice, that of Aristotle, the "first" analyst of the "value form." "There can be no exchange," Marx quotes Book 1 of the *Ethics,* "without equality, and no equality without commensurability." Commensurability "is, however, in reality, impossible" (Aristotle), "foreign to the true nature of things" (Marx), but this does not gainsay its becoming "a makeshift for practical purposes" (151). The "intercourse" that is the essence of human existence can performatively overcome the lack of rational ground for exchange, leaping into the realm of the practical by acting as if exchange were not ungrounded. Though Aristotle discovers real impossibility and therefore implicitly discovers the necessary disavowal of it, he falls short of discovering that aesthetic form itself sublimates this impossibility: the value that is relationality is purely formal. Marx offers a very specific cause for this oversight. Artistotle's social context made the analysis of form unrealizable: because of legitimized slave labor, Greek society remained in the realm of explicit "inequality"—whereas "only in a society . . . where the concept of human equality had acquired permanence" (where the notion of abstract equality had become hegemonic) could it become possible for the "form of value" to appear (152). This means not only that capitalism is for Marx absolutely inextricable from the theoretical equality espoused in democracy, but also that the critique of political economy is simultaneously a theory of aesthetics, the conditions of sensuous perception.

And yet, no sooner has this incisive determination of historical specificity been asserted than it is retracted: in the very next sentence, Marx recurs— "But (hegemonic equality) is first only possible in a society where the commodity form is the general form of the labor product" (152). We have therefore a loop, an end that is its own beginning: the abstract equality of the commodity arrives only with the equality of humanity, which arrives only with abstract equality of the commodity. Undecidable formulations of retroactivity like this are the signature figure of the text, paradoxes that propel the narrative's continuous leaps over the contradictions (real impossibilities) that are its object.[32] In this way the narrative texture itself becomes the site of the critique's engagement with the problem of the "makeshift for practical purposes." The text comes to know its object not linearly, but formally.

One arc of formal knowledge occurs in the reversing gesture of isolating the commodity as an elemental form, only to discover that there is nothing elemental about it. The reversal is not coincidentally one of the most oft-quoted lines in the book: "a commodity appears at first sight an extremely obvious, trivial thing. But its analysis brings out that it is a very strange thing, abounding in metaphysical subtleties and theological niceties" (163). In the sway of this vertiginous passage from the elemental to the metaphysical, the narrative compulsively pursues the even more obscure region of theology: "we must take flight into the misty realm of religion" (*müssen wir in die Nebelregion der religiösen Welt flüchten*) (165). Tackling the commodities on their own terms, in the language with which they alone are familiar, on their own turf, in their own world, becomes still yet more marvelous and contradictory, and the only way to land this flight into religion, to conclude this foray into fetishism, is with the flourish of the most inscrutable literary allusion in the text. Arriving at "the peculiar circumstance that the use value of a thing is realized without exchange . . . while inversely value is realized within exchange," the narrative throws up its hands: "who would not call to mind at this point the advice given by the good Dogberry to the night-watchman Seacoal?" (177). With that rhetorical question highlighting its invocation, the text exits with a quote from *Much Ado About Nothing*: "to be a well-favoured man is the gift of fortune; but to write and to read comes by nature." In what possible sense does this amount to "advice" so indispensable that it is spontaneously called to mind? Shakespeare's speaker is plagued by terminal malapropism, and the purity of heart behind his errors of tongue functions as a kind of foil for the varieties of deception explored in the play: deceit as a means can yield good or bad ends. Dogberry, dogged by grandiloquence, speaks this befuddling apposition, erroneously naturalizing written language. Marx's elusive allusion to this chaos in the guise of solving the double result of value within and without exchange effects metalepsis at multiple levels: for double result, he substitutes confounded language; for contradiction he substitutes chaos; for innate value he substitutes innate writing; for the misty realm of religion he substitutes the ironic realm of literature.

From the throes of this propulsive figurative machine, it is not surprising that again "we must take flight." And so we begin again: after the concluding Shakespearean allusion, the second chapter commences by redirecting the line of inquiry. "Commodities cannot themselves go to market and perform exchanges in their own right. We must, therefore, have recourse to their guardians, who are the possessors of the commodities" (178).[33] Having spent so much time in the commodity world, this recursive transition back to the world of guardians is belabored and confounded by imagery recollecting the vicissitudes of personification: "Commodities are things, and therefore lack the power to resist man. If they are unwilling, he can use force, in other words, he can take possession of them" (178). Within these two sentences the movement back and forth between commodities-qua-things and commodities-qua-persons ("unwilling") complicates and undermines the recourse to the world of the guardians. Indeed, no sooner have guardians been established as forceful and agential possessors than we find that their world too is contrived by personification: "Here the persons exist for one another merely as representatives . . . of commodities . . . in general, the characters who appear on the economic stage are merely personifications of economic relations; it is as the bearers of these economic relations that they come into contact with each other" (179). The priority of the person over the commodity is asserted, but almost instantly the commodity's personhood resurfaces, and with it the thing-hood of the person who is only a "representative" or "bearer," who exists "merely" (repeated twice) as personification.

The movement from the elementary form to the metaphysical form, from the commodity to the guardian (and back again), cannot rest with the elementary form of the guardian, but must rather take as its point of departure the arena of relations, the forum of exchange. Thus proceeds the next propulsive gesture: "Let us now accompany the owner of some commodity, say our old friend the linen weaver, to the scene of action, the market" (199). In the market, the arena arrived at by the metaleptic movement of the search for value within its varying forms of appearance, it becomes possible to observe the strange offspring of the commodity's promiscuous exchanging of body and soul: the exchange of bodies changes the body; the commodity effects a "metamorphosis." This "troublesome" "transubstantiation," as it is elsewhere repeatedly called, is not a passive process undergone by the commodity, but an active one, requiring "the leap" "from the body of the commodity into the body of the gold" (200). Marx is at pains to mark this leap sufficiently, to name it adequately: now it is "metamorphosis," now it is "transubstantiation," now it is the *"salto mortale."* The very proliferation of names for this process performs the metaleptic momentum it delineates, the suspension of one figure by another, the substitution of one figure (commodity, figure of value) for another (gold, figure of commodity, hence figure of abstract value).

Thus when the mystery of the commodity form is found to inhere in a leap, for which the text uses the striking image of *"salto mortale,"* the finding is most effectively disclosed by the recurrence of the same leap within the narrative structure itself. The *salto mortale* happens twice—once on the part of the commodity, and again on the part of the narrative: "Capital must have its origin both in circulation and not in circulation. We therefore have a double result. These are the conditions of the problem: *hic rhodus, hic salta!*" (269). A challenge to leap in the here and now, Marx's evocation of Aesop recalls Hegel's prescription for philosophy in the here and now.[34] Thus concludes the chapter on "Contradictions in the General Formula for Capital"—but these contradictions have not been solved so much as displaced; and so the next chapter commences on the other side of the abyss cleared in the leap. The duplicitous origin of value both within and without circulation is ostensibly addressed after the leap by the discovery of a reiterated duplicity, "a commodity whose use-value possesses the peculiar property of being a source of value" (270). Labor derives its use-value as a commodity from its embodiment in concrete ontological form of the otherwise ontologically inconsistent value. This ontological oscillation animates labor—*it is more than it has.* Its value is "in it more than it"; its use-value is this valorizing capacity of its value.[35]

It is this excessive potentiality of labor—this fact that labor is in excess of itself—that complicates any grounding of value in labor, for how can something so dynamic furnish a fixed ground? And so indeed no sooner has labor been introduced as a figure for the "makeshift" grounding of exchange than it is supplanted by a metonymically linked notion: labor-time. Labor as such cannot ground value (ultimately there is no ground for the ungrounded); and so a related figure replaces it, "labor-time," the abstract, universal, putatively comparable unit of expenditure of labor. But even then, labor-time is itself supplanted by the figure of "social labor-time" (as opposed to "abstract labor time"), for it is only *after* labor-time has been subject to "quantitative determination" and *after* it has been sold that it can precipitate the value it is purported to ground. This retroactive grounding means, as Karatani astutely underscores, that nothing is guaranteed:

> A commodity cannot express its value—no matter how much labor time is expended to produce it—if it is not sold. Seen *ex post facto* the value of a commodity could be considered as existing in social labor time, while in *ex ante facto,* there is no such guarantee.[36]

Value without guarantees. Value after the fact, but not before. This is the instability of the capitalist metaphysic, the retroactive traction of an abstraction. After the fact of selling it can be said that labor, nay labor-time, nay social labor-time, grounds value, but this ground can only be achieved by the leap—the leap of the sale, the leap of the commodity, the leap across the chasm of impossibility. In order to represent this leap, the text of *Capital* takes its own leap, *hic Rhodus, hic salta!* The narrative momentum of *Capital* is described by these propulsive leaps: the movement from labor to labor-time to social labor-time to the leap—a movement I have been calling metalepsis—here enfolds within the text of *Capital* a rhythmic performance of its own concept. With each contradiction, each double result, each fathoming of abyssal foundationlessness, the narrative leaps.

Across the books of *Capital* this leap rebounds, the text becoming, like *Scorpion and Felix* before it, an echo of *Tristram Shandy*'s frenetic digressive energy. The propulsion of the leap reverberates in numerous correlative images of "throwing," "flinging," and "hurling" (*werfen, einwerfen, schleudern*), the "incessant" but "alternating rhythm" of spurts and jumps, wages and waste, banishment and abandon.[37] It is by this motion of leaps that Marx depicts "the enormous power" of capitalist "expansion," its "elasticity, a capacity for sudden extension by leaps."[38] Active and passive, compulsive and controlled, these verbs effect the jerking (*stossweise*), unstable disequilibrium of the leap, formalizing the automatic repetitive tick of drive.

No wonder, then, that the only conclusion possible for such a book is the union of the leap and of drive:

> But the accumulation of capital presupposes surplus-value; surplus-value presupposes the availability of considerable masses of capital and labor-power in the hands of commodity producers. The whole movement, therefore, seems to turn around in a glitching circuit (*fehlerhaften Kreislauf*), which we can only get out of by assuming a primitive accumulation which precedes capitalist accumulation; an accumulation which is not the result of the capitalist mode of production but its point of departure (873).[39]

The glitching circuit distills the topos of drive as a lurching, incomplete circulation propelled forth by its own failure to approach its object. We arrive at the end of a lengthy journey, only to find ourselves back at the beginning. Later Marxist reformulations of primitive accumulation as a constant feature of capitalism, rather than a stage, make explicit what unfurls implicitly in this image of the glitching circuit.[40] The looping motion of the narrative whose end is its own beginning, which can only find its beginning at the end, mimes the metaphysic of capital, its positing its own preconditions:

> Just as the heavenly bodies always repeat a certain movement, once they have been flung into it, so also does social production, once it has been flung into this movement of alternate expansion and contraction. Effects become causes in their turn, and . . . the whole process . . . always reproduces its own conditions (786).

Effects become causes in their turn. We have seen such momentum to surge at the moment of finance, when the fictitious becomes the real. Realizing capital poses a "case of metaphysics," which finally signifies this self-positing system, a process producing its own conditions of possibility. The turn we have noted of financial journalism and bourgeois political economy toward psychologism symptomatizes this metaleptic metaphysic; Marx's own discourse discloses it. All the metaleptic movement of the narrative strives at representing this worldly metalepsis, capital's own substitution of effect for cause.[41] If this ungroundedness is the key to Marx's grasp of capital's dynamism, it has been most dexterously formulated by the dynamic motion of the figurative texture of *Capital* itself.

Personification and metalepsis are but two of the many tropes that structure *Capital,* just as structuring tropes are but one of the many features *Capital* shares with the Victorian novel. Figurative reading accesses the conceptual agency of literary form, opening onto the many ways in which *Capital* realizes its insights not argumentatively, but aesthetically. Reading Marx's Victorian novel is only one way to encounter his text, but it magnifies the verve of his critique—that we may more spiritedly, more materially, advance it.

6.   *Psychic Economy and Its Vicissitudes*

Freud's Economic Hypothesis

Psychic economy: a notion so ubiquitous, a conceit so familiar, it ranks as one of modernity's reigning tropes. Within the languages of psychoanalysis and psychology, "psychic economy" is first among proper names for substantifying the workings of desire, sexuality, the psyche, and even the conscious mind, finally designating the foundational structure of psychosocial life. Alongside these proprietary discourses of the psyche, other disciplines—from sociology to education, economics to literature—pepper their frameworks with assured references to this foundation. "Economy," this casual ubiquity evinces, warrants no explanation; it aptly encapsulates the structure of subjectivity and opportunely portends the structural continuity between individuals and sociopolitical macro-economy.[1]

The preceding chapters have argued that the construct of psychic economy has a history—issuing from the discourses of Victorian psychology and political economy amid financialization—and a function: dispelling the riddles of the "case of metaphysics" roused by realizing capital. Assembling that history enables us to appreciate the complexities of the intellectual field against which the novels of Dickens, Eliot, and Trollope emerge, affirming the dexterity with which literature engages the supreme fictions of the nonliterary world. Moreover, the reading of major Victorian novels in light of this history illuminates the unsavory consequences of widespread fascination with "psychic economy": minimizing ethical obligations, economizing personal relationships, realizing capital. Taking its impetus from this literary concern with the world-making power of metaphor, this book has aimed to defamiliarize the metaphoric conjunction of subjectivity and economy. I want to conclude, therefore, by introducing a disjunction between this strange notion and its reputed origin, Freudian psychoanalysis. Although the twentieth-century consensus that there exists a thing we can usefully denote with "psychic economy" happily credits Freud with patenting this denotation, the nineteenth-century history of the metaphor exposes a different origin. In light of my investigation of that history, I contend that Freud neither consecrates a concept nor coins a term, but rather experiments with the metaphor, contemplating its uses and abuses, tracing the mechanisms of its over-determination. In the tradition of the Victorian novels he so relished, Freud breaks with the ideological supposition of Victorian prose thinkers that desire is the truth of capital, instead making explicit that "economy" is merely a figure for the psyche—in principle, one potential figure among others. His economic logics disturb the stasis of reification; his interpretations keep figures in motion.

Far from the founding inscription of "psychic economy," Freud's economic thought amounts rather to a translation and reworking. Economic imagery absolutely anchors Freud's wide-ranging work—it provides rhetorical architecture for his first attempts to outline psychoanalysis and buttresses major revisions to the principles of psychoanalysis—and he consistently built it up, grading "the economic" essential to his "metapsychology." Along with the "topographic," which maps regions of the psyche (conscious, unconscious, preconscious, and later, id, ego, superego), and the "dynamic," which models repression (regulating the expression of psychic ideas in and across the different topographic regions), the "economic" is the third of Freud's metapyschological hypotheses, metaphorizing the "distribution" of psychic resources. Arguably, "the economic" stands less as one of three than as a *meta*-metapsychology, for it conditions the other two: psychic topography and psychic dynamism both derive from psychic equilibrium. Psychoanalysis thus accords a determinate priority (we might even say "economic determinism") to "the economic," from the first to the last instance: the inaugural *Project for a Scientific Psychology* (1895) all the way through the ultimate *Civilization and Its Discontents* (1934) equally stipulate fixity of psychic resources and systematic psychic organization.

Yet even with this undeniable centrality of the economic hypothesis to Freudian psychoanalysis, "economy" is no unambiguous signifier for Freud. Thus there are competing scholarly attempts to historicize one or another vector of his economics—such as his enrollment in physics courses or his enmeshment in bourgeois Vienna.[2] My turn to Freud returns to the texture of his own economic language to take stock of the whole shape of his economic thinking and thereby achieve a more nuanced interpretation of what psychic economy might signify in psychoanalysis. To do so, I heed the lead of the Victorian novelists, whom, after all, Freud read deeply, and whom he credited with discovering psychoanalysis before him.[3] Freud's careful reflection on metaphoric language partakes of the realist novelists' animating investigation of metaphor and reference, and just as we have followed that investigation by closely reading novelistic rhetoric, here I will pay close attention to Freud's economic language.

Inspired by Victorian novels, the endeavor to read Freud closely also stems from the work of Freud's closest reader, Jacques Lacan. For Lacan Freud's thought inheres in his twists and turns, reformulations and new topographies, and thus "the poetics of Freud's work" open "the first entryway into its meaning."[4] In the wending and winding inspirations and revolutions of Freud's economic language, I find a richness and complexity of meanings that mirror the Victorian novel's dual concern with the ungroundedness of economy and with the problematic ground laid by psychic economy. When Freudian theory presented psychoanalysis as something radically other than psychology, it broke with much that was Victorian. Yet since, as I have argued, major realist novels cast particular aspersions on the Victorian psychic economy matrix, Freud's discarding of Victorian psychology's reified psychic economy may be seen as maintaining allegiance to Victorian novels. Freud's idea of economy, I argue, is multidimensional, multisemic, and, above all else, metaphoric: a metaphor that never loses sight of its own metaphoricity, a metaphor that splices the terms it also entangles. As metaphor, as self-consciously experimental thinking, Freud's economy performatively discloses the essentially open, antagonistic, and dynamic nature of any given economy. I propose that this sensation of economy as figurative succession (to recall the definition of metalepsis from Chapter 1)—and not Freud's alleged naturalization of "investor psychology"—constitutes the seminal psychoanalytic contribution to the critique of political economy. By emphasizing the openness of economy and the contingent constitutions of economic life, psychoanalysis elaborates the *political* dimension of political economy, the impossibility that any particular mode of economy is immanent to the psyche.

The Economic Base

When in 1895 a young Freud first set out to devise a radical alternative to psychology, the potential benefits of some sort of economic figuration immediately intrigued him. He wrote in a letter to Fliess, "I am tormented (*mich quälen*) . . . to discover what form the theory of psychical functioning will take if . . . a kind of economics (*eine Art Oekonomik*) . . . is introduced into it."[5] Psychoanalysis might benefit from and indeed require a kind of economics, because, in Freud's view, all science, whether physics, chemistry, biology, or psychology, necessarily employed what he called "figurative language" (*Bildersprache*), for "we could not otherwise describe the processes in question at all, and indeed we could not have become aware of them."[6] "It is only from analogies," Freud asserts, "that we shall find the courage to set up the hypotheses necessary for throwing a more penetrating light upon" psychic life.[7] In psychoanalysis as in science, figurative language is indispensable and perhaps even desirable: since the unconscious speaks in figures, theorizing the unconscious best proceeds through figures.

Out of its primal demand to name the unnamable, psychoanalysis appropriates "a kind of economics."[8] As generative as this importing of economics might be for the nascent theory, for the incipient theorist it is inseparable from "torment." Across Freud's oeuvre, torment unsettles almost every reference to the economic, betraying the fixed edges of this figurative prism, much the way the qualifying "kind of" surveys the insurmountable chasm between what is wished for and what is attained. Freud held open this gap, warning that the economy image only amounted to "a rather vague expression" and constantly marking the image with scare quotes, self-reflexive confessions, qualifications, and adverbial circumlocutions like "so to speak," "so called" (*sozusagen, sogenannte*).[9] Freud couples his economic expressions with consistent and considered indication of the speech acts that generate them. All this conscientious circumspection dissolves the coherence of "psychic economy" consecrated by Victorian psychologists and political economists and puts to shame the casual evocations that abound in contemporary discourse. We epigones have long since settled into a colloquial comfort with psychic economy, but we would do well to mark the vexation, conscientiousness, and complexity that attend Freud's formulations.

For the Victorian psychologists who preceded him, the rhetoric of psychic economy functioned as an answer, not as a question. As we have seen, Alexander Bain, Herbert Spencer, George Henry Lewes, and William Stanley Jevons, fathers of psychology and modern economics both, authored their own economic hypotheses in which the language of exchange, distribution, and money described the mental functioning that comprised the macroeconomic desire theory of value. "Psychic economy" for these thinkers secured the ground of the otherwise ungrounded financial economy, realizing capital. Contrary to this reification, Freud chartered economic language experimentally, cautiously, speculatively. It is this note of caution that allies him to his beloved Victorian novelists, who, I have argued, astutely explore the costs of that metaphor—its misconstruing of intimate relations, its foreclosing of ethical obligations, its securing a ground where there is none. Freud's affiliate investigation takes a different shape: probing the performative effects of the metaphor, he asks anew what, in a speculative gambit rather than ideological reification, metaphors can do.

In this radical inquiry into the potentialities of metaphor, Freud experimentally engages "economy" in many aspects. For our project to defamiliarize the metaphor of "psychic economy," the first thing to note is that this experimentation destabilizes the thingliness of psychic economy. Indeed, quite strikingly, the Freudian syntax features the noun "psychic economy" exceedingly rarely—perhaps five times in the entire oeuvre.[10] James Strachey's translations have considerably muddied matters: he insistently inserts the English noun "economy" in numerous instances in which Freud stakes other holdings. To take just two examples, in *Dora: An Analysis of a Case of Hysteria,* Freud uses "psychic household (*psychischen Haushalt*)," but Strachey opts for "domestic economy of the mind"; in the essay "Libidinal Types," Freud writes "household of the soul (*seelischen Haushalt*)," while Strachey overwrites "libidinal economy."[11] In the context of Freud's relentless caution with economic language, Strachey's hasty consolidations seem problematically insensitive and misleading.

Despite the overarching importance of the economic hypothesis to the metapsychology, no nominative "psychic economy" predominates. Indeed, rather than to a concept or thing, Freud's appeal to "the economic" refers to a "point of view" (*Gesichtspunkt*), a consideration (*Betrachtung*), a perspective, a prism.[12] The economic signals a way of seeing, a "figurative language" with which to describe and to know—but a figure born of a torment, a figure that holds at a distance what it also brings into focus. "The economic," Freud repeatedly cautions, "leads us to one of the most important, but unluckily one of the most obscure, regions of psychoanalysis."[13] Ferried by metaphor into obscure realms, Freud even has a dream of finding himself on a train, moving confusedly between different cars, unable to determine whether he is the owner of a copy of Adam Smith's *The Wealth of Nations. The Interpretation of Dreams* reports that dream strangely, leaving it only partially interpreted—powerfully conveying the ongoing enigma of unaccountable crossings under the seminal sign of political economy.[14] As a point of view, as a figurative language, as a disoriented guide on shaky transport to obscure regions, "economy" inumbrates as much as it elucidates, dissimulates as much as it conceptualizes.

Where, for the Victorian psychological tradition and the hegemonic paradigm it installs, "psychic economy" designates a natural object, "the economy" heralds desire as its cause, and capital serves as the unique and adequate signifier of desire, for Freud "economy" does not occur naturally. Inextricably bound up with obscurity and torment, all it can signify is denatured objects and inadequate figures. If this means that psychoanalysis offers no immediate insights into economics, no sanctification of the marginal utility revolution's desire theory of value, and no naturalization of capitalism, this is so much the better for the psychoanalytic contribution to the critique of political economy. To get at that contribution, we must read Freud's economic images in the manner he himself demands they be read: figurally. Around the signifier "economy" circulate manifold modalities that cannot be reduced to "market" or "capitalism." As we shall see, at alternating junctures the language of economy evokes the *nomos* of the *oikos,* the law of the arrangement of life; a closed equilibrium; fixed material resources; a "system of writing"; and the disequilibrium of drive. It is to this very complexity and evasiveness of the figure of economy that we must look for Freud's greatest economic insights. The diversified economic figures in the Freudian portfolio attest to the fundamental polyvalence of "economy," what Marxian thought hails as its essentially *political* character. Freud's various formulations perform the essential deferral of the grounding of economy: *there is no given economy;* no hypostatized—or literally capitalized—Economy.[15] Economy as such is obscure; any instantiated economy *must be made,* designed, planned.

Households of the Soul

One connotation of economy stands out in Freud's thought—not for its simplicity or fundamentality, but for his unhesitating invocation of it:

> The motive of human society is in the last resort an economic one; since it does not possess enough provisions to keep its members alive unless they work, it must restrict the number of its members and divert their energies from sexual activity to work. It is faced, in short, by the eternal, primaeval exigencies of life, which are with us to this day. (*Das Motiv der menschlichen Gesellschaft ist im letzten Grund ein oekonomisches . . . die ewige, urzeitlich . . . Lebensnot.*)[16]

So many temporal adjectives underscore the immutability of the economic. In this instantiation, "economic" demarcates the insuperable base of existence, not the effect but the cause of human sociality—as Freud remarked in a letter to Roman Rolland: "I myself have always advocated the love of mankind not out of sentimentality or idealism but for sober, economic reasons: because in the face of our instinctual drives and the world as it is I was compelled to consider this love as indispensable for the preservation of the human species as, say, technology."[17] Over the course of his career, Freud returns several times to this unqualified, untormented reference to "the economic," indexing this ineluctable materiality that must be encountered, managed, formed into any particular economy—a formation that is always the object of political antagonism.[18] In this way Freud recalls the Aristotelean conception of the *oikos* as the arena of eating and drinking, dwelling and laboring, whose every constitution under a *nomos* is contingent.[19] It is this necessity-contingency polarity that galvanizes the enigmas of existence and enjoyment. "Economy" in this instance names the necessary fact *that there is economy*—a fact in excess of any definite articles or defining predicates.

When Freud then repeatedly conjures a "psychic household" (*psychischen Haushalt*), his image entails not only a mental space for carrying out "work" and managing the "stuff of life" (*Lebensmittel*), but also an analogously inexorable and contingent arrangement of the psychic: there is no immanent order of the mind.[20] This idea of arrangement founded on the household image fundamentally frames Freud's notion of the psyche, which is why he prefers the noun "household" to "economy." As Lacan observes:

> If the psyche has any meaning, if there is a reality which is called psychic reality, or, in other words, if living beings exist, it is in so far as there is an internal organization (*organization interne*) which up to a certain point tends to oppose the free and unlimited passage of forces and discharges of energy, such as we may assume to exist, in a purely theoretical way, intercrossing in the inanimate reality.[21]

Economic language facilitates Freud's depiction of this reality: if life must be made from available materials and happy accidents, then so must the psyche. Libido is "something that should be differentiated—an amount of affect, a sum of excitation—something having all the attributes of a quantity, although we possess no means of measuring it."[22] The material stuff whose intersection with the signifier is the object of psychoanalytic interpretation presents itself obliquely—in dreams, jokes, and symptoms. Economic language—"production, increase or decrease, distribution and displacement" and "investments and withdrawals"—helps to make such an intersection available to analytic discourse.[23] Indeed, the initial clinical encounter with hysteria and obsession inspired this "quantitative conception," which was "derived directly" from the problems of "excess" that such pathologies evince: psychic energy manifesting as hysterical excess must have been displaced by repressive subtraction elsewhere in the topography of the subject.[24] If "a kind of economics" lends structure to the emergent libido theory, this loan is entirely analogical: it is, in the interest of accounting for the systematicity of an as yet unidentified system, a borrowing of the vocabulary and relationships of another system. In repayment, by providing an interpretative procedure for economic dynamics in the psyche, psychoanalysis might offer itself as a model of a structural analysis of any particular given economy.[25] But for all this mutual interpretative benefit, within Freudian thought it is quite clear that there is no grounding function between the two systems: while the Victorians sought to present psychic economics as the basis of capitalist economics, Freud does not avow that agenda. Rather, his is a thought in process, a thought in search of its object and of the tools of its search, and a thought that espouses its own status as both under construction and experimentally metaphorical.

One of the most common errors leading to the confusion of Freud's economic thought with a naturalization of capitalism is the translation of *Besetzung* as "investment." Strachey proposed "cathexis," but most regularly used "investment"—a translation I find highly ideological, for it has played no small role in the reception of Freud as a universalizer of a particularly capitalist subjectivity.[26] To reapproach Freud's slippery term, we can start with the notion of "arrangement of resources" consequent upon the household image. The appeal of the verb *besetzen* rests precisely in its domestic ubiquity, its manifold quotidian denotations. It encompasses "to put," "to place," "to cast," "to occupy," and many other open-ended functions. Freud deliberately opted to root his idea in this polysemous verb, activating an unusual noun to substantialize an everyday, everywhere, ongoing process of organizing, putting something to use in a certain way.[27] That deliberate choice explains numerous facts of textual and translation history. For starters, he resisted Strachey's invention of "cathexis" and did not even use the word *Besetzung* anywhere in the paper from which Strachey took one of his main connotations, an "electric charge."[28] Over the course of time he mobilized diverse, context-dependent expressions when making English translations of his own work, selecting verbs like "colored" or "toned" where Strachey uses "cathected" or "invested."[29] And finally, he declined to ever fix the definition of the term. All of these factors comprise Freud's repeated affirmation of the intrinsically dynamic character of *Besetzung*. It was an economic tenet for him: material must be put to use, but how that use is valorized remains an open question. If there is an economy of the psyche, it is the arena not of any particular mode of production, but of vivacious, adaptive use. Both the homogenization of "cathexis" and its standard incautious translation into "investment" totally eclipse Freud's careful convictions about the complexity of psychic functions, egregiously inflating the capitalist economic parallels. In the sway of these translations, and in the swell of the Victorian rubric, it becomes very difficult to hew rigorously to the subtlety of Freud's insights and the polysemy of his language. But close scrutiny of the corpus reveals that "investment" occludes the diversity of processes at work; characterizing the Freudian subject as an "investor" and thus a typical bourgeois agent of finance dangerously reduces the intricacy of Freud's ideas.[30]

Alongside his interest in arrangement and relative intensity, Freud experimented with the "working hypothesis" of "quantity," a tentative heuristic for experimentally apprehending this material and intensity.[31] At times Freud suggested that "quantitative" might be a preferable synonym for "economic" in his thought, and quantity jumps to the forefront in those discussions of the economic metapsychology that seek to explain Freud's economic language as a reflexive mirroring of his study of the works of Fechner and Helmholtz.[32] Here, too, that explanatory gesture under-reads the dynamic and generative aspects of Freud's conscientiously figurative language. Freud adamantly maintained not only that "quantity" was a figure, but that it was an instrumental figure, a useful figure, to which he gave the unusual compound name *Hilfsvorstellung*—a "helping image" (like a "helping verb").[33] The insufficiency of this help never falls out of focus: Freud deems quantity a figure for something else, "something which possesses all the attributes of a quantity though we have no means of measuring it."[34] Terms like "increase" or "decrease," "yield" or "withdrawal" belong to this experimental framework, adding further dimension even as they propagate its inexactitude—hence Freud's caution that such quantifiers connote something "relative" rather than absolute.[35]

An alert ear always discerns the approximate, insufficient timbre of these images, and Freud asserts repeatedly that quantity is merely a proxy for the qualitative determinations that remain utterly elusive.[36] He writes almost plaintively, in *The Economic Problem of Masochism,* for instance, of the unsuitability of quantity:

> Pleasure and unpleasure therefore cannot be referred to an increase or decrease of a quantity ... they depend, not on some quantitative factor, but on some characteristic of it which we can only describe as a qualitative one. If we were able to say what this qualitative characteristic is, we should be much further advanced in psychology. Perhaps it is the rhythm, the temporal sequence of changes, rises in falls in the quantity of stimulus. We do not know *(wir wissen es nicht)*.[37]

Quantity is a tool, a makeshift of last resort, a figure in the service of grasping at what "we do not know." Later critics often cling to quantity as the basic meaning of Freud's economic thought, referring it to the thermodynamic and physical models Freud studied in his youth and citing it as a foundational analogy attesting to a fundamental continuity. Deleuze and Guattari punctuate this tendency: "Just as Ricardo founds political or social economy by discovering quantitative labor as the principle of every representable value, Freud founds desiring-economy by discovering the quantitative libido as the principle of every representation of the objects and aims of desire."[38] But the nature of the thought-experiment was that helping-images could be used, tested, and rejected, and so Freud took creative license with physics allusions, and then discarded conservation models as early as 1905.[39] "We have long since abandoned the most obvious and simplest view of this economy," he wrote in reference to the conservation image. Freud's insistence on the dynamism symbolized and performed by his economic language allows for this conceptual flux and agility.

Substitutive Representations

To the extent that "quantity" augurs finite intensities, what it helps to image is not scarcity, but the lump sum: the psyche insists on its own complete integrity. Its will to make itself known compels it, where complete expression is internally prohibitive or externally prohibited, to seek out substitute expressions. Dreams, parapraxes, fantasies, and symptoms all come to be thought of as "substitutive representations."[40] The unconscious insists, but does not directly exist—it must be reckoned with through representation.[41] Significantly, Freud conceived this representation as a "system of writing" that he opposed to a "language," elevating the pictorial, graphic, and material dimensions of representation above its referential or signifying function.[42] And just as the psyche commissions successive figurative expressions to make itself known, psychoanalysis crafts figurative language to make itself know—a figurative language that, Freud's tireless reservations about metapsychology remind us, is always in flux.[43] Thus in 1925 Freud expands "the economic factor" to exceed "quantity" and incorporate this agency of insistent substitutive figuration—and he retroacts this expansion all the way back to *Studies on Hysteria*.[44]

Indeed, Freud had already obliquely formulated "economy" as a forum of "substitutive representations" with his analogy between obsession and currency in "Notes on a Case of Obsessional Neurosis" (1909). I want to linger over this case of the Rat Man, one whose insights Freud suffers more than narrativizes, and which we have yet to assimilate. Surprisingly, the Rat Man is not addressed by major critical works on Freud's economic thought such as Goux's *Symbolic Economies* or Lyotard's *Libidinal Economy*.[45] In *The Post Card,* Derrida alludes to this unaddressable quality of the Rat Man, registering in his initial section of postal messages (which he recommends be read "as the preface to a book that I have not written") the density and dream-like quality I am referring to: "Yes, I was speaking to you of the Rat Man. Nothing about it has been understood yet, or so I feel . . . the passage is essential, constitutive, irreducible. Not a step of Freud's which does not come back to it."[46] For all this essential importance, then, the case of the Rat Man remains strangely under-encountered. One of the great enigmas of Freud's archive, his singular act of retaining the Rat Man's original case notes (it was his habit to destroy raw material after working through it), attests to this unencountered status.[47]

The Rat Man, let us recall, is a patient who experiences obsessional fantasies about rats—specifically, the enactment of a military torture regimen. In his fantasies, his father and his fiancée are subjected to the torture, suffering anal penetration by rats. Analysis of the fantasies educes associations of "rats" with torture and authority, with vermin and filth, with offspring and penises, and, finally, with money, loans, debts, and compounds. Within the case study this polysemic proliferation ensnares analysand and analyst alike, for Freud not only hunts the rats in the Rat Man's language, such as his upcoming marriage (*Heirat*), he also furrows around in a wealth of associations in his own analytic discourse. Fantastically playing with verbs, gerunds, adjectives, and nouns with "*Rat*" at their root, he calls the case a *Rätsel* (riddle) and deems the process by which "Rat" has acquired so many associations *"hinzutraten"* (accumulating). No wonder then that the Rat Man himself, remarking the homophone between *"Ratten"* (the plural "rats") and *"Raten"* (the plural "rates") and *"raten"* (the verb "to counsel"), arrives at a formula for the analytic exchange: "so many gulden, so many rats." The Rat Man comes to analysis *to work,* and for that privilege he pays, *twice,* in gulden and in rats—and receives, in return, more rats.[48] For his part Freud notes that in this transaction the Rat Man purchases (*erwerben*) ever more associations for "Rat," and he concludes that through the logic of his neurosis the Rat Man "had coined a regular rat currency" (*eine förmliche Rattenwährung eingesetzt*).[49] Freud's ratting around in puns betokens the particular formation of economy at stake in this case: however much "Rat" symbolizes to the analysand, to the analyst "Rat" symbolizes above all else the sheer possibility of symbolization, the possibility upon which currencies capitalize.[50]

Economy may be incarnated as a system for symbolic substitution, conjuring the abstraction "value" to ground exchange, coining currency to symbolize value, commissioning paper to substitute for precious metal. The psyche may be understood as a forum of substitutive mechanisms—as indeed Freud had already elaborated in his interpretation of dreams, symptoms, and parapraxes. With the Rat Man case and the currency metaphor, Freud analogizes these two modes of substitution. In this case, then, Freud introduces yet another connotation of "economy" into his overall project: next to "household" and the dispensation of quantity, a network of symbolic representation much like the notion behind the discourse of fictitious capital. At the same time, his thought here opens onto the possibility that psychoanalysis, as the theory of symbolic substitution, might apprehend structures of substitution beyond the subject. The repetition of formal structures in multiple aspects of human social life (in, say, the unconscious as well as in capitalism) becomes an object of inquiry for psychoanalysis, which vigilantly restrains itself from accounting for this repetition as a naturalization of capitalism. Quite to the contrary, in discovering the structures of exchange dispersed throughout human culture, psychoanalysis helps illuminate how capitalism need not monopolize differential symbolization. Capitalism, everyone from nineteenth-century financial journalists to twentieth-century philosopher-critics might say, is inextricable from symbolization.[51] In the Rat Man case and beyond, Freud authorizes a radical qualification of this argument: while capitalism presents itself as coeval with symbolization, symbolization has priority.

As my emphasis on the unencountered oddity of the Rat Man case is meant to convey, Freud's quick, quipping currency analogy functions here much more as a symptom than an analysis, a rat chasing its own tail. Much like the torment that inspires psychoanalysis, the analogy between neurosis and currency in the Rat Man gnaws at Freud. That unsettling opacity powerfully evinces that something in this mode of economy-qua–perpetual symbolization proves recalcitrant to accounting—an incisive point about capital if ever there was one.[52] And it equally confirms that not all of Freud's economic thought can be assimilated to economy-qua–symbolic substitution—that not all of what Freud grasps under the sign "economy" is continuous with capital.

Capital Analogies

Crucially, we must tender the same observation about the "not all" of Freudian economy apropos the most notorious moment of economic language, Freud's analogy between an unconscious wish and a capitalist. Since the analogy multiplies and slides, it is necessary to quote at length:

> I am now in a position to give a precise account of the part played in dreams by the unconscious wish . . . worry alone could not have made a dream. The *motive force* (*Triebkraft*) which the dream required had to be provided by a wish; it was the business of the worry to get hold of a wish to act as the motive force of the dream.
>
> The position may be explained by an analogy (*um es in einem Gleichnis zu sagen*). A daytime thought may very well play the part of *entrepreneur* for a dream; but the entrepreneur, who, as people say, has the idea and the initiative to carry it out, can do nothing without capital; he needs a *capitalist* who can afford the outlay, and the capitalist who provides the psychical outlay for the dream is invariably and indisputably, whatever may be the thoughts of the previous day, a *wish from the unconscious*. Sometimes the capitalist is himself the entrepreneur, and indeed in the case of dreams this is the commoner event: an unconscious wish is stirred up by daytime activity and proceeds to construct a dream. So, too, the other possible variations in the economic situation that I have taken as an analogy have their parallel in dream-processes. The entrepreneur may himself make a small contribution to the capital; several entrepreneurs may apply to the same capitalist; several capitalists may combine to put up what is necessary for the entrepreneur. In the same way, we come across dreams that are supported by more than one dream-wish.

The tertium comparationis in the analogy that I have just used—
the quantity put at the disposal of the entrepreneur in an appropriate
amount—is capable of being applied in still greater detail to the purpose of
elucidating the structure of dreams. In most dreams it is possible to detect a
central point which is marked by peculiar sensory intensity . . . if we undo
the displacements brought about by the dream-work, we find that the *psychical* intensity of the elements in the dream-thoughts has been replaced by
the *sensory* intensity of the elements in the content of the actual dream. . . .
Thus the wish-fulfillment's power of brining about representation is diffused over a certain sphere surrounding it, within which all the elements—
including even those possessing no means of their own—become empow-
ered to obtain representation.[53]

Enthusiasts of "psychic economy" as a link between psychological subjectivity and capital always cite this analogy as their ultimate trump card, so let us
tease out its actual logic. As is Freud's habit, the analogy is introduced not
casually, but deliberately and self-consciously. Strachey uses "explain" where
Freud in fact writes "to say it in an analogy." Freud, like the daytime worry,
is looking for a means of expression. He turns to analogy for that means.
The analogy offers the new terms "entrepreneur," "capital," "capitalist," and
"outlay." "Entrepreneur" represents the daytime thought (the worry in this
instance); "capital" represents the "means" of representation; "capitalist" represents the unconscious wish; and "outlay" represents the material signifiers
and images that, by way of condensations and displacements, will afford the
unconscious wish and the daytime thought representation. This very proliferation of terms in Freud's analogy itself illustrates the diversity of linguistic
means by which a dream is made.

In aiding Freud to depict the processes of distortion, derivation, and over-
determination that produce the dream, the capital analogy works in a very
specific way. Far from signaling unconscious desires for investment or a drive
for accumulation, this analogy ultimately boils down again to the "helping
image" of "quantity," the place where Freud concludes. Here as elsewhere,
quantity remains marked as itself an analogy, a way of grasping the multi-
variable intensity and the pulsating insistence of the unconscious on making creative use of signifiers to externalize itself. Capital is not the stuff of
desire, nor even the most efficient symbol of desire, but rather the dynamic
means of representing unconscious dynamics, which desire itself represents.
The Victorian construct in which capital expresses desire and the economy

booms and busts as desires vacillate is here reversed: capital is no special issue, but merely an image Freud crafts conscientiously, even hesitantly, to signify the linguistic (metaphoric, metonymic, metaleptic) operations of unconscious thought.

What can be said of the connections between capital and the unconscious is here far from formulatable, and the unfinished business dramatically propels an archival oddity that rivals Freud's enigmatic retention of the Rat Man case notes: Freud committed quite bizarre, unadorned self-citation of this *Triebkraft*-capital(ist) analogy on two occasions, acknowledging a kind of compulsion to repeat. In *Fragment of an Analysis of a Case of Hysteria,* he inserts:

> I have made one or two observations in my *Interpretation of Dreams* on the relation between the waking thoughts which are continued into sleep (the "day's residues") and the unconscious wish which forms the dream. I will quote them here as they stand, for I have nothing to add to them (*die ich hier unverändert zitieren werde, denn ich habe ihnen nichts hinzuzufügen*).[54]

And again, in *Introductory Lectures on Psychoanalysis:*

> I have made use of an analogy for the relation of the day's residues to the unconscious wish, and I can only repeat it here (*den ich hier nur wiederholen kann*).[55]

Crystallizing the torment around the helping-images of economy, the compulsive repetition of this analogy challenges as much as it confirms. Beneath the veneer of analogical aptitude lies an obduracy that cannot be confronted. This is no confident, triumphant suture of psyche and capital, but a strange stutter. Something—it tries to say—*something* of a relation between capital and dreams exists. In the end it is the compulsory repeating of the image that tells us more about the idea than the image itself: dreams, like capital, like repetition compulsions, are substitutive image engines—in the idiom of our inquiry, dreams and capital, machines of metalepsis both.

Unlike his contemporaries and predecessors, Freud's economic language did not work to ground economic phenomena in the psyche. Rather, by maintaining a strictly analogical relationship and by proceeding from the clinic outward to the metapsychology, Freud tentatively worked to explain economic phenomena as structures. By refusing psychological causality and instead illuminating economic structurality, the metapsychology renders an analysis of economic modes. Just as we have seen Marx's metaleptic formulation of the drive to constitute one of his greatest insights into capital, Freud's metaleptic economic hypothesis too begins to sketch an alternative, critical psychic economy construct that ought to be forcefully opposed to the reification of psychic economy-qua-naturalization of capital that I have argued defines much of Victorian discourse. Not surprisingly, it is also to the thought of drive where we must look for this radical alternative.

(D)riven Economies

Freud often reverentially limns the opacity and complexity of the drives, deeming them "mythical entities, splendid in their indefiniteness."[56] Essential but opaque, inevitable, yet variable, drives share the radical ontological openness of economy; the language of economy around drives captures this. Thus when Freud discovers the death drive, his first choice for how to frame the discovery is as an economic mystery. Indeed, the opening paragraphs of *Beyond the Pleasure Principle* reiterate that the economic metapsychology's emphasis on quantity and constancy is the closest Freud's thought can come to "the obscurest and least penetrable region of psychic life," the definition of pleasure. But as heuristically valuable as quantity and constancy have been up to this point, it has emerged from analytic experience that, however much the subject has a goal of pleasure, "the tendency toward the goal does not imply the attainment of it, and in general the goal is only approximately attainable."[57] The book elaborates this approximation of goals, hailing for the first time a structure of "short circuit" and "circuitous routes to a direct and substitutive satisfaction"—that is, introducing the contour of circuit to the paradigm of substitution Freud deems "currency."[58]

That effect reverberates in the narrative rhythm of *Beyond the Pleasure Principle,* whose argument progresses by staging three successive examples of failures of the principle (traumatic war neuroses, *fort-da* game, negative therapy), thereby performing the motion of circuitry: each incomplete idea gives way to another reiteration that is itself still incomplete. *Beyond the Pleasure Principle* thereby becomes a text whose recursive structure formalizes the topology of the "short circuit" that it identifies in psychic life. It opens with a discussion of the importance of the "economic" (set off by quotation marks also in the original). Freud claimed a reassessment of the economic axis as the occasion for that text, whose avowedly "speculative" gestures usher in the topos of "short circuit," those "circuitous routes to substitutive satisfaction" that the psyche follows instead of simply attaining its goals directly.[59]

For our purposes it is important to note that these insights inhere aesthetically, not just deictically. The theory of drive emerges more in the metaleptic structure of the text than in its enunciations—Freud does not rest with the articulation of repetition compulsion; the disturbance compels him to ever more formulations, subverting every attempt to specify it completely. The inadequacies of the successive examples of the repetition compulsion stir Freud to theorize drive, but the very inability to formulate the theory completely is already implicated in the structure of the drive itself. The topos performed by the argument presents the economic as a system that maintains itself "after its own fashion," circuitously, indirectly, through paradoxically generative failures. This text formalizes the disequilibrium of economy, the suspension of successive figures, the inevitably circuitous achievement of ends. Every *oikos,* because of its necessary and contingent *nomos,* will pursue its ends "in its own fashion," "after its own way."

As *Beyond the Pleasure Principle* works to become a theory of circuits, of how "the organism wishes to die only in its own fashion," this concept of indirection enfolds the pleasure principle itself into a more overarching "death drive" and expands economy from a closed-system to an internally riven, spastically driven anti-system.[60] The economy of drive is disequilibriate because drive names the excess in the subject beyond its systematicity, beyond its self-interest, beyond its own life. Drive is the enigmatic impulsion out of stasis and into dynamism, an enigma that paradoxically entails the ineluctable inertia back toward stasis, death, inorganicity. Death drive, "a function whose business it is to free the mental apparatus entirely from excitation or to keep the amount of excitation in it constant or to keep it as low as possible,"[61] mandates a return to an inorganic state. Here again we find cause for concern with Strachey's scientizing translation of *Trieb* as "instinct" rather than as "drive," for it has occluded an essential Freudian distinction. While instinct is directed outward, toward an external object that would satisfy it, drive is directed inward and remains objectless. In contrast to instinct, drive finds satisfaction through its very movement, the excessively repetitive circuit that yields still more excess. Without drive there is no enjoying subject, but the enjoying subject is not the drive's product (strictly speaking, drive has no product) so much as the *residue* of its movement. As this indirect circuit, the death drive paradoxically denominates the momentum of life, even though this is not its goal. When the subject, as we have seen in Marx's language, is capital, the accretion of this excess appears as its own end, to reap accumulation from ever more circulation, to turn debts into profits, to extract surplus from destruction. Capitalism endeavors to turn excess to account, whereas the ultimate motion of the drive is ontologically unaccountable.

Discovering that repetition compulsion lends a circuitous topos to enjoyment and a "short-circuit" shape to life, Freud also discovers this unaccountability of drive, and that disequilibrium is a truer form of economy. *Beyond the Pleasure Principle's* narration of "repetition compulsion" complements the earlier notion of an economic tendency toward constancy by another economic quality, that of continuous repetitive circuits. From a notion of an efficient, self-contained equilibrium, the economic hypothesis shifts, now encompassing a suspensive oscillation between excitation and release, expansion and contraction, excess and efficiency, what Freud terms a "vacillating rhythm" (49). Freud's understanding that "the aim of all life is death" is leavened with the formulation that "the living organism struggles most energetically against events (dangers, in fact) which might help it to attain its life's aim rapidly—by a kind of short-circuit" (47). The figure "short-circuit" opens the closed conception of economy-qua–equilibrate system, installing instead the conception of economy-qua–disequilibrate, paradoxically productive failure.

Freud framed the discovery of drive as a revaluation of his economic point of view, and any utilitarian resonance of the purposeful pursuit of pleasure is dissipated by the form of "circuitous routes" the subject follows instead of attaining its goals directly. Drive therefore animates another register of the economy figure: the suspensive oscillation between the pleasure principle and the movement beyond the pleasure principle. This additional valence of economy invites us to conclude that no simple expository project operates through the figurative language of economy; no unitary concept is enshrined. Therein lies the force of psychoanalytic economic thought. The sheer density and polyvalence of Freud's economic figures—the household, the closed system, the network of substitutions, the disequilibrium of drive—disclose the radical openness of economy and the antagonism that founds every contingent economic order. Driven by this openness, psychoanalysis signifies and resignifies economy at every turn, from the *Project* to *Civilization and Its Discontents,* premising a mode of reading and an experimental science upon the metaleptic inconsistency, rather than the reified positivity, of its object.

In the simplest sense, of which we need remind those critics who make so many mountains of a single capital analogy, Freud's economic metapsychology departs from the Victorian rubric, since he omits claims about capitalist economy as the fulfillment of human nature.[62] More strikingly, a radical distinction emerges from Freud's unwavering emphasis on the *figurative* tenor of his economic thought. Against the long durée of ideological literalizations, Freud's economic thought advances figuratively: "economy" itself functions as a figure, a figure whose referent cannot be reliably determined, a figure that divulges just how much referential unreliability is crucial to economic relations. Psychologism occludes this antagonism and forecloses this contingency, forsaking structural analysis of financial leverage for dissembling platitudes about insatiable desire, reifying "psychic economy" to forcibly naturalize the capitalist mode of economy. What is proper to Freud, by contrast, is the torment that incites psychoanalysis, the helping-images with which it develops its revolutionary inquiry, the radical questioning by which psychoanalysis transcends psychology, and the condensation of all of these things in the economy that knows itself as figure.

Epilogue   *The Psychic Life of Finance*

Although this book focuses on Victorian thought in the past, Victorianism remains alive in the present. In our epoch of global financial turmoil, we have not only to reckon with collateralized debt obligations, toxic assets, and zombie banks, but also with the obfuscating din of economic discourses that explain away the contradictions of capital as merely psychological phenomena. When Federal Reserve Chairman Benjamin Bernanke testified before the United States Congress about the causes of the economic meltdown of 2008, he pled lack of expertise: "Senator, you asked me my opinion as an economist," he said with a smile, "but unfortunately this is a matter for psychology."[1] With his coy disclaimer Bernanke crystallized the commonly invoked psychology defense for economics: the buck stops with the subject of fickle desires. From the *New York Times* to the Brookings Institution to Yale and UPenn, talking heads have widely intoned this mantra: "irrational exuberance was the fundamental cause" of the Great Recession.[2] Not the structures of finance, but the structures of feeling economists claim precede them are enshrined as the ultimate ground of the economy. Even those economists and politicians who sufficiently entertain structural analysis to forgo the language of flagging confidence and identify failing regulations *still* posit an underlying psychology as the root of economic volatility. One economist put the case best: "over-arching all these other pieces (excessive leverage, weak regulation) is psychology. If it weren't for psychological issues, even with all of that in place we wouldn't have the fiasco we have now."[3]

As widespread appeals to the depth psychology of crisis attest, the discipline of psychology offers not only a set of tropes for economic phenomena ("mania," "panic," "depression"), but also a matrix of causality within which systemic inconsistencies of capital such as the futurity of credit and the specularity of value are displaced onto the psychological idiosyncrasies of individuals. Interpreted through this matrix, the chimerical instruments of finance appear as inevitable and innate flows of affect: unstable financial instruments are traded for an unstable mass psychology—a foundationless house of cards for playing without a full deck.

This trade—the displacement of structure by psychology, what I have called "psychologism"—has a history that might arguably be dated to as early as Adam Smith's immanent rule of the inadvertent beneficence of "immense desires" and that, as Bernanke's successful exculpatory testimony indicates, will continue to unfold tomorrow. This book has been less a survey of that history than a sketch of an episode of rhetorical torsion, an episode of psychologism as it came to subvert a reigning paradigm of structure. That episode transpires in the late 1850s and early 1860s, at a moment when explosive financial growth, cataclysmic financial crisis, and the emergence of secular psychology converged in a bourgeoning awareness of crisis as systemic, regular, and traumatic, and in a flourishing cross-pollination between the language of psychology and the language of economics. The nexus of these ideas eventually eclipsed what had been a powerful account of the structural, logico-temporal instabilities of finance—the critique of fictitious capital. With the advent of psychologism in economic thought, the system of capitalism falls out of focus, and the passions (irrationality, improvidence, greed) hog the spotlight. Foreclosing the possibility of systemic change and decontextualizing the forces of personification and metalepsis that contour the passions, the hypostasization of "psychic economy" ideologically sutures antagonisms past and present.

Bernanke's disclaimer is thus only the most crystalline instance of a century-old project of academic economics to dispel that which in capital is impervious to quantification or scientization—its metaphysics in which the fictitious is the real. If Bernanke and Shiller are the heirs apparent to the psychologism that arose from the shadow of that Victorian eclipse, and if too much contemporary theory unthinkingly ventriloquizes the metaphor of psychic economy designed by Victorian financial journalists, psychologists, and political economists, it remains the case that the Victorian novel bequeaths an alternate inheritance, one to which Marx and Freud make strategic claim. Through its inventive engagement with the ungroundedness of finance and its unrelenting suspicion of psychic economy as a metaphor upon whose strength we "act fatally," the Victorian novel realizes the critique of fictitious capital, disclosing the comprehensive proliferation of economic tropes from the regime of financial poiesis. Its insights into the figurative power of capital are not presented linearly, nor can we trace them to the novel's iteration of other discourses. We owe such luminosity rather to the counterfactual vitality of an aesthetic that thinks and that, as the brightest future of our current crisis, awaits us in the past.

Notes

Introduction. "A Case of Metaphysics": Realizing Capital

1. Exactly when financialization begins is subject to varying interpretations in economic history and Marxist historiography. In the wake of the 2008 economic crisis, the term has enjoyed widespread usage as a name for the qualitative and structural economic transformations since 1973 (the end of Bretton Woods), but it is also used more generally by the highly influential historian Giovanni Arrighi to name a particular and *recurrent* phase in the capitalist cycle of accumulation (beginning in Genoa in the fifteenth century); see Arrighi, *Long Twentieth Century*. In between these two usages are thinkers as disparate as the cultural materialist philosopher Walter Benjamin, *The Arcades Project,* and the literary historian Mary Poovey, who both characterize the nineteenth century as fundamentally constituted by the flows of capital and the development of institutions, protocols, and epistemologies comprising "the financial system"; Poovey, ed., *Financial System.* My own usage aligns with this middle point, identifying the Victorian era as the crucible of qualitative transformation, while nonetheless maintaining a structural Marxian framework within which all capital is thought to be finance capital, transcendentally if not empirically. I elaborate this distinction later. For a discussion that typifies the recent usage of the term, see Postone, "Theorizing the Contemporary World."

2. The phrase "shocked disbelief" comes from Federal Reserve Chairman Alan Greenspan's testimony to the United States Congress on 23 October 2008 about the rarity and unpredictability of crisis; Scannell and Reddy, "Greenspan Admits Errors."

3. For one of the earliest definitive histories, see Andreadēs, *History of the Bank of England.* More comprehensive are Crouzet, *Victorian Economy,* and Doubleday, *Financial, Monetary, and Statistical History;* see also Matthews, *Study in Trade-Cycle History;* Collins, *Banks and Industrial Finance;* and Morgan, *London Stock Exchange.*

4. This concept was first enunciated in the epoch of financialization, but has two important precursors: the use of the image of economy to refer to the concrete physical system of the body and the conjuring of ideas of a harmonious confluence of psychical and material interests, not yet deemed "the economy."

On "economy" in the anatomical and medical discourse of the seventeenth and eighteenth centuries, see Rabinbach, *Human Motor;* and Barker-Banfield, "Spermatic Economy," 47–70. It is only in the nineteenth century, when, as historians like Appleby, *Economic Thought,* and Schabas, "Victorian Economics," 72–93, argue, "economy" undergoes "abstraction," emerging as an autonomous realm exempted from political and ethical determination, that the word "economy" itself shifts toward "reference to immaterial things," as the OED notes regarding Darwin's *On the Origin of Species.* Thus Adam Smith's seminal idea of a field of aggregate desires attaining equilibrium—an idea elaborated in both *The Wealth of Nations* and *The Theory of Moral Sentiments*—is named by the force of coordination, "the invisible hand," but does not yet congeal in an image of the economy of desire.

5. Lukacs, "Reportage or Portrayal" and "Realism in the Balance." Alex Woloch draws attention to this balancing act in arguing that "depth psychology and social expansiveness" comprise "two contradictory generic achievements" (19); Woloch, *The One Vs. the Many.*

6. On this idea of "unrolling," George Eliot's companion, George Henry Lewes, instructively defined realism as "economy of art," highlighting this exposure of tropes; realists in the Victorian moment understood their aesthetic project in part as the foregrounding of tensions between figurative and referential language; Lewes, *Literary Criticism of George Henry Lewes,* 91. Paul de Man defines irony as the thematization of this tension; de Man, *Blindness and Insight,* 209.

7. Levi-Strauss, *Structural Anthropology,* 206-31.

8. In *Allegories of Reading,* de Man regards literary language as an incitement to discern the tense conjunctions of the literal and the literary, the material and the speculative, the real and the fictitious. He ultimately distinguishes between reading for metaphor and reading for allegory: "The paradigm for all texts consists of a figure (or a system of figures) and its deconstruction. But since this model cannot be closed off by a final reading, it engenders, in its turn, a supplementary figural superposition which narrates the unreadability of the prior narration. As distinguished from primary deconstructive narratives centered on figures and ultimately always on metaphor, we can call such narratives to the second (or the third) degree *allegories.* Allegorical narratives tell the story of the failure to read, whereas tropological narratives, such as the *Second Discourse,* tell the story of the failure to denominate. The difference is only a difference of degree, and the allegory does not erase the figure. Allegories are always allegories of metaphor and, as such, they are always allegories of the impossibility of reading—a sentence in which the genitive 'of' has itself to be 'read' as a metaphor" (205). In this model the literary framing of a problem carves new facets, but does not fix the problem in place, much less solve it.

9. Leatham, *Letters on the Currency,* 44 (italics original). Leatham was a Yorkshire banker whose report cautioned the government that the inordinate numbers of economic transactions conducted with bills of exchange were of indeterminate value: "It is impossible to decide what part arises out of real *bona fide* transactions,

such as actual bargain and sale, or what part is *fictitious, and mere accommodation paper*—that is, where one bill is drawn up to take another running, in order to raise a fictitious capital, by creating so much currency. In times of abundance, and cheap money, this I know reaches an enormous amount . . . and it is full of rottenness and unsoundness, and a great source of speculation and failure."

10. These hypercreditized protocols of the London Stock Exchange were routinely exposited in the Victorian financial press, and just as routinely decried. For exemplary expository essays, see "The Stock Exchange," in *The Chambers Journal,* 366-68, and Francis, *Chronicles and Characters of the Stock Exchange.*

11. On promises that create new states of affairs, see Austin, *How to Do Things with Words.* On the materiality of performatives, see Tom Cohen and Barbara Cohen, eds., *Material Events,* and Mario Ortiz-Robles, *The Novel as Event.*

12. Macleod, *Theory and Practice of Banking,* 1:258; italics original.

13. The *New York Times* made special note of the phrase "the real economy" when it became a motto of the 2010 World Economic Forum in Davos; thereafter the paper adopted the phrase into its regular usage, as did Federal Reserve Governors and U.S. officials. At Davos and elsewhere, the phrase is intended to differentiate goods and services from financial instruments; Smale, "Bankers Put Focus on 'Real Economy.' "

14. This romance is especially prevalent in the recent global crisis, and at times enchants even astute readers of Marx, like Harvey, a great popularizer of the concept of fictitious capital, who aligns it with a postmodernity "dominated by fiction, fantasy, the immaterial (particularly money), fictitious capital, images, ephemerality"; Harvey, *The Condition of Postmodernity,* 339. See also Richard Godden's opposition between financial "fantasy" and "actual production": Godden, *Fictions of Capital,* 185–86. For helpful arguments in an opposing tradition, see Bajorek, *Counterfeit Capital,* and Mieszkowski, *Labors of Imagination.*

15. Marx, *Capital: A Critique of Political Economy,* 1:151.

16. For further philosophical elaboration of this projection of *ex post facto* achievements onto *ex ante facto* thinking, see Kojin Karatani's brilliant exposition of the Kantian transcendental illusion in Karatani, *Transcritique.*

17. De Man, *Allegories of Reading,* 108.

18. "Belief producers" is Mary Poovey's phrase; Poovey, *Genres of the Credit Economy,* 249.

19. J. G. A. Pocock's seminal formulation that in the credit economy "property . . . has ceased to be real and has become not merely mobile but imaginary" has inspired a generation of critics; Pocock, *Virtue, Commerce, and History,* 112. I take the phrase "epistemological malaise" from Sherman, *Finance and Fictionality,* 3.

20. Baucom, *Specters of the Atlantic,* 17, 67. Shifting the frame from belief to action owes much to the Althusserian theory of ideology: socioeconomic cohesion does not require belief—it requires only action; Althusser, "Ideology and Ideological State Apparatuses." Slavoj Žižek offers a helpful note on this formula, which resonates with our discussion of metalepsis: "When Althusser repeats, after Pascal,

'Act as if you believe, pray, kneel down, and you shall believe, faith will arrive by itself,' he delineates an intricate reflexive mechanism of retroactive 'autopoetic' foundation . . . the external ritual performatively generates its own ideological foundation"; Žižek, *Metastases of Enjoyment,* 58.

21. Žižek's project to radicalize the possible connections between Marxism and psychoanalysis and renew the critique of ideology has been based in no small part on this distinction between belief and action, discourse and displacement. In his theory ideology is not a set of ideas, but a set of practices constituting reality and preconditioned by fantasy. "The fundamental level of ideology is not of an illusion masking the real state of things but that of an (unconscious) fantasy structuring our social reality itself"; Žižek, *The Sublime Object of Ideology,* 33. Displacement and condensation are the master tropes of dreamwork identified by Freud; I invoke them here as figures opposed to the often literal way in which Foucauldian discourse is thought to operate, disseminating ideas that are directly adopted as beliefs by the subjects of power; Freud, *The Interpretation of Dreams,* Chap. 6.

22. I mean "psychologism" here in the broadest sense in which the critique of philosophy has employed it: the conflation of nonpsychological entities with psychological ones, the displacement of logic by psychological naturalism. For an argument that pyschologism originates with the Victorian philosopher John Stuart Mill, see Godden, "Psychologism in the Logic of John Stuart Mill," 115–43.

23. In *The Form of Victorian Fiction,* J. Hillis Miller describes this secular ontology: "The situation which they (Victorian novelists) confront may most properly be described not as the disappearance of God but the death of God," which involves "first, a vanishing of any extrahuman foundation for man, nature, society" and results in a "situation in which human subjectivity seems to become the foundation of all things, the only source of meaning and value in the world" (31–32).

24. Hirschman, *The Passions and the Interests.*

25. Pocock, *Virtue, Commerce, and History,* but also Lynch, *The Economy of Character;* Thompson, *Models of Value;* and Finn, *The Character of Credit.* See also Collini, *Public Moralists:* "an economic world in which reputation played a powerful part: to be known as a man of character was to possess the moral collateral which would reassure potential business associates or employers" (106). For the phrase "reputationally intensive," see Morrison and Wilhelm, *Investment Banking,* 125.

26. Poovey, "Discriminating Reading," 10–35.

27. Victorian financial journalism, I argue in Chapter 1, is far more likely to criticize finance or to perform the logical contradictions of finance than to exposit it. On another point: my argument reverses the claim that "sexology and psychoanalysis borrowed much of their aura of scientificity from the putatively objective discourses of thermodynamics and economics"; Bennett, "Desire as Capital," 105. Pointing instead to the historical situation of contest, debate, and anxiety about the science of economics and the economic practices of finance, my research suggests that the relationship of putative objectivity functioned in the other direction:

Political economists promoted the economic language in psychology because psychology was shoring up the scientificity of economics.

28. Althusser, "A Letter on Art," in *Lenin and Philosophy*, 152.

29. I echo here Frederic Jameson's observation that the realist novel is "the privileged instrument of the analysis of reality"; Jameson, *Marxism and Form*, 195.

30. J. Hillis Miller, *Form of Victorian Fiction*, 35.

31. Watt, *Rise of the Novel*, 30. The notion of this reifying function founds the dominant paradigm in Victorian studies, as well as in studies of literature and money more generally. Patrick Brantlinger, *Fictions of State*, formidably contends that while "realistic fiction is often highly critical of such generalized social evils as avarice and materialism . . . its rhetorical conventions and structures involve the reification of the status quo" (146).

32. "As money became more representational, representation became more real"; Vernon, *Money and Fiction*, 7.

33. Baucom, *Specters of the Atlantic*, 17. Belief-production is a repeated refrain in Poovey's work; see especially *Genres of the Credit Economy*, 249.

34. In work by Lukacs, Fredric Jameson, and others, realism wields force as a sociological record of capital's transgressions; see Lukacs, "Art and Objective Truth," 25–60, and "Realism in the Balance," 28–59; Jameson, "Cognitive Mapping."

35. Lukacs, *A History of the Evolution of Modern Drama*. Similarly important here is Marc Shell, who remarks apropos painting that "the participation of economic form in painting . . . is defined neither by what painting depicts (sometimes money, sometimes not) nor by why painting depicts it (sometimes for money, sometimes not) but rather by the interaction between economic and aesthetic symbolization and production"; Shell, *Art and Money*, 4.

36. For just a few examples of this dominant indexical approach, see Freedgood, "Banishing Panic," 180–95, and Crosby, "A Taste for More," 251–61; see also Shrimpton, "Even These Metallic Problems," 17–38; Henry, " 'Ladies Do It?' "; McGann, "Literary Realism," 133–56; and Wagner, *Financial Speculation*.

37. "Literary history's function is to tirelessly restore referentiality; it produces such referentiality and forces such recognition from the text. Literary history thus contrives the belief that the text articulates the real. In this fashion it transforms the text into an institution"; de Certeau, *Heterologies*, 32.

38. On the prevailing literary criticism whose "sole purpose is to do away with reading entirely," see de Man's *Resistance to Theory*, 31.

39. De Man, *Allegories of Reading*, 66–67, 137.

40. On this anti-hermeneutic in the case of psychoanalysis, see, in addition to the entire oeuvres of Freud and Lacan, specific admonitions against hermeneutics in Freud, *The Interpretation of Dreams*, Chap. 6, and Lacan, *The Four Fundamental Concepts of Psychoanalysis*, Chap. 1. For a systematic and cogent argument, see Jean La Planche's thesis that psychoanalytic interpretation is not translation, but "detranslation," "with no pre-established codes," and that the only possible syntheses

are "purely spontaneous, and above all, individual"; La Planche, "Psychoanalysis as Anti-Hermeneutics," 8.

41. The inquiry into connections between literature and capitalism known as "the new economic criticism" emphasizes, as I do, the synergy between the modern novel and industrial and financial development. Poovey's work in particular has delineated an archive of primary financial events and sources that constitute a backdrop for the very idea of literary value; that archive is also engaged here. Catherine Gallagher has explored, as I do, the mutual concerns of Victorian novels and the discipline of political economy. Where the prevailing thesis among the scholars identified with the new economic criticism is that Victorian fiction ideologically supported the financial economy by accurately representing it, I argue that novels criticized finance precisely by uncoupling it from accurate or referential representation. I identify a rapidly changing matrix of cultural representations of finance, desire, and metaphoricity itself that novelists actively engaged, rather than passively reflected. I encounter the economic interests of the realist novel neither by fact-checking literature's references to actually existing capitalism nor by taxing how much Dickens got paid per word. In particularly rejecting such emphasis on the business aspects of publishing and authorship, I maintain that the mid-Victorian realists were sensitive to economic meaning, economic form, and economic representation in ways that vastly exceeded their self-interests as commercial agents. Just as I do not limit my selection of economically astute novels to those with verisimilitudinous plots, I do not equate the economic consequentiality of novels with the professionalization of novelists. Amanpal Garcha has recently argued that the obsession in Victorian literary critical circles with the construction of the author as a commercially viable professional is more a projection of contemporary anxieties of career competition in the American academy than an impartial examination of Victorian quandaries; Garcha, "Careerist Theory."

42. In his discussion of Austen, for example, Woloch concludes of the asymmetrical distribution of character space that "the disturbing recession of equality to the invisible horizon of Austen's narrative shows the profound and perhaps unique way in which she grasped the emergent structure of modern capitalism and represented it on the literary plane"; Woloch, *The One Vs. the Many,* 124. In his analysis, then, the character system as an organizing structural principle of the novel is itself the materialization "on the literary plane" of capitalism's organizing structural principle of asymmetry and inequality.

43. Levine, "Strategic Formalism," 640; Woloch, *The One Vs. the Many,* 124.

44. Levine, "Strategic Formalism," 632. On this distinction between referring to the world and disclosing the craft of worlding, see Paul de Man's analysis that "a theory of constituting form is altogether different from a theory of signifying form"; de Man, *Blindness and Insight,* 232.

45. See the discussions of those texts and others in editor Francis O'Gorman's compendium, *Victorian Literature and Finance* (Oxford: Oxford University Press, 2007), as well as in Wagner, *Financial Speculation.*

46. These two options representing, respectively, Marxist literary criticism and historicism.

47. Ruskin, *Modern Painters*, 43.

48. In 1852 *The Spectator* succinctly imparted this performative: "in the picture of society as it is, society as it ought to be is implied"; "Thackeray's *Esmond*," 1066.

49. While I take the phrase "conceptual agency" from Susan J. Wolfson's discussion of literary form, she intends "the way form shapes perceptions and critical thinking," but I am after the way form thinks; Wolfson, "Reading for Form," 16. In this endeavor I am indebted to Julia Reinhard Lupton's formidable models of "thinking with" literature, especially as developed in Lupton, *Thinking with Shakespeare*.

50. Here too I break with Poovey. To be sure, Evans and Bagehot were prominent financial essayists, but I find nothing expository about their discourse, and certainly nothing sufficiently expository as to justify Poovey's identification of them as the managers of public trust in finance. Theirs is a language and a corpus demanding fastidious reading, full of contradictions, paradoxes, supernatural images, dream sequences, mysteries, and a staggering incapacity to enumerate the fundamentals of finance.

51. This general sense is developed by Bloom, *A Map of Misreading*.

52. "We promote some to the status of knowing (tenured?) readers by envisioning a group of very differently endowed 'normal' readers to whom the ruses we are able to decode are in the first instance directed"; Shaw, *Narrating Reality*, 34 (parenthesis original).

1. Fictitious Capital / Real Psyche: Metalepsis, Psychologism, and the Grounds of Finance

1. Evans, *Commercial Crisis of 1857–1858*, v.

2. See Poovey, *Genres*; Alborn, "Creating Capitalism: Joint-Stock Enterprise in British Politics and Culture 1800–1870 (Review of *Creating Capitalism*, by James Taylor)," *Victorian Studies* 50, no. 1 (2007): 147–49; Wagner, *Financial Speculation*.

3. Evans, *Commercial Crisis of 1857–1858*, v, 11, 42.

4. Evans, "The Great Banking Forgeries," 107. Alborn impressively discusses this position that "the fictional mercantile sins concocted by novelists were child's play compared to goings-on in the real world of capitalism"; Alborn, "The Moral of the Failed Bank," 212.

5. Images of "unsoundness" recur throughout *The Commercial Crisis of 1857–1858*, 36, 99, 203, and passim. "Apologists for the credit economy" is Poovey's phrase from her Introduction to *Financial System*. She levies this charge repeatedly: see also Poovey, "Writing about Finance," and Poovey, *Genres*, 246.

6. Evans's article "Alarming State of Trade" registered that the 1833 Charter Act "introduced a new element, that of fictitious capital." The year 1833 stands as a financial watershed moment because it saw the Bank of England Charter Act,

which, in addition to authorizing the bank to sell shares in itself as if it were a corporation, repealed bans on usury. By overturning millennia of longstanding—even biblical—condemnations of the "monstrous" "birth of money from money" (Aristotle, *Politics and the Constitution of Athens*), the act paved the way for an economy in which money buys and sells itself nearly autonomously (1258B). In his *History of the Commercial Crisis of 1857–1858*, Evans also referred to the credit system as "monstrous development" (32). Eventually framing his own discussion of fictitious capital as the offspring of "interest bearing capital, the mother of all insane forms," Marx echoed the diagnosis in the Victorian press; Marx, *Capital* 3:596. On the evolution of usury discourse, see Nelson, *Idea of Usury*.

From 1833 onward the financial press regularly referred to "too great a facility in obtaining credit—in creating fictitious capital" ("What Would Be the Effect of Abolishing All Laws Related to Debtor and Creditor?" *Fraser's Magazine*) and to the ways that "fictitious capital has stimulated trade to an unhealthy state"; Chubb, "Bank Act and the Crisis of 1866," 179. By 1845 the question "What meaning do you attach to the expression 'fictitious capital?'" was, along with basics like "Define price" and "Define value," part of a required template for the Masters of Arts examinations in Political Economy at what is now University College London; Taylor and Taylor, *London University Calendar*, 208.

Like Evans's history after it, Arthur Smith's history of the 1847 crisis, *The Bubble of the Age*, refers to "fictitious capital" throughout its book-length discussion. *Fraser's Magazine* summed up the concerns about fictitious capital: "Our system of credit, though propped up by writs, imprisonment without limitation, an increasing pestilent race of common law attorneys, with ruin and misery in their train, is all false and hollow . . . to whom, then, is this system of credit useful? To the speculator—to the man so desirous of profit, that the slow and silent increase by fair trade is laughed at—by the monopolist, who wishes to grasp all he can . . . by this fictitious credit speculations are made, commodities produced in quantities above the steady demand; and, though the speculators are benefited by an increase of wealth, the community is injured by the effects"; "What Would Be the Effect?" 549.

Apropos the 1866 crisis, Hammon Chubb argued, "For more than three years the speculative propensities of the public have been stimulated by the manufacture of finance bills for millions upon millions. This paper, which ought never to have been admitted within the walls of a respectable bank or discount establishment on any terms whatever, no matter what might have been the character of its endorsements, was taken freely in all directions . . . every contractor who wanted to make a railway, or build a city, had only to go to a finance concern, pay them an enormous bonus, and be furnished with what was called "money" in the shape of bills drawn by himself and accepted by the company. . . . Such a man has been trading on fictitious capital. . . . The speculative trader is always anxious to individualize himself, and yet to be of the nation. 'Give me,' he says 'the means I want. I have nothing to do with these national crises.' But he cannot separate himself thus. He has been swelling the volume of fictitious capital; he has been doing his utmost to force into circulation an unreal currency; he has been eating up the temporary fruits of it, and with the break-down of these, he must suffer with the rest"; Chubb, "The Bank Act and the Crisis of 1866."

7. On "breakdown," see "The Interior of the Royal Bank of Liverpool," in the *Economist;* see also "The reduction of the fictitious value to the real value is indispensable," in "Iron and Coal Trades"; also in the *Economist.*

8. Quintilian, *Institutes of Oratory,* Book 8, Chap. 6, Para. 37–39; Genette, *Narrative Discourse.*

9. Genette, *Narrative Discourse,* 234–35, and Genette, *Narrative Discourse Revisited,* 88; Bloom, *A Map of Misreading,* 74.

10. Quintilian, *Institutes of Oratory,* Para. 38: "For the nature of metalepsis is that it is an intermediate step, as it were, to that which is metaphorically expressed, signifying nothing in itself, but affording a passage to something."

11. The phrase "animal spirits" became crucial in economics after John Maynard Keynes used it to name economically consequential feelings such as "consumer confidence"; Keynes, *General Theory of Employment,* 161–62. In the wake of the crisis of 2008, professional economists looking to deepen the theory of "irrational exuberance" have elevated the term to new levels of popularity and prominence; see renowned academics Akerlof, *Animal Spirits,* and Shiller, *Irrational Exuberance.*

12. Marx, *Capital* 3:525–26.

13. "The very existence of the Stock Exchange, as at present constituted, almost depends upon speculations" . . . "operations of the greatest magnitude, founded, not on actual necessities, but solely on speculation" do not require "actual money or bona fide business." "If bargains in the public securities were obliged to be settled in hard cash, or even in bank notes, the business could never be got through; whereas by the existing system, millions of money may change hands without the necessity of calling into requisition a single current coin of the realm"; Evans, *The City,* 36, 40.

14. "This they are sometimes enabled to do by the employment of *fictitious capital;* that is, by the issue of more bills or promises to pay money, than they have *real capital* to meet"; "Capital in Trade," 63.

15. "Banking Morality," 446.

16. "Poetry of Banking," 151; "Banking and Poesy"; "National Debt." *The Era* decried "the poetry of banking, but verily, Joint Stock Banking is a fiction altogether"; "Money Market, City, Friday." See also the "poetry of stock-jobbing" ("National Debt," 669), and "all the artifices, whether of rhetoric or of finance" ("Accounts of the Credit Mobilier"). Dickens made the connection between fictitious capital and technologies of writing: "raise a fictitious capital at the commencement of your business by the stroke of a pen"; Dickens, "Bankruptcy in Six Easy Lessons," 210.

17. Dickens, "Bankruptcy in Six Easy Lessons," 151.

18. Eden, *The Semi-Detached House*, 159. See also the description in *Chambers's Journal* that "inside the House . . . a perfect babel was heard" ("The Stock Exchange," 366–68). As Dickens observed of financial men, "many men understand the true art of figures: viz, to conceal the truth" ("Bankruptcy in Six Easy Lessons," 210). The *Economist* less satirically indicted this collusion of figures and finance, cataloguing "all the artifices, whether of rhetoric or finance" by which men conduct business; "Accounts of the Credit Mobilier." Journalists made efforts to compile glossaries of this specialized language.

19. Evans, *The City*, 92. Apparently utterly lacking in irony, the journalist Leo Hartley Grindon published a book-length series of reports on Manchester banking that celebrated this command of metaphor by identifying bankers as poets. For example:

> Mr. James (a Manchester banker) was a man of remarkably pure mind, and gifted, at the same time, with that inestimable intellectual blessing—imagination. Somehow there have been more men of imagination in the higher levels of the Manchester and Salford Bank than perhaps in any other in the town, a circumstance to which may be ascribed, in no slight measure, the happiness of its inner life, and its unalloyed prosperity. For the men of imagination, the men whose temperament is of the species called poetic, not only enjoy the privilege of seeing into the depth and the significance of things —it is these who especially sympathise, their sympathies giving birth to kindness and considerateness, forbearance and generosity, the auxiliaries best of all to rely upon when men are desirous of success, in whatever walk of life it may be sought. Mr. James was a poet; Grindon, *Manchester Banks and Bankers*, 287.

20. "Banking," 428–29. The diaphanous insubstantiality and insipid ubiquity of shares is famously invoked in a narratorial screed in Dickens's *Our Mutual Friend*:

> The mature young gentleman is a gentleman of property. He invests his property. He goes, in a condescending amateurish way, into the City, attends meetings of Directors, and has to do with traffic in Shares. As is well known to the wise in their generation, traffic in Shares is the one thing to have to do with in this world. Have no antecedents, no established character, no cultivation, no ideas, no manners; have Shares. Have Shares enough to be on the Board of Direction in capital letters, oscillate on mysterious business between London and Paris, and be great. Where does he come from? Shares. Where is he going to? Shares. What are his tastes? Shares. Has he any principles? Shares. What squeezes him into Parliament? Shares. Perhaps he never of himself achieved success in anything, never originated anything, never produced anything! Sufficient answer to all; Shares. O mighty Shares! To set those blaring images so high, and to cause us smaller vermin, as under the influence of henbane or opium, to cry out night and day, "Relieve us of our money, scatter it for us, buy us and sell us, ruin us, only we beseech ye take rank among the powers of the earth, and fatten on us!" (114).

21. "Many people regard the creation of a bill, without the most remote thought of its payment at maturity, simply as an ordinary business transaction; that it is a simple financial operation, rather to the benefit of the nation than not; and that the meeting a bill when due, should not be effected by the vulgar device of its payment, but by recourse to further financial operations"; Chubb, "Bank Act and the Crisis of 1866," 187.

See also Hollingshead, "The City of Unlimited Paper": "as fast as one payment falls due another loan is obtained, and the whole system is kept up like the brass balls which the juggler tosses in the air" (2).

22. "The very nature (of credit instruments) intensifies the mystery. Are they not pieces of paper, lines in books, mystic words uttered in bank parlours,—and yet are not the fortunes of private men and of nations made or broken by these thin yet omnipotent nothings?"; Price, "Credit and Crises."

23. "Banking and Poesy," 355.

24. Evans, *The City*, 32 and passim; see also Francis, *Chronicles and Characters of the Stock Exchange*, 329-30.

25. Although my book does not undertake readings of Victorian poetry, it certainly seems worth noting that in the moment of "the poetry of banking" and perpetual financial upheaval, poetry wrote itself into crisis: sales plummeted, experiments proliferated, Robert Browning murdered lyric, and cultural-political authorities like Matthew Arnold and Benjamin Disraeli declared "the reign of poesy (is) over" (85). Disraeli, *Vivian Grey*.

26. "To compare money with language is not less erroneous. Language does not transform ideas, so that the peculiarity of ideas is dissolved and their social character runs alongside them as separate entity, like prices alongside commodities. Ideas do not exist separately from language. Ideas which have first to be translated out of their mother tongue into a foreign tongue in order to circulate, in order to become exchangeable, offer a somewhat better analogy; but the analogy is then not with language, but with its foreignness." (*Das Geld mit der Sprache zu vergleichen ist nicht minder falsch . . . bieten schon mehr Analogie; die Analogie liegt dann aber nicht in der Sprache, sondern in ihrer Fremdheit*); Marx, *Grundrisse*, 162 [English]; *Gesammelte Werke* 42:96 [German].

27. Marx, *Capital* 3:531. See also "By and large, money now functions only as a means of payment, i.e., commodities are not sold for money, but for a written promise to pay at a certain date"; ibid., 3:525.

28. For the technical discussion of linguistic performatives, see Austin, *How to Do Things with Words*. Writing of the performative, the philosopher of language John Searle uses this example of legal tender; see Searle, *Speech Acts*. On the importance of the performative for Marx, though not specifically on the question of money, see J. Hillis Miller, "Promises, Promises."

29. Marx, *Capital* 1:284.

30. Bajorek, *Counterfeit Capital*, 48.

31. Marx, *Collected Works* 34:485.

32. Leatham, *Letters on the Currency,* 44 (italics original). The same stroke introduces the concept and the problem of its indeterminacy—a simultaneity that seems to allude rather strikingly to the unthought centrality of the fictitious to Marx's structural analysis of capital.

33. "To Readers and Correspondents" (544).

34. "A large part of this year's rise in certain more speculative securities implies no real change of credit, but is only the result of the ordinary multiplying power of good or bad influences which belongs to the mechanism of the Stock Exchange. That the improvement is also nursed by combination and other arts so as to create a fictitious credit, is a necessary accompaniment of the situation. Hence it happens that the change from the depression of last year and early spring to the buoyancy of the present moment, in the cases where collapse has not proved to be definite, may be explained in great part without raising any doubts as to the justice of last year's discredit"; "The Recent Rise in Foreign Securities and the New Turkish Loan."

35. "National Debt." Evans also registered this problem of closure, dramatically concluding one of his books with, "Where will all this end?"; Evans, *The City,* 201.

36. This anteriority also constitutes the difference between speculation and investment, as Chancellor argues: "The line separating speculation from investment is so thin that it has been said both that speculation is a name given to a failed investment and that investment is the name given to a successful speculation"; Chancellor, *Devil Take the Hindmost,* xi.

37. Harvey, *Limits to Capital,* 266.

38. This contrast between empirical and structural is a variation on that between phenomenological and transcendental that Kordela makes apropos capital's virtuality; Kordela, "Marx's Update of Cultural Theory," 45.

39. Evans, *The City,* 34. *Fraser's Magazine* printed the common sentiment, "What credit is, where it dwells, what are the peculiarity and the essence of its strength, are questions which not only the commercial, but even the philosophical mind finds it hard to answer"; Price, "Credit and Crises."

40. As reported in Rivington, *Annual Register,* 11–12.

41. Evans, *The City,* 61. He also remarks elsewhere on limited popular knowledge: "The operations of the speculator, the business of the broker, and the situation of the jobber, all with their different tendencies, have puzzled the public in the investigation of the secret, especially in relation to the several phases of affairs. That fortunes are lost and won by the result of the movements of the dealers, appears to be the extent of knowledge the majority of the public have on the subject" (26).

42. Marx, *Capital* 3:595–99.

43. *Commercial Crisis of 1847–1848.* For Evans's own evolving psychological interests, he had begun to write of "the ruling passion," the "desire to make money easily and in a hurry" that "cannot endure any delay to gratification"; Evans, *Facts, Failures, and Frauds,* 3–5.

44. Houghton, *Victorian Frame of Mind,* 61.

45. "Report from the Commissioners" cited in Bucknill, *Manual of Psychological Medicine,* 83.

46. "Shadowless Men," 295, 297.

47. "The Stock Exchange," 366-68.

48. Hollingshead, "City of Unlimited Paper," 4.

49. Evans, *Speculative Notes,* 53. See also: "Inside the House (Stock Exchange), during business-hours, all is bustle, stir, and noise; a perfect babel of voices is heard, and jobbers, brokers, and clearks are rushing in, and out, like greaves in a tallow tub. It is a restless mob eddying to and fro; old and young, rich and poor, grave and gay, are the persons before us"; "The Stock Exchange."

50. "The Stock Exchange."

51. Evans, *Speculative Notes,* 39.

52. Ibid., 36.

53. Francis shares Evans's view: "The history of the railway mania of 1845 is not the least remarkable among those delusions which from time to time arise to throw aside legitimate trade and paralyse national commerce. . . . A desire to speculate grew . . . and England was seized with her ancient phrenzy. For some time it was legitimate and confined within its proper sphere, but the desire spread; the contagion passed to all, and from the clerk to the capitalist the fever reigned uncontrollable and uncontrolled"; Francis, *History of the Bank of England,* 118.

54. The Fed seems particularly fond of Bagehot; see Anderson, "Bagehot on the Financial Crises," 1–2, and Madigan, "Bagehot's Dictum." To this day the *Economist* still prints a column entitled "Bagehot's Notebook." Bagehot's *Lombard Street* is required reading at UC Berkeley in Economics 210A.

55. "I venture to call this Essay 'Lombard Street' and not the 'Money Market'; or any such phrase, because I wish to deal, and to show that I mean to deal, with concrete realities"; Bagehot, *Lombard Street,* 1.

56. Andreādēs, *History of the Bank of England,* 324.

57. "Similarly, we are all in our various departments of life in the habit of assuming various probabilities as if they were certainties. In Lombard Street the dealers assume that 'Messrs. Baring's acceptance at three months' date is sure to be paid,' and that 'Peel's Act will always be suspended in a panic'"; Bagehot, *The Works and Life of Walter Bagehot* 5:338. "And the familiarity of such ideas makes it nearly impossible for any one who spends his day in Lombard Street to doubt of them. But, nevertheless, a person who takes care of his mind will keep up the perception that they are not certainties." See also "A sanguine man will believe with scarcely any evidence that good luck is coming, and a dismal man that bad luck is coming. As far as I can make out, the professional "bulls" and "bears" of the City do believe a great deal of what they say, though, of course, there are exceptions, and though neither the most sanguine "bull" nor the most dismal "bear" can believe all he says"; Bagehot, *The Works and Life of Walter Bagehot* 5:332.

58. Bagehot, *The Works and Life of Walter Bagehot,* vol. 8, *Physics and Politics,* Sect. 3.

59. Derrida comments from both points of view: "Everything is act of faith, phenomenon of credit or credence, belief and conventional authority in this text which perhaps says something essential about what here links literature to belief, to credit and thus to capital, to economy and thus to politics. Authority is constituted by accreditation, both in the sense of legitimation as effect of belief or credulity, and of bank credit, of capitalized interest. . . . Accredited in this way, a "true" corpus is still, perhaps, counterfeit money; it may be a ghost or a spirit, the spirit of the body and of capital (for a title, a heading, is a capital)"; Derrida, *Given-Time,* 97.

60. Bagehot alludes to the anxiety of tolerating an unanswered question: "credit is a set of promises to pay; will those promises be kept?"; Bagehot, *Lombard Street,* 22. "What credit is, where it dwells, what are the peculiarity and the essence of its strength, are questions which not only the commercial, but even the philosophical mind finds it hard to answer"; Price, "Credit and Crises."

61. Bagehot, *Lombard Street,* Chap. 7, Para. 41.

62. Baeghot, *Lombard Street,* 51. Bagehot's dictum was printed and reprinted across the contemporary United States financial press and blogosphere after 2007. See, for instance, "From Bagehot to Bernanke" and Chancellor, "Look Out: This Crunch Is Serious." The Federal Reserve Bank of Dallas even held a conference on crisis, for which program the sentiment was emblazoned as epigraph; see Robinson, "The Federal Reserve."

63. Bagehot, *Lombard Street,* Chap. 17.

64. This formula of the circuit of panic was printed as early as two days after the climax of the 1866 crisis, the failure of Overend, Gurney, and Co., in the *Examiner:* "It is of no use to dwell upon the fatal effects of that general rush of panic which creates the ruin from which it would fly"; "The Panic in the Money Market."

65. Bagehot, *Lombard Street,* Chap 7, Para. 41, and Bagehot, *Physics and Politics,* 138.

66. Bagehot, *The Works and Life of Walter Bagehot* 1:128.

67. Physiologists say, on a priori ground, that if you spend nervous force in one direction, you will not have as much to spend in another. . . . Of any particular total of nervous force, what is expended in one way will not remain to be expended in another; in any given case, to use the well-known phrase, "what is gained in children will be lost in mind"; Bagehot, *Economic Studies,* 118–19. "The principle way in which capital increases in England now, is by abstinence from enjoyment. We receive our incomes in money, and either we spend them on our enjoyments, in which case capital is not increased, for our incomes are all gone and no new productive thing is made, or we abstain from enjoyment and put our money into trade ourselves, supposing that we are in trade, and supposing that we are not in trade, lend it to those who are. The productive part of wealth—the wealth which creates other wealth—is augmented mainly by our not enjoying our incomes"; Bagehot, *Economic Studies,* 142, 209.

68. Bagehot, *Collected Works* 9:272–75.

69. Loyd, *Reflections,* 44.

70. There was a prevalence of discussions about psychology in the periodicals of the time, including the *Westminster Review,* the *Contemporary Review,* and the *Fortnightly Review;* Small, *Conditions for Criticism,* 70.

71. Language from Spencer, *Principles of Psychology,* and Bain, *Senses and Intellect;* pronouncement from William James, *Principles of Psychology* 2:240.

72. Spencer, "Philosophy of Style," 2:93.

73. Spencer, *Principles of Ethics,* 200. "When, some fifty years ago, Milne-Edwards gave to this principle of development in animals the name 'physiological division of labor,' he recognized the parallelism between vital economy and social economy; and this parallelism has been since growing ever clearer."

74. In 1876 Bain became a founding editor and Spencer a founding contributor for the journal *Mind,* whose preface promised to promote psychology as "common ground whereon thinkers of widely different schools may meet" ("Prefatory Words," 5). By its third volume *Mind* would print an essay on political economy redefining the field with psychological precepts at its core: "a moral science which considers *the resources of human nature for the satisfying of human wants*" (Cunningham, "Political Economy," 379, italics original) conceives that "value is not a quality, but a relation—a relation between this object and desirable things in general" (370), that "the thing in-itself has no value, only pleasure in the thing" (374), and that therefore "exchanged commodities are not themselves the embodiment of any pleasure, but rather of abstinence from enjoyment" (374).

75. "The progressive evolution of emotions of higher complexity and greater power, produces other emotions than those which arise by the simple aggregation. . . . There is an evolution of emotions that are not only more complex, but also more abstract. Of this, the love of property supplies an example. When the intelligence is so far developed that time and locality are in some degree cognizable; and when, by consequence, a portion of food beyond what can be eaten at one time, can, when hunger next makes nascent the psychical states that accompany eating, be remembered as having been left in a particular place; there will, by a repetition of these experiences of a satiated hunger, and a subsequently recurring hunger that prompts a return to the remaining food, be established an organized connection between the consciousness of such remaining food and the various states of consciousness produced by a return to it: and there will thus be constituted an anticipation of a return to it—a tendency to perform all such actions accompanying return to it as are not negatived by the present satiety—a tendency, therefore, to take possession of it. By an analogous process there will be established a tendency to take possession of some habitual place of shelter; and afterwards to take possession of things serving for artificial shelter and for clothing"; Spencer, *Principles of Psychology* 2:1034. As is the case when mental abstraction is exemplified by "love of property," for Spencer the best example of the psychical activity of aggregation of abstraction is money, which symbolizes love of property in aggregate: "By a gradual transition, things indirectly connected with personal

welfare must come to be included: as, for example, the club used for a weapon; the impressions produced by which will make nascent the various impressions that have accompanied its use, and the conception of further use. And by a carrying of the same process to still higher complications, there will arise a propensity to take possession not only of various weapons and appliances of daily life, but also of the tools and materials required to make such weapons and appliances; afterwards of the materials required to make such tools; and so on to all degrees of remoteness: until the things accumulated for one purpose or other become extremely numerous and varied. But now observe that in proportion as these things become extremely numerous and varied; and in proportion as the acts of acquiring them and preserving them become frequent; there will, in conformity with the general law, be established a great variety of different excitements in connection with the act of taking possession or holding possession: and hence this act will itself become a source of excitement. And as the excitement thus caused, must be more habitual than that caused by any particular order of object; as, further, the special excitements attaching to special objects possessed, must, in virtue of their variety, prevent the excitement of possession from being connected with any one of them in particular; it results that the excitement of possession becomes one of a new kind, holding a great variety of excitements to which it ministers, in an accumulated but vague aggregation. And when, in the course of civilization, money comes to be the representative of value in general—value as abstracted from special objects—we see, in the miser, how the desire of possession in the abstract, may become almost independent of those from which it arose; and may become stronger than any one of them individually"; Spencer, *Principles of Psychology* 2:1034. Here it is the psychical engine of desire, compounded by the mental capacity for abstraction, that generates hierarchies of value among commodities, money, and beyond. Bain: "The pleasure of *money* is a remarkable instance of associated feeling. The sum total of purchasable enjoyments becomes linked in the mind with the universal medium of purchase, and this medium grows into an end of pursuit. In the first instance, we are stimulated by these other pleasures, but an affection is often generated at last for money itself. This transfer is brought about when we allow ourselves to be so engrossed with the *pursuit* of wealth, that we rarely advert to the remote ends or the purchasable pleasures; the mind dwelling solely on the one object that measures the success of our endeavors. A moderate pursuit of gain that leaves the mind free to dwell upon the pleasures and advantages that money is to bring, does not generate that intense affection for gold as an end constituting the extreme form of sordid avarice"; *Senses and Intellect,* 398. Money stems from the mind's "interest in remote means substituted for direct ends"; Lewes, *Problems of Life and Mind,* 172.

76. On the desire of Victorian political economists to appear more scientific and less political, see Schabas, "Victorian Economics," 76.

77. Jennings, *Natural Elements,* 34.

78. Gagnier adroitly provides a critical narrative of this revolution. She argues that Jevons's thought could only be possible at a certain stage of industrial devel-

opment: "as the basic needs of subsistence were satisfied, humankind's desire for variety in shelter, food, dress, and leisure grew limitlessly, and thus the idea of needs, which were finite and the focus of political economy, was displaced by the idea of tastes which were theoretically infinite"; Gagnier, *Insatiability of Human Wants,* 4, 59–60, 93–94. My argument provides a parallel claim: the material history that made Jevons's ideas possible is as much financial as it is industrial; the very notion of desire as a source of economic value stems as much from the history of ideas as it does from corporeal satiety. Also relevant here, though opposed by Gagnier, is Lawrence Birken's defense of Jevons as affirming liberation, aligning the marginal utility revolution with a kind of sexual revolution; Birken, *Consuming Desire.*

79. Jevons, *Theory of Political Economy,* 1.

Jevons spends the bulk of his revolutionary text trying to argue for the legitimate mathematical basis of quantifying desire: "Now there can be no doubt that pleasure, pain, labor, utility, value, wealth, money, capital etc. are all notions admitting of quantity; nay the whole of our actions in industry and trade certainly depend upon comparing quantities of advantage or disadvantage. Even the theories of moralists have recognized the quantitative character of the subject. Bentham's *introduction to the principles of morals and legislation* is thoroughly mathematical in the character of the method. . . . But where, the reader will perhaps ask, are your numerical data for estimating pleasures and pains in PE? I answer, that my numerical data are more abundant and precise than those possessed by any other science, but that we have not yet known how to employ them. The very abundance of our data is perplexing. There is not a clerk nor book-keeper in the country who is not engaged in recording numerical facts for the economist. The private-account books, the great ledgers of merchants and bankers and public offices, the share lists, price lists, bank returns, monetary intelligence, Custom-house and other Government returns, are all full of the kind of numerical data required to render Economics an exact mathematical science" (7–10). On the revolutionary status of Jevons's thought, see Blaug, *Economic Theory in Retrospect,* 309, who also contextualizes Jevons's discoveries alongside his nearly simultaneous Austrian and Swiss counterparts, Carl Megner and Leon Walras.

80. "Ruskin's Remedy for Inundation," 32.

81. John Stuart Mill, *Principles of Political Economy,* 270; Jevons, *Theory of Political Economy,* 7.

82. Jevons, *Theory of Political Economy,* 11.

83. Wicksteed, *Palgrave's Dictionary,* 767.

2. Investor Ironies in Great Expectations

1. Dickens, *Great Expectations,* 252; hereafter cited parenthetically.

2. The ubiquity of this claim is captured by its appearance on the first page of the scholarly introduction by Trotter: "In its most immediate aspect, *Great Expectations* is a story of moral redemption"; Introduction, Great Expectations, vii.

3. Among others, Buckley (*Season of Youth*) and Moretti identify *Great Expectations* as the paradigmatic English *Bildungsroman:* "The *Bildungsroman* as the 'symbolic form' of modernity. . . . A specific image of modernity: the image conveyed precisely by the 'youthful' attributes of mobility and inner restlessness. Modernity as a bewitching and risky process full of 'great expectations' and 'lost illusions'"; Moretti, *Way of the World,* 5.

4. De Man, *Blindness and Insight,* 209.

5. For the classic analysis of the colonial interests of *Great Expectations,* see Said, *Culture and Imperialism,* xvi.

6. Initially introduced with reference to Wemmick's rings (*Great Expectations,* 201), "portable property" is used to refer to other kinds of possessions, and to the general condition of the propertied ("I judged her to stand possessed of portable property" [294], and the unfortunate "unpossessed of portable property" [369]), and to the documents of wealth (deeds, bank notes, and bank account registers) that Magwitch has brought with him. Wemmick's advice takes on a callous edge when he cautions Pip to try to extract the portable property from Magwitch ("Avail yourself of this evening to lay hold of his portable property. You don't know what may happen to him. Don't let anything happen to the portable property" [372]) and when he ultimately laments the forfeiture of the wealth upon Magwitch's arrest ("I do not think he could have been saved. Whereas, the portable property certainly could have been saved. That's the difference between the property and the owner, don't you see?" [452]).

7. Forster, *Life of Charles Dickens* 2:285.

8. It seems apposite here that Eliot's only first-person text, *The Lifted Veil,* explores the horrors of too much insight, and that Trollope's, *The Struggles of Brown, Jones, and Robinson,* deals with a limited liability partnership.

9. Woloch writes that *Great Expectations* "is the story of a first-person narrator stuck in a third-person narrative world—a world in large part shaped by the structures and logic of Dickens's own earlier omniscient novels"; Woloch, *The One Vs. the Many,* 178.

10. Brooks, *Reading for the Plot,* 116.

11. For the difference between sovereign chartered partnerships and corporations and on the transition to corporations, see the excellent study by Alborn, *Conceiving Companies.*

12. The metaphysical considerations were mentioned by the Duke of Argyll, an MP at the time of the passage of the Acts; Loftus, "Limited Liability," 80. I emphasize what Oliphant calls the "abstract being" of the corporate person in order to attend to the way the Victorians apprehended this person as a continuation of the Stock Exchange in general and therefore as figurative or tropological in excess of fictional; Oliphant, "Autobiography of a Joint Stock Company." That is, in the Victorian context, the fictionality of the corporate person is equaled by its poeticity, its construction from the trope of personification and even prosopopoeia. This strikes

me as slightly different from the wholesale interest in fictionality that Walter Benn Michaels has argued characterizes the later American context; Michaels, *The Gold Standard,* 202.

13. "Banking Morality," 445–47.

14. Creative texts soon seized upon this tension, with first-person narration eventually proving a popular mode of lampooning the corporate person by the time of "The Autobiography of a Joint-Stock Company (Limited)," a satire on the rhetorical character of this "abstract being" penned by *Household Words* correspondent Laurence Oliphant in *Blackwoods Magazine* in 1876; reprinted in Poovey, *The Financial System,* 355. The text begins, "In a few days my brief and stormy career will finally close. I can calmly, and even thankfully, contemplate this premature existence of an existence which has ruined reputations, shattered fortunes, and carried want and misery into thousands of humble homes"; Poovey, *The Financial System,* 328–29. The precise commencement on the deathbed is typical of an analeptic narration that situates its own time of enunciation and reason for being—and in this, as I discuss later, it follows the paradigm that Dickens so starkly avoids.

15. Trotter's Introduction to *Great Expectations* helpfully outlines this textual history (vii–xx).

16. Prince, *Dictionary of Narratology,* 5.

17. This formula of irony is offered by de Man before he subjects it to "auto-critique" in favor of a model I discuss later; de Man, *Aesthetic Ideology,* 169. See also his suggestion, in "The Rhetoric of Temporality," that irony arises from self-presentation, that "in speaking of irony we are dealing not with the history of an error but with a problem that exists within the self . . . ironic language splits the subject into an empirical self that exists in a state of inauthenticity and a self that exists only in the form of a language that asserts the knowledge of this inauthenticity . . . the ironist invents a form of himself that is 'mad' but that does not know its own madness; he then proceeds to reflect on his madness thus objectified"; de Man, "Rhetoric of Temporality," 211, 214, 216.

18. On the complexities of narrative temporality, see Genette, *Narrative Discourse.*

19. Ibid.

20. In brilliantly mining the psychoanalytic valence of the plot's structuring repetitions, Brooks, in *Reading for the Plot,* has convincingly illuminated the novel's connections between plotting and repression. I would like to attend a bit more closely to the connections between the novel's circular structure and its overarching investigation of figures of economy.

21. Bain, *Emotions and the Will,* 441–44.

22. The national debt was one of the main vehicles for investment in the mid-Victorian period. Its liquidation, in addition to requiring some new sources of national revenue, would entail moderately profitable repayment to a large class of investors, those who would have "personal participation in the treasure"; see Michie, *London Stock Exchange,* 37–69.

23. For the best example, see Cohen's "Manual Conduct in *Great Expectations.*" A more subtle inquiry into Pip's excessive feelings is Andrew Miller's discussion of the novel as "a description and performance of shame"; Miller, *Burdens of Perfection,* 182.

24. "National Debt." If the capital is fictitious, so are the dividends—if the dividends are fictitious, so is the currency that represents them—if the currency is fictitious, all prices valued in that currency must be fictitious also. In fiction, therefore, we move, live, and have our financial being. When will this fiction end? See discussion of this lament in Chapter 1 of this volume.

3. The Economic Problem of Sympathy: Parabasis and Interest in Middlemarch

1. See, for example, Chase, *Eros and Psyche;* Kucich, *Repression in Victorian Fiction;* and Rylance, *Victorian Psychology.*

2. On theater, see Marshall, *Figure of Theater;* on visualization, see Jaffe, *Scenes of Sympathy;* on narrative, see Courtemanche, *"Invisible Hand."*

3. Carlyle, *Past and Present,* 123.

4. Eliot, "Thomas Carlyle," 343. For an argument that more than one novelist so responded, see Carlisle's exploration of the common conception of audience that motivated Carlyle, Eliot, Dickens, and Thackeray; Carlisle, *Sense of an Audience.* Albeit with less nostalgia for feudalism, Friedrich Engels resoundingly approved of *Past and Present,* while disparaging the promise of novelistic realism to fulfill that charge: "All the multi-volume novels with their sad and amusing intricacies . . . you may with an easy conscience leave unread. . . . Carlyle's book is the only one that strikes a human chord, presents human relations and shows traces of a human point of view"; Mark and Engels, *Marx, Engels Collected Works* 3:444.

5. See the important address: "For not having a lofty imagination, as you perceive, and being unable to invent thrilling incidents for your amusement, my only merit must lie in the truth with which I represent to you the humble experience of ordinary fellow-mortals. I wish to stir your sympathy with commonplace troubles—to win your tears for real sorrow: sorrow such as may live next door to you"; Eliot, *Scenes of Clerical Life,* 46.

6. The first maxim comes from a letter to Charles Bray dated 5 July 1859, in Haight, *Selections from George Eliot's Letters.* The second and third are both from Eliot, "The Natural History of German Life," in *Selected Essays, Poems and Other Writings,* 110. For Redfield the general association between sympathy and the aesthetic indicates a limitation of sympathy: "sympathy is always already an aesthetic experience, one that can only take place within the realm of fiction, mimesis, representation, and reproduction"; Redfield, *Phantom Formations,* 136. Nazar points out that Eliot's emphasis on sympathy distinguishes her aesthetic from earlier modes: "It situates its discourse of representation not only by reference to feeling, as the aesthetic tradition more generally does, but also, in distinction from the aesthetic

tradition, by reference to a feeling for social others"; Nazar, "Philosophy in the Bedroom," 294. On the visual and spectatorial dimensions of this aesthetic, see Jaffe, *Scenes of Sympathy*. On sympathy as metaphor, see Albrecht, "Sympathy and Telepathy." On sympathy as a novelistic project, see Ablow, *Marriage of Minds*.

7. Marx, *Capital* 1:255.

8. In focusing on Adam Smith, I should like to invite the critical liturgy on the philosophical sources and biographical experiences behind Eliot's sympathy to be more responsive to the economic context and ramifications of her ethics. For discussion of Rousseau, Wordsworth, Feuerbach, and Comte as sources for Eliot's sympathy, see Anger, *Victorian Interpretation;* Argyros, *"Without Any Check";* Purdy, "'The One Poor Word'"; and Nazar, "Philosophy in the Bedroom." On the biographical sources of this philosophy and its manifestation in Eliot's personal ethical and religious praxis, see Bodenheimer, *Real Life of Mary Ann Evans.*

9. Eliot, *Adam Bede,* 172; Eliot, *Daniel Deronda,* 306.

10. For this Levinasian position, see both Albrecht ("Sympathy and Telepathy") and Ermarth ("George Eliot's Conception of Sympathy"), who both explore Eliot's understanding of sympathy as "a difficult psychic negotiation between self and other" (Ermarth, "George Eliot's Conception of Sympathy," 23). I submit that Eliot's conception of these difficulties was less an abstract outline of "the other" not to be transgressed and more a concrete confrontation with what she and other Victorians saw as material limits to the affections of the self. As a good exception to the fascination with alterity, Lane's recent study of antisocial feelings obliquely broaches the question of exhaustion by highlighting a foundational "misanthropy" that Eliot at once admits and "smothers"; Lane, *Hatred and Civility,* 134–35.

11. Eliot, "Natural History of German Life," 111.

12. Ibid, 110.

13. Thinkers ranging from Alexander Bain to Samuel Smiles extended the image of "economy" from its eighteenth-century anatomical connotations to depict processes of consciousness and sentiment; see, for a small selection, Bain, *Senses and the Intellect;* Jevons, *Theory of Political Economy;* Lewes, *Problems of Life and Mind;* Smiles, *Self Help;* and Spencer, *Principles of Psychology.*

14. On the evolution of usury discourse and its corollary social estrangement, see Nelson, *Idea of Usury.* For details of the 1833 Act, see Francis, *History of the Bank of England.* For a Victorian analysis of usury, see Mill, *Principles of Political Economy.* For more recent analysis of 1833 as a watershed moment, see Alborn, *Conceiving Companies.*

15. For Schlegel, irony is "permanent parabasis," a perpetual undoing of levels of narrative or lines of meaning; cited in de Man, "Concept of Irony," 179. For de Man, "irony is the permanent paresis of the allegory of tropes," the disruption of "systematicity" or "coherence"; see "The Concept of Irony," 163–84.

16. In linking *Middlemarch's* shift from sympathy to interest to developing financial capitalism, I will undoubtedly echo the seminal claims of Albert Hirschman

that "from idea of counter-vailing passions, interests emerge as tamers, passions as those to be tamed"; Hirschman, *Passion and the Interests,* 32.

17. The phrase comes from Eliot's essay "Debasing the Moral Currency," in *Impressions of Theophrastus Such,* 81–87.

18. Lewes, *Literary Criticism of George Henry Lewes,* 91.

19. Lewes, *Principles of Success in Literature,* 167.

20. Ibid., 166.

21. Ibid., 167.

22. Spencer, "The Philosophy of Style."

23. Ibid., Para. 3.

24. Ibid., Para. 47.

25. Ibid., Para. 59.

26. Haight, *George Eliot Letters* 8:245.

27. Eliot, *Middlemarch,* 441; hereafter cited parenthetically by page number.

28. "This alternation between exuberance and apology, expansion and shrinking, utterance and scribble, was to govern Eliot's literary production throughout her life: she lived it as a rhythm of fluctuating excitement and discouragement while she was working on her novels, followed by deep gloom when each was completed. At a number of climactic moments the play of expansion and shrinking reappears, but the rhythm is broken, lifted out of the interior life of a single character and distributed to a pair of characters, one of whom is seen expanding in loving recognition of the other, who is commonly figured as shrunken or shrinking from contact"; Hertz, *George Eliot's Pulse,* 26.

29. See Woloch, "Characterization and Distribution."

30. For a distillation of this schema (realism: metonymy:: romanticism: metaphor), see Jakobson, *Fundamentals of Language,* 92–95.

31. On realism as particularization, see Lukacs, *Studies in European Realism.* More recently and specifically regarding Eliot, see Gallagher, "George Eliot: Immanent Victorian."

32. Beer, *George Eliot,* 192.

33. "Money Market, City, Friday," 3.

34. Eliot, *Selected Essays.* 128. "The social affections" is a phrase I take from Eliot's beloved Ruskin, *Unto This Last,* 167, 180, passim.

35. The notion of this reifying function founds the dominant paradigm in Victorian studies, as well as in studies of literature and money more generally. Patrick Brantlinger formidably contends that while "realistic fiction is often highly critical of such generalized social evils as avarice and materialism . . . its rhetorical conventions and structures involve the reification of the status quo"; Brantlinger, *Fictions of State,* 146. John Vernon similarly pursues an "analogy (that) is the comparison between the novel's claim to represent reality and paper money's claim to represent things of enduring value: gold and silver"; Vernon, *Money and Fiction,* 7. These critical assessments of Victorian realism of course owe much to Ian Watt's seminal study of realist reification, "Robinson Crusoe, Individualism, and the Novel."

36. See, paradigmatically, J. Hillis Miller's "Narrative and History," in that he argues that the second half of the sentence forms the novel's central deconstructive principle, but entirely ignores that principle's context within the sentence as a whole, and therefore underestimates its political stroke, or Albrecht's use of the second half of the sentence as epigraph for a section of his argument devoted to the ethical dangers of metaphor as a mode of imaginative relation, for "recourse to metaphor (is) a framing of the relation to the other as a similarity, not as irreducibly differential" (452).

37. Haight, *Selections from George Eliot's Letters.*

38. Ibid., To Julia Cameron, 17 January 1871.

39. Caleb Garth "could not manage finance: he knew values very well, but he had no keenness of imagination for monetary results in the shape of profit and loss"; Eliot, *Middlemarch,* 236. Fred Vincy must learn that credit comes perilously close to theft: "people who spend a great deal of money on themselves without knowing how they shall pay, must be selfish. They are always thinking of what they can get for themselves, and not of what other people may lose" (239). While Lydgate must learn to be less profligate, his wife Rosamund must learn that money does not grow on trees: "think no unfair evil of her, pray; she had no wicked plots, nothing sordid or mercenary; in fact, she never thought of money except as something necessary that other people would always provide" (252). And, of course, much of the subplot between Will and Bulstrode, the only financial official in the novel, revolves around the banker's avaricious and dishonest amassing of wealth (677).

40. My focus on Adam Smith takes its cue not from Eliot's letters or library, but from the references in *Middlemarch* itself and from the remarkable formal resonances between Smith and Eliot. In a rare treatment of Eliot and economic philosophy, Coovadia has linked Eliot's notion of social totality and Adam Smith's notion of social interrelatedness, but while Coovadia sees a conceptual resonance between Smith's invisible hand and Eliot's web (see Coovadia, "George Eliot's Realism and Adam Smith"), I emphasize here the ethical and economic consequences of a formal resonance between Smith's sympathy and Eliot's. David Marshall has found that *Daniel Deronda* "acts as a dramatization" of Smith's theory, but his focus is entirely thematic, on the similarities between what he interprets as the theatrical paradigm in Smith's theory and the spectatorial aspects of the interaction of Eliot's characters; Marshall, *Figure of Theater,* 221.

41. Adam Smith, *Theory of Moral Sentiments,* 12.

42. Marshall shows that Smith's mentor, Lord Kames, held this view of spontaneous feeling and associates Smith's departure from it with "Defoe's view of radical separateness, isolation, and solitude of people"; Marshall, *Figure of Theater,* 170.

43. Smith, *Theory of Moral Sentiments,* 11.

44. Ibid., 58.

45. Adam Smith, *The Wealth of Nations,* 572.

46. From the time of *Middlemarch*'s publication in 1871 through the present, a spectrum of readers has found Will an unsuitable suitor for Dorothea, often

concluding that their marriage mars an otherwise impeccable novel. Writing in the *Spectator* in 1872, Richard Holt Hutton called Will "altogether uninterest-ing . . . petulant and small" (Hutton, "Review of Middlemarch," 1554), finding him even less appealing than Dorothea's first husband, Edward Casaubon, and almost a hundred years later Barbara Hardy found Will so "inadequate" as to be the emblem of the novel's "incompleteness"; Hardy, *Appropriate Form,* 128. The broad consensus in more recent criticism has been succinctly captured by Ringler: "Why, when Eliot herself was able to defy social tradition and achieve her own epic life, did she relentlessly consign Dorothea to the unmitigated mediocrity of a conventional marriage to Will?"; Ringler, "Middlemarch: A Feminist Perspective," 57. Even critics more interested in Dorothea's agency, like feminists Gilbert and Gubar, have interpreted her choice to be "subversive" of the ossified patriarchy of "The Dead Hand" of Casaubon, but have still found Will an unsuitable suitor—"a baby" with little to offer; Gilbert and Gubar, *Madwoman in the Attic,* 550. And again quite recently, David Kurnick deemed the marriage a "failure of epic proportions"; Kurnick, "An Erotics of Detachment," 589.

47. "The Dead Hand" is the title of Book 5 in the middle of *Middlemarch.*

48. Since the late nineteenth century this missing link has been known as "das Adam Smith Problem" after a group of German intellectuals identified an ap-parent contradiction between the importance of sympathy in *The Theory of Moral Sentiments* and the importance of self-interestedness in *The Wealth of Nations.* In the late twentieth century a variety of solutions to the problem have been formulated, which often come down to asserting that virtue or ethics remained important counterparts to self-interest. I am here asserting that *Middlemarch* solves the prob-lem in a different way by revealing how much self-interest was always at the core of the metaphoric operation of sympathy. For a helpful overview of the history of approaches to the problem, see Teichgraeber, "Rethinking Das Adam Smith Problem."

4. *"Money Expects Money": Satiric Credit in* The Way We Live Now

1. See Herbert's assessment that Trollope is "determined . . . to remain within the idiom of stringent realism": Herbert, *Trollope and Comic Pleasure,* 189; Wall's easy "photographic realism": Wall, "Trollope, Satire, and the Way We Live Now," 43; Henry James's "a more copious record of disagreeable matters could scarcely be imagined, for instance, than *The Way We Live Now*": Henry James, "Anthony Trollope," 4; and Harold James's estimation that "Part of the charm of this genre of novel is the exact depiction, almost anatomization, of an arcane world": Harold James, "Literary Financier," 255. See also Cecil's seminal judgment that "of style . . . Trollope has none at all"; Cecil, *Early Victorian Novelists,* 199.

2. Henry James, "Anthony Trollope," 2. At times Trollope endorsed this finding, going so far as to quote, in his own *Autobiography* (144), Nathaniel Hawthorne's echo of James: "[Trollope's novels] precisely suit my taste—solid and substantial,

written on the strength of beef . . . and just as real as if some giant had hewn a great lump out of the earth and put it under a glass case."

3. See Skilton's position that Trollope's "work seems more strikingly transparent than almost any other": Skilton, *Anthony Trollope and His Contemporaries,* 138; Kendrick's formula that "Realist writing, for Trollope, is absolutely literal, not metaphoric": Kendrick, *Novel-Machine,* 6; and Tanner's approval that "Trollope's apparent lack of rhetoric was a distinct advantage": Tanner, "Trollope's *The Way We Live Now,*" 260. See also Tanner's sense that Trollope's prose amounts to "reporting," "rather than inventing," and that "Trollope uses fewer metaphors and images than any novelist I can recall . . . he works so exactly with the illusion of factual authenticity . . . to read it is to assent to its high degree of plausibility" (260). More colloquially, of course, the critical consensus manifests in the conviction that Trollope is boring.

4. Lewes, *Principles of Success in Literature,* 91.

5. "Vitriolic satire" is the phrase of Iva Jones (*Amid Visions and Revisions*). Our fondness today for heralding its "massive social indictment" (Sutton, "Affront to Victorian Dignity," 93) is just this side of history from the major reception of the novel in its day as an odiously powerful satire. The *Spectator* thought it stank: "an atmosphere of sordid baseness which prevents enjoyment like an effluvium," and contended with disgust that readers should sooner visit a "sewage farm" in search of "a breath of fresh air, as read *The Way We Live Now* for entertainment"; quoted in Hall, *Trollope,* 397. The *Saturday Review* was annoyed with the relentlessness of the satire, calling in its loan: "Satire, of course, naturally turns upon its shams and pretences, but its credit and presentableness as such, its decorums and reserves, its fair show to the world, whether false or not, become in the course of time stupid and irritating to the jaded imagination"; quoted in Hall, *Trollope,* 399. More recently, Trollope biographer Hall calls it his "most sustained satire" (384), and the early comprehensive commentator Sadleir refers to it as a "long and trenchant satire . . . a sour and pitiless picture of a sordid scene"; Sadleir, *Anthony Trollope,* 396–99. Comparing the text to Thackeray's *Vanity Fair,* Jumeau finds it animated with "savage indignation"; Jumeau, "The Way We Live Now," 65. While Wall notes that the satire falters into "a kind of sympathy" ("Trollope, Satire, and the Way We Live Now," 49), he focuses on Trollope's *personality,* finding him "constitutionally unable" to hold up the whip of satirist. By contrast, my reading attributes the shift to a formal impasse. Delany is exceptional in declining to identify *The Way We Live Now* as a satire, finding it instead "an elegiac novel, a lament for the passing away of the old prestige order where identity depends on one's rank" (Delany, *Literature, Money, and the Market,* 19), but his historical and thematic concerns disincline him from formal analysis. Kincaid explores the satire's alloy with more conventional comedy and interprets the marriages at the end as evidence of these comedic features; Kincaid, *Novels of Anthony Trollope.*

6. Trollope, *Autobiography,* 354–55; Letter of 4 April 1873 to Alfred Austin, in Trollope, *Letters of Anthony Trollope.*

7. Pope, *Epilogue to the Satires* 1:212–13, 216–19; Trollope, *Autobiography*, 355.

8. For an elegant argument about temporal immanence in the Gothic mode, see Law, "Being There."

9. Delany, *Literature, Money, and the Market*, 19.

10. The plans are reproduced in Sadleir, *Anthony Trollope*, 423.

11. Trollope, *The Way We Live Now*, 57; hereafter cited parenthetically.

12. Smalley, *Trollope*, 399.

13. Freud identified condensation as the chief technology of jokes in his *Jokes and Their Relation to the Unconscious*.

14. Smalley, *Trollope*, 399.

15. Dickens, "Bankruptcy in Six Easy Lessons," 210.

16. Evans, *Commercial Crisis of 1857–1858*, 1.

17. The unattributed impersonal knowledge that makes the story go around illustrates that mental speculation is constitutive of the experience of literary realism, for we speculate all along about what the characters might do and feel and wait for the omniscient narrator to confirm our speculations. In her seminal study of gossip, Spacks has intimated as much by using "speculation" to describe the work of readers and of characters: "We, as readers, speculate about Eleanor; so do the people who know her, within the fiction. Only the narrator need not speculate: he *knows*"; Spacks, *Gossip*, 194. Within Trollope's satire, however, speculation constitutes the narrative voice as much as it does the readers' experience.

18. Bagehot, *Lombard Street*, 24–28. Focusing on journalism rather than rumor, Poovey has also explicated "the financial system's extreme susceptibility to the influence of representation" in the introduction to her compendium of nineteenth-century financial documents: "Because the operations of the financial system are extremely sensitive to the circulation of information (or rumors), efforts to understand the system—to represent and dramatize its parts—could actually affect the system itself. . . . This mutually provocative interaction is also evident in the financial panics that punctuated the nineteenth century"; Poovey, *The Financial System*, 5.

19. Evans, *Commercial Crisis of 1847–48*, 71.

20. Frye, *Anatomy of Criticism*, 224.

21. Smalley, *Trollope*, 414. The *Examiner* ran a similar review: "Mr. Trollope does not seek to throw a transforming imaginative veil over his world. . . . The intricate schemings and plottings in which social ambition is wont to show itself—the methods of unscrupulous financiers, the details of Parliamentary candidature, together with all the petty splendours of balls and dinner parties, are here given as with the semblance of absolutely perfect knowledge"; see Smalley, *Trollope*, 410–11. See also the *Spectator*: "Mr. Trollope is so rarely inaccurate that we suppose that somewhere there is a world like that which he describes," quoted in Tanner, "Trollope's *The Way We Live Now*," 257.

22. The *Times*, 24 Aug 1875, quoted in Hall, *Trollope*, 388.

23. Frye, *Anatomy of Criticism*, 224.

24. For an argument that satiric narration was an "experiment" and a "mistake" for Trollope, see Kincaid, *Novels of Anthony Trollope*, 145. While Kincaid focuses on something like Trollope's ethics as an author as they shape his narratorial persona, I am trying to capture the formal impossibility of a satire of finance.

25. "Mr. Trollope's Last Novel," 139.

5. *London, Nineteenth Century, Capital of Realism: On Marx's Victorian Novel*

1. Wheen, *Karl Marx*, 304.

2. Briggs, *Marx in London*, 53.

3. Quotes from such reports fill the pages of *Capital*. On their role for the fellow novelists, see Sheila Smith, "Blue Books and Victorian Novelists."

4. Marx, *Capital* 1:802; hereafter cited parenthetically.

Marx's son-in-law, Paul Lafargue, went one step further: "only in England could Marx become what he has become . . . in such an economically undeveloped country as Germany was until the middle of this century, Marx could not have arrived at his critique of bourgeois economy and at a knowledge of capitalist production any more than this economically undeveloped Germany could have had the political institutions of economically developed England"; Lafargue and Liebknecht, *Extracts from Reminiscences of Karl Marx*, 42.

5. Letter to Engels, 31 July 1865, in Marx and Engels, *Collected Works*, vol. 42.

6. Lafargue reported that the story left "a deep impression" on Marx; Lafargue and Liebknecht, *Extracts from Reminiscences of Karl Marx*, 16.

7. Balzac, "Le Chef d'Oeuvre Inconnu": "*Il y a tant de profondeur sur cette toile, l'air y est si vrai, que vous ne pouvez plus le distinguer de l'air qui nous environne. Où est l'art? Perdu, disparu! . . . Rien, . . . Jen e vois là que des couleurs confusément amassées et contenues par une multitude de lignes bizarres qui forment une muraille de peinture.*"

8. Afterword, Marx, *Capital*, second German edition, 1873, reprinted in *Capital* 94: "The mealy-mouthed babblers of German vulgar economy fell foul of the style of my book. No one can feel the literary shortcomings in *Das Kapital* more strongly than I myself. Yet I will for the benefit and the enjoyment of these gentlemen and their public quote in this connexion one English and one Russian notice. The *Saturday Review* always hostile to my views, said in its notice of the first edition: The presentation of the subject invests the driest economic questions with a certain peculiar charm. The *St. Petersburg Journal* (Sankt-Peterburgskie Viedomosti), in its issue of 20 April 1872, says: The presentation of the subject, with the exception of one or two exceptionally special parts, is distinguished by its comprehensibility by the general reader, its clearness, and, in spite of the scientific intricacy of the subject, by an unusual liveliness. In this respect the author in no way resembles . . . the majority of German scholars who . . . write their books in a language so dry and obscure that the heads of ordinary mortals are cracked by it."

9. Marx and Engels, *Marx Engels Collected Works* 1:616.

10. Marx, *Capital* 1, Chap. 29.

11. Letter to his father, 10 November 1837, in Marx and Engels, *Marx Engels Collected Works* 1:10.

12. Gellert, *Karl Marx's "Capital" in Lithographs;* Eisenstein. On talking commodities, see Hamacher's excellent "Lingua Amissa" and Derrida's *Specters of Marx.* On sensationalism, see Cvetkovich, *Mixed Feelings.* On literary allusions, see Hyman, *Tangled Bank.* A passing reference likens *Capital* to a *Bildungsroman* in Heinzelman, *Economics of the Imagination,* 182.

13. On the reality effect, see Barthes, *Rustle of Language.* For another good example from *Capital,* see also the stupendous list of specialized works involved in making a watch; *Capital* 1:462.

14. For this definition of melodrama, see Brooks, *Melodramatic Imagination.*

15. Such a perspective was, of course, openly advocated by Dickens, Eliot, and others, and is a critical commonplace, as in, for example, Levine's concise remark that "Nineteenth-century writers sought to represent reality accurately not simply for the sake of mimetic perfection, but because a secure knowledge of the real *mattered.* Realists wanted their readers to know the way the world worked so that they would understand how to act in that world"; Levine, *Serious Pleasures of Suspense,* 138. For an admirable book-length study shining bold new light on this question, see Ortiz-Robles, *Novel as Event.*

16. Lukács, "Critical Realism and Socialist Realism," 93–135. See also the exemplary, though not economically focused, discussion of typicality in Gallagher, "George Eliot: Immanent Victorian."

17. I take the phrase "conceptual agency" from Wolfson's discussion of literary form, though by it she intends "the way form shapes perceptions and critical thinking," while I am after the way form thinks; Wolfson, "Reading for Form," 16. In this endeavor I am indebted to Lupton's formidable models of "thinking with" literature, especially as developed in her *Thinking with Shakespeare.*

18. My reading is limited to the first volume of *Capital,* as that is the only volume Marx saw to completion.

19. Dickens, *Bleak House:* "What connection can there be between the place in Lincolnshire, the house in town, the Mercury in powder, and the whereabout of Jo, the outlaw with the broom, who had the distant ray of light upon him when he swept the churchyard step? What connection can there have been between many people in the innumerable histories of this world, who, from opposite sides of great gulfs, have, nevertheless, been very curiously brought together!" (16). In emphasizing the way in which the Dickensian narrator's question prompts synthesis of plots, settings, and characters as all of one "curious" whole, I mean in part to underscore that *Capital* is read here as a specifically *Victorian* novel, one that asserts its own wholeness.

20. Karatani, "Capital's Drive," 200–11, and Žižek, *Parallax View,* 60–65. Žižek's work often *refers* to drive in discussing capitalism, but rarely explores the idea. It seems nonetheless possible to glean from his work that a properly thorough exploration of drive will be the final and urgent ground of psychoanalytic Marxism. For

indications in this direction, see Kordela, "Marx Condensed and Displaced." Also salient here is Johnston's remarkable elucidation of a materialist account of drive, though this is only momentarily developed with respect to Marx; Johnston, *Time Driven*, 329–30.

21. Marx, *Capital* 1:92. "*Zur Vermeidung möglicher Missverständnisse ein Wort. Die Gestalten von Kapitalist and Grundeigentümer zeichne ich keineswegs in rosigem Licht. Aber es handelt sich hier um die Personen nur, soweit sie die Personifikation ökonomischer Kategorien sind, Träger von bestimmten Klassenverhältnissen und Interessen*"; *Marx Engels Werke* 23:16. All German quotations hereafter cited parenthetically.

22. Maritornes being a whorish servant girl in *Don Quixote*.

23. See Hamacher, "Lingua Amissa." Also noteworthy: J. Hillis Miller, "Promises, Promises," and Žižek's formidable "How Did Marx Invent the Symptom?"

24. Marx, *Grundrisse*, 162: "To compare money with language is not less erroneous. Language does not transform ideas, so that the peculiarity of ideas is dissolved and their social character runs alongside them as separate entity, like prices alongside commodities. Ideas do not exist separately from language. Ideas that have first to be translated out of their mother tongue into a foreign tongue in order to circulate, in order to become exchangeable, offer a somewhat better analogy; but the analogy is then not with language, but with its foreignness." "*Das Geld mit der Sprache zu vergleichen ist nicht minder falsch . . . bieten schon mehr Analogie; die Analogie liegt dann aber nicht in der Sprache, sondern in ihrer Fremdheit*"; *Marx Engels Werke* 42:96.

Prominent contemporary brokers of this analogy, not always with sufficient attention to Marx's correction, include Derrida, *Given Time* 1; Goux, *Symbolic Economies;* Goux, *Coiners of Language;* Shell, *Economy of Literature;* and Karatani, *Architecture as Metaphor.*

25. Marx, *Capital* 1:254, 265, 342, 423, 424, 739, 765, 991, 1003, 1015, 1020, 1025, and passim.

26. Ibid., 1:252, 254, 255, 259, 320, and passim. Eventually, about halfway through the text, the self-reflexivity of this expression, "the valorization of value," precipitates the substitute expression "self-valorization," furthering the personifications; ibid., 1:449, 486, 557, 644, 669, 756 and passim.

27. "*Wissenschaftliche Analyse der Konkurrenz ist nur möglich, sobald die innere Natur des Kapitals begriffen ist, ganz wie die scheinbare Bewegung der Himmelskörper nur dem verständlich, der ihre wirkliche, aber sinnlich nicht wahrnehmbare Bewegung kennt*"; *Marx Engels Werke*, 23:335.

28. It does not appear in *Grimm's Deutsches Wörterbuch*, Marx's contemporary dictionary; it does not appear in *Duden*.

29. "*Dieser Widerspruch zwischen der quantitativen Schranke und der qualitativen Schrankenlosigkeit des Geldes treibt den Schatzbildner stets zurück zur Sisyphusarbeit der Akkumulation*"; *Marx Engels Werke* 23:147.

30. On this distinction in psychoanalysis, see Lacan, *The Four Fundamental Concepts of Psychoanalysis,* 168; see also Johnston, *Time Driven*, 191.

31. David Harvey's recent companion constructs a graphic chart of these dualities, mapping the dual value of the commodity, the dual forms of exchange value, the dual positions in the market, and the dual function of money; Harvey, *Companion to Marx's Capital,* 109.

32. On diverse logics of contradiction in capitalism, see Kordela, "Political Metaphysics."

33. *"Wir müssen uns also nach ihren Hütern umsehen, den Warenbesitzern"*; *Marx Engels Werke* 23:99.

34. Fowkes, translator of the Penguin edition of *Capital,* has a helpful footnote highlighting this resonance. Marx's reference is to a passage in Aesop's fables also quoted by Hegel in the Preface to *Philosophy of Right* to underscore that the philosophical imperative is to describe what is rather than prescribe what should be; see Marx, *Capital* 1:269.

35. I paraphrase here Lacan's notation of the uncanny excess within a subject that activates love: "I love something in you more than you"; *The Four Fundamental Concepts of Psychoanalysis,* 269.

36. Karatani, *Transcritique,* 217.

37. The text of *Capital* is saturated with images of throwing: *Capital* 1:208, 216, 223, 231, 249, 251, 262, 267, 299, 301, 445, 567, 617, 709, 723, 754, 936, and passim; for "Alternating rhythm," see *Capital* 1:723.

38. Marx, *Capital* 1:579–80; *"ürhaupt die der grossen Industrie entsprechenden allgemeinen Produktionsbedingungen hergestallt sind, erwirbt diese Betriebsweise eine Elastizität, eine plötzliche sprungweise Ausdehnungsfähigkeit . . . Die ungeheure, stossweise Ausdehnbarkeit"*; *Marx Engels Werke* 23:476.

39. *"Diese ganze Bewegung scheint sich also in einem fehlerhaften Kreislauf herumzudrehn, aus demn wir nur hinauskommen, in dem wir eine der kapitalistischen Akkumulation vorausgehende "ursprüngliche" Akkumulation ("previous accumulation" bei Adam Smith) unterstellen, eine Akkumulation, welche nicht das Resultat der kapitalistischen Produktionsweise ist, sondern ihr Ausgangspunkt"*; *Marx Engels Werke* 23:471.

40. On primitive accumulation as a constant rather than a phase, see David Harvey's discussion of what he calls "accumulation by dispossession," in Harvey, *New Imperialism,* 137–83.

41. Here, too, we might remark the Hegelianism of Marx's procedure: figural relations in the text are relations in the world itself.

6. Psychic Economy and Its Vicissitudes: Freud's Economic Hypothesis

1. Wicksteed, in his entry for *Palgrave's Dictionary of Political Economy,* framed this continuity most definitively for the Victorians: "The economist must from the first to last realize that he is dealing with psychological phenomena, and must be guided throughout by psychological considerations" (767). And Deleuze pronounced the same for the twentieth century and beyond: "political economy and libidinal

economy are finally one and the same"; Deleuze, "Preface." See also Seem's Introduction to *Anti-Oedipus:* "While Deleuze and Guatttari quote frequently from Marx and Freud, it would be an error to view *Anti-Oedipus* as yet another attempt at a Freud-Marx synthesis. For such an attempt always treats political economy (the flows of capital and interest) and the economy of the libido (the flows of desire) as two separate economies. . . . Deleuze and Guattari, on the other hand, postulate one and the same economy, the economy of flows. The flows and productions of desire will simply be viewed as the unconscious of the social productions. Behind every investment of time and interest and capital, an investment of desire, and vice versa"; Deleuze, *Anti-Oedipus,* xviii.

    2. Breithaupt, "Homo-Oeconomicus"; Birken, *Consuming Desire;* Bennett, "Desire as Capital."

    3. Freud loved and cited Austen, Dickens, Eliot, Kipling, Meredith, Wilde, and other Victorian novelists, prescribed novel reading to patients such as the Rat Man and the Wolf Man, and gifted Martha Bernays *David Copperfield* as a wedding present. He repeatedly attributes psychoanalytic insight to these novels. "The description of the human mind is indeed the domain which is most his (the creative writer's) own; he has from time immemorial been the precursor of science, and so too of scientific psychology"; Freud, *Standard Edition* 9:43; hereafter SE. See also "creative writers are valuable allies and their evidence is to be prized highly, for they are apt to know a whole host of things between heaven and earth of which our philosophy has not yet let us dream. In their knowledge of the mind they are far in advance of us everyday people, for they draw upon sources which we have not yet opened up for science"; SE 9:31. "The fact is that local diagnosis . . . leads nowhere, whereas a detailed description of mental processes such as we are accustomed to find in the works of imaginative writers enables me, with the use of a few psychological formulas, to obtain at least some kind of insight"; SE 2:159. And additionally, "Up till now we have left it to the creative writer to depict for us the necessary conditions for loving which govern people's choice of an object. . . . It becomes inevitable that science should concern herself with the same materials whose treatment by artists has given enjoyment to mankind for thousands of years, though her touch must be clumsier and the yield of pleasure less"; SE 11:164.

    For arguments that Victorian fiction provided foundational assumptions for Freud, see Lukacher, *Primal Scenes,* 330–38; Thomas, *Dreams of Authority,* 1–16; and Dever, *Death and the Mother.* On non-Victorian literature, see Reinhard and Lupton, *After Oedipus.* For literature in general, see de Certeau's idea that it is "the theoretical discourse" "which allows it (psychoanalysis) to be thought"; de Certeau, *Heterologies,* 18.

    4. Lacan, *Écrits,* 267, 102. In his own close reading of Lacan, Fink is a vigilant reminder of this insistence; see Fink, *Lacan to the Letter,* 67.

    5. Letter 24, 25 May 1895, in Freud, *Letters of Sigmund Freud* (English*);* Letter 64 in Freud, *Briefe an Wilhelm Fleiss* (German), 130.

6. SE 18:60.

7. SE 15:59.

8. See, for just a couple examples, SE 2:391; SE 14:151; and *Gesammelte Werke* 11:389 (hereafter GW).

9. In one of the early usages, in his essay in French on the heredity and aetiology of neuroses, he refers to the image of "l'economie nerveuse" as a "rather vague expression" ("l'expression un peu vague"); SE 3:150; GW 1:414. For "What we may call an economic" and just a few of the circumlocutionary gestures, see SE 15:274, 355, 377, passim.

10. SE 12:236; SE 18:391; SE 20:149, 232; SE 21:218. Posthumous essays published only in English tend to use the noun formulation an additional three or so times.

11. GW 5:203; SE 7:42 "psychichen haushalt" is rendered "domestic economy of the mind," quite an unfortunate inflation given Freud's care when directly employing the word "oikonomie." This happens again in SE 21:220, where *seelischen Haushalt* is translated "libidinal economy," as well as in SE 12:235. A parallel problem assails Freud's *Jokes and their Relation to the Unconscious*. Numerous times in that text, Strachey repeatedly renders as "economy" what Freud describes as a saving, "*Einsparung.*"

12. SE 18:228; SE 18:7; SE 23:226; SE 21:161; SE 16:374. *Betrachtung:* SE 16:274.

13. SE 16:355: "The *economic*. This leads us to one of the most important, but unluckily also, one of the most obscure, regions of psychoanalysis." See also the caution that "we now have a suspicion of an economy in the far more comprehensive sense of psychical expenditure in general; and we must regard it as possible that a closer understanding of what is still the very obscure concept of "psychical expenditure"; SE 8:117.

Freud's disquietude about the metapsychology materializes in his archive, which mysteriously disappears seven of the twelve papers on metapyschology from 1915.

First use of "psychoanalysis" is in a French essay; Freud, "L'hérédité et l'étiologie des névroses," in SE 3:143.

14. "I was suddenly in another compartment, in which the upholstery and seats were so narrow that one's back pressed directly against the back of the carriage. I was surprised by this, but I reflected that I might have changed carriages while in a sleeping state. There were several people, including an English brother and sister. A row of books was distinctly visible on a shelf on the wall. I saw *The Wealth of Nations* and *Matter and Motion,* a thick volume and bound in brown cloth. The man asked his sister about a book by Schiller, whether she had forgotten it. It seemed as though the books were sometimes mine and sometimes theirs"; SE 4:55.

15. On the historically specific hypostatization of "the" economy, see Appleby, *Economic Thought.*

16. SE 16:311; GW 11:322.

17. Letter 217, 29 January 1926, *Letters of Freud.*

18. See also "okonomie des Menschenlebens" in SE 14:276 and GW 10:325, and "satisfaction (of the instinctual dispositions) is the economic task of our lives" and "laws of economic necessity," in SE 21:95, 103.

19. See Aristotle's *Politics.* Perhaps not coincidentally, Freud's most direct commentary on economic systems, his discussion of Soviet communism in *Civilization and Its Discontents,* strongly makes this point about the ineluctability of antagonism in social relations; SE 21:112. See also Arendt's discussion in *The Human Condition.*

20. He used the formulation "psychic household" or the variations "household of the soul" or "libido household" regularly, in contrast to the rare use of "economy" as a noun that I have already noted; see, for example, GW 5:203; GW 8:37; GW 14:500; GW 14:511, 512; and GW 15:88, 105.

21. Lacan, *Ego in Freud's Theory,* 60. For Lacan's use of the term "organization interne," see Lacan, *Le Séminaire Le Livre II: Le Moi dans la theorie de Freud et dans la technique psychanalytique* (Paris: Éditions du Seuil, 1978), 78.

22. SE 3:59.

23. "We thus reach the idea of a quantity of libido, to the mental representation of which we give the name ego-libido, and whose production, increase, or diminution, distribution and displacement should afford us possibilities for explaining the psychosexual phenomena observed"; SE 7:217 ("*libidoquantums, dessen psychische Vertretung wir die ICHLIBIDO heissen, dessen production, Vergrosserung oder Verminderung, Verteilung und Verschiebung*") (emphasis capitalized in original). See also the idea of libidinal increases, *libidosteigerung,* where "*steigerung*" is the economic name for sales increase or production increase; SE 10:210, GW 7:436. On "the great reservoir," see Strachey's explanatory note, SE 19:62.

24. As Freud writes in the *Entwurf:* The quantitative conception "derived directly from pathological clinical observation especially where excessively intense ideas were concerned—in hysteria and obsessions, in which, as we shall see, the quantitative characteristic emerges more plainly than in the normal"; SE 1:294.

25. This would be a variation on Žižek's elemental point about the "homology" of procedure between Freud and Marx; Žižek, *Sublime Object of Ideology,* Chap. 1.

26. See, for example, Birken, *Consuming Desire;* Bennett, "Desire as Capital"; Zaretsky, *Secrets of the Soul.* Notably, none of these authors cite Freud's German. For a rebuttal to such arguments, see Gay's "Human Nature in History," 78–115.

27. His first usages of it involve scare quotes; GW 1:215.

28. Strachey acknowledges his invention of the term in "Obituary for Joan Riviere." The electric charge image occurs in Freud's 1894 "Neuropsychoses of Defense"; SE 3:41–60. On the term in Austrian context and its distortion by Strachey, see Ornston, "Invention of 'Cathexis,'" 392.

29. See, for example, "eines mit Affekt besetzen seelischen," "a mental process which is emotionally colored" or "eine Gruppe von zusammengeboerigen, mit Af-

fekt besetzen Vorstellungselementen," "a group of ideas which belong together and have a common emotive tone"; Erwin, *Freud Encyclopedia, 72.*

30. Bennett, "Introduction: Psychoanalysis, Money, and the Economy"; introductory address at the Freud Museum in London in 2010.

31. For Freud's use of the term "intensity," see SE 3:130.

32. "The economic, or, if you prefer, the quantitative factor, which is intimately linked to the pleasure principle, dominates all its processes"; SE 22:73.

33. SE 3:60. *"Ich will endlich mit wenigen Worten der Hilfsvorstellung gedenken, deren ich mich in dieser Darstellung der Abwehrneurosen bedient habe";* GW 1:73.

34. SE 3:59.

35. "The outcome of such situations will entirely depend upon economic considerations—of the relative magnitudes of the trends which are struggling with one another"; SE 19:152.

36. Derrida has commented on this elusiveness of the qualitative as part of the "speculative," and therefore not philosophical, tenor of Freud's thought; Derrida, *Post Card,* 279 and passim.

37. SE 19:159.

38. Deleuze, *Anti-Oedipus,* 329.

39. On the inconsistency of Freud's references to physics, see Bass, "Status of an Analogy."

40. "Substitutive representation"; SE 19:150. This is a regularly recurrent idea; see "the multiplicity of developmental dispositions which give repressed impulses the opportunity of breaking through into substitutive structures" (SE 13: 174), or "Repressed impulses . . . succeed in making their influence felt in the mind by circuitous paths, and the indirect or substitutive satisfactions of repressed impulses thus achieved are what constitute neurotic symptoms"; SE 20:267.

41. Freud maintained that the substitutes, as representations, were not able to dispose entirely of the substance they represent. "In our discussion so far we have dealt with the repression of an instinctual representative, and by the latter we have understood an idea or group of ideas which is cathected with a definite quota of psychical energy (libido or interest) coming from an instinct. Clinical observation now obliges us to divide up what we have hitherto regarded as a single entity; for it shows us that besides the idea, some other element representing the instinct has to be taken into account, and that this other element undergoes vicissitudes of repression which may be quite different from those undergone by the idea. For this other element of the psychical representative the term quota of affect has been generally adopted. It corresponds to the instinct in so far as the latter has become detached from the idea and finds expression, proportionate to its quantity. From this point on, in describing a case of repression, we shall have to follow up separately what becomes of the idea, and what becomes of the instinctual energy linked to it"; SE 14:152.

42. "If we reflect that the means of representation in dreams are principally visual images and not words, we shall see that it is even more appropriate to compare

dreams with a system of writing than with a language. In fact the interpretation of dreams is completely analogous to the decipherment of an ancient pictographic script such as Egyptian hieroglyphs. In both cases there are certain elements which are not intended to be interpreted (or read, as the case may be) but are only designed to serve as 'determinatives,' that is to establish the meaning of some other element. The ambiguity of various elements of dreams finds a parallel in these ancient systems of writing; and so too does the omission of various relations, which have in both cases to be supplied from the context. If this conception of the method of representation in dreams has not yet been followed up, this, as will be readily understood, must be ascribed to the fact that psycho-analysts are entirely ignorant of the attitude and knowledge with which a philologist would approach such a problem as that presented by dreams"; SE 13:176. For a formidable discussion of the consequences of this distinction, see Derrida, "Freud and the Scene of Writing."

43. See, for instance, "In the total absence of any theory of the instincts which would help us to find our bearings, we may be permitted, or rather, it is incumbent upon us, to start off by working out some hypothesis to its logical conclusion, until it either breaks down or is confirmed. . . . But I shall be consistent enough [with my general rule] to drop this hypothesis if psycho-analytic work should itself produce some other, more serviceable hypothesis about the instincts"; SE 14:77.

44. In *An Autobiographical Study,* Freud clarified that the "economic factor" (*einen ökonomischen Faktor*) arose conceptually from early clinical "regard (for) the symptom as the product or equivalent of an amount energy which would have otherwise been employed some other way." He added in parentheses directly thereafter, "This latter process was described as conversion." The very idea of quantity is subordinated to the idea of conversion, substitution; SE 20:22.

45. Goux, *Symbolic Economies;* Lyotard, *Libidinal Economy.*

46. Derrida, *Post Card,* 68, 3.

47. "Editor's Notes to Rat Man," SE 10:154.

48. Dany Nobus has a remarkable project in progress on this conception of psychoanalysis as paying for the privilege of working; Nobus, "What Are Words Worth?"

49. SE 10:212; GW 7:433.

50. However much he emphasizes the similarities between dreams and symptoms, Freud also maintains a distinction between them, precisely, as Lacan points out, on economic grounds (where "economic" connotes the insistence of integrity): "there is an absolutely fundamental economic difference between the symptom and the dream. All they have in common is a grammar. That's a metaphor, don't take it literally. They are as different as an epic poem is from a work on thermodynamics. The dream makes it possible to grasp the symbolic function at play, and it is, on that account, capital for understanding the symptom. But a symptom is always part of the overall economic state of the subject, whereas the

dream is a state localized in time, under extremely specific conditions"; Lacan, *Ego in Freud's Theory,* 122.

Goux has formidably argued that the psychic and monetary logics of substitution amount to one and the same "the global mode of symbolizing . . . reproduced in each register"; Goux, *Symbolic Economies,* 139.

51. See, paradigmatically, Ibid.

52. We might even ask whether, when confronted with a displacement machine, meta-language is desirable or even technically feasible. Karatani makes a formidable observation: "It is absolutely impossible to control capitalism from the meta-level, because capitalism itself is deconstructive"; Karatani, *Architecture as Metaphor,* 67. In the case of psychoanalysis, we might say that psychoanalysis refuses to operate as metalanguage, because it seeks a form adequately open to, rather than structurally closed against, its object, the unconscious.

53. SE 3:559–61; all italics original.

54. SE 7:86; GW 5:249.

55. SE 15:225; GW 11:231.

56. SE 22:95.

57. SE 18:10; Freud citing Fechner.

58. SE 18:10, 37, 38 and passim.

59. SE 18:10, 37, 38 and passim.

60. SE 18:38.

61. Freud, *Beyond the Pleasure Principle,* 76.

62. His only direct address of specific economic systems comes in *Civilization and its Discontents,* where he is keen to disabuse a certain strand of Communist praxis of the fantasy that abolishing private property will alleviate all social antagonism, but equally keen not to make pronouncements about the desirability of particular economic modes. Far from an apology for capitalism, this seems a finely observed Marxian point.

Epilogue: The Psychic Life of Finance

1. United States Congress Joint Economic Committee Hearings of 23 September 2008, as reported in "Does Treasury Need $700 Billion All At Once?" *Wall Street Journal,* 24 September 2008.

2. Robert Shiller, the Yale economist who authored a book "motivated" by the famous speech of Bernanke's predecessor, Alan Greenspan, boldly declares as much on the first page of his new 2009 preface to his influential book: "The policy response was inadequate because of a failure to understand the origins of the crisis and the irrational exuberance that was the fundamental cause"; Shiller, *Irrational Exuberance,* xi. The University of Pennsylvania hosted an April 2009 conference, "Crisis of Confidence: The Recession and the Economy of Fear," after which the university's renowned Wharton School of Business issued a press release affirming

the conference consensus that "psychological factors are at work behind the crisis"; "Hope, Greed, and Fear: The Psychology behind the Financial Crisis," http:// knowledge.wharton.upenn.edu/article.cfm?articleid=2204.

3. Professor of Economics Hersh Shefrin, as reported in "Financial Crisis Illustrates Influence of Emotions, Behavior on Market," PBS Online News Hour, 8 October 2008.

Works Cited

Ablow, Rachel. *The Marriage of Minds: Reading Sympathy in the Victorian Marriage Plot.* Stanford: Stanford University Press, 2007. Print.

"The Accounts of the Credit Mobilier for the Last Two Years." *Economist,* 26 September 1857. Print.

Akerlof, George A. *Animal Spirits: How Human Psychology Drives the Economy, and Why It Matters for Global Capitalism.* Princeton: Princeton University Press, 2009. Print.

Alborn, Timothy L. *Conceiving Companies: Joint-Stock Politics in Victorian England.* London: Routledge, 1998. Print.

——. "Creating Capitalism: Joint-Stock Enterprise in British Politics and Culture 1800–1870 (Review of *Creating Capitalism,* by James Taylor)." *Victorian Studies* 50, no. 1 (2007): 147–49. Print.

——. "The Moral of the Failed Bank: Professional Plots in the Victorian Money Market." *Victorian Studies* 38, no. 2 (1995): 199–226. Print.

Albrecht, Thomas. "Sympathy and Telepathy: The Problem of Ethics in George Eliot's The Lifted Veil." *ELH* 73 (2006): 437–63. Print.

Althusser, Louis. *Lenin and Philosophy, and Other Essays.* New York: Monthly Review Press, 2001. Print.

Althusser, Louis, and Étienne Balibar. *Reading Capital.* London: Verso, 1997. Print.

Altick, Richard Daniel. *The Presence of the Present: Topics of the Day in the Victorian Novel.* Columbus: Ohio State University Press, 1991. Print.

Anderson, Richard. "Bagehot on the Financial Crises of 1825 . . . and 2008." *Economic Synopses* 7 (2009): 1–2. Print.

Andreadēs, Andreas Michaēl. *History of the Bank of England, 1640 to 1903.* 4th ed. New York: A. M. Kelley, 1966. Print.

Anger, Suzy. *Victorian Interpretation.* Ithaca: Cornell University Press, 2005. Print.

Appleby, Joyce. *Economic Thought and Ideology in Seventeenth-Century England.* Princeton: Princeton University Press, 1978. Print.

Arendt, Hannah. *The Human Condition.* Chicago: University of Chicago Press, 1998. Print.

Argyros, Ellen. *"Without Any Check of Proud Reserve": Sympathy and Its Limits in George Eliot's Novels.* New York: Peter Lang, 1999. Print.

Aristotle. *Aristotle: The Politics and the Constitution of Athens.* Trans. Stephen Everson. Cambridge: Cambridge University Press, 1996. Print.

Arrighi, Giovanni. *The Long Twentieth Century: Money, Power and the Origins of Our Times.* London: Verso, 2010. Print.

Austin, J. L. *How to Do Things with Words.* 2nd ed. Cambridge, Mass.: Harvard University Press, 1975. Print.

Bagehot, Walter. *The Collected Works of Walter Bagehot.* Cambridge, Mass.: Harvard University Press, 1965. Print.

———. *Economic Studies.* London: Longmans, Green, 1902. Print.

———. *Lombard Street: A Description of the Money Market.* London: Dodo Press, 2006. Print.

———. *Physics and Politics; or, Thoughts on the Application of the Principles of "Natural Selection" and "Inheritance" to Political Society.* Boston: Beacon Press, 1956. Print.

———. *The Works and Life of Walter Bagehot.* 10 vols. London: Longmans, Green, 1915. Print.

Bain, Alexander. *The Emotions and the Will.* London: John W Parker and Son, 1859. Print.

———. *The Senses and the Intellect.* London: John W Parker and Son, 1855. Print.

Bajorek, Jennifer. *Counterfeit Capital: Poetic Labor and Revolutionary Irony.* Stanford: Stanford University Press, 2009. Print.

Balzac, Honoré de. "Le Chef d'Oeuvre Inconnu." In *Oeuvres Completes de Honoré De Balzac.* Paris: Michel Lévy Freres, 1870, 15:305–31. Print.

"Banking." *Household Words,* 17 May 1856, 427–32. Print.

"Banking and Poesy." *City Jackdaw,* 21 September 1877, 355. Print.

"Banking Morality." *London Review,* 29 April 1865, 445–47. Print.

Barker-Banfield, G. J. "The Spermatic Economy: A Nineteenth-Century View of Sexuality." In *Pleasure or Procreation? Sexual Attitudes in American History.* Malabar, Fla.: Robert E. Krieger, 1983, 47–70. Print.

Barthes, Roland. *The Rustle of Language.* New York: Hill and Wang, 1986. Print.

Bass, Alan. "The Status of an Analogy: Psychoanalysis and Physics." *American Imago* 54 (1997): 235–56. Print.

Baucom, Ian. *Specters of the Atlantic: Finance Capital, Slavery, and the Philosophy of History.* Durham: Duke University Press, 2005. Print.

Beer, Gillian. *George Eliot.* Brighton: Harvester, 1986. Print.

Benjamin, Walter. *The Arcades Project.* Cambridge, Mass.: Belknap Press of Harvard University Press, 1999. Print.

Bennett, David. "Introduction: Psychoanalysis, Money, and the Economy." Introductory address, conference proceedings, Freud Museum, London, 2010. Print.

———. "Desire as Capital: Getting a Return on the Repressed Libidinal Economy." In *Metaphors of Economy.* Amsterdam: Rodopi, 2005, 95–112. Print.

Birken, Lawrence. *Consuming Desire: Sexual Science and the Emergence of a Culture of Abundance, 1871–1914*. Ithaca: Cornell University Press, 1988. Print.

Blaug, Mark. *Economic Theory in Retrospect*. 4th ed. Cambridge: Cambridge University Press, 1985. Print.

Bloom, Harold. *A Map of Misreading*. Oxford: Oxford University Press, 1980. Print.

Bodenheimer, Rosemarie. *The Real Life of Mary Ann Evans: George Eliot, Her Letters and Fiction*. Ithaca: Cornell University Press, 1994. Print.

Brantlinger, Patrick. *Fictions of State: Culture and Credit in Britain, 1694–1994*. Ithaca: Cornell University Press, 1996. Print.

Breithaupt, Fritz. "Homo-Oeconomicus: The Rhetoric of Currency and a Case of Nineteenth-Century Psychology." *Nineteenth-Century Prose* 32 (2005): 6–26. Print.

Briggs, Asa. *Marx in London: An Illustrated Guide*. London: Lawrence and Wishart, 2008. Print.

Brooks, Peter. *The Melodramatic Imagination: Balzac, Henry James, Melodrama, and the Mode of Excess*. New Haven: Yale University Press, 1995. Print.

———. *Reading for the Plot: Design and Intention in Narrative*. New York: A. A. Knopf, 1984. Print.

Buck-Morss, Susan. "Envisioning Capital: Political Economy on Display." *Critical Inquiry* 21, no. 2 (1995): 434–67. Print.

Buckley, Jerome Hamilton. *Season of Youth: The Bildungsroman from Dickens to Golding*. Cambridge, Mass.: Harvard University Press, 1974. Print.

Bucknill, John Charles. *A Manual of Psychological Medicine: Containing the History, Nosology, Description, Statistics, Diagnosis, Pathology, and Treatment of Insanity, with an Appendix of Cases*. Philadelphia: Blanchard and Lea, 1858. Print.

"Capital in Trade." *School Master*, 1832, 63. Print.

Carlisle, Janice. *The Sense of an Audience: Dickens, Thackeray, and George Eliot at Mid-century*. Brighton: Harvester Press, 1982. Print.

Carlyle, Thomas. *Past and Present*. London: Chapman and Hall, 1843. Print.

Cecil, David. *Early Victorian Novelists: Essays in Revaluation*. London: Penguin, 1948. Print.

Cervantes Saavedra, Miguel de. *Don Quixote*. New York: Penguin Books, 2003. Print.

Chancellor, Edward. *Devil Take the Hindmost: A History of Financial Speculation*. Basingstoke: Macmillan, 1999. Print.

———. "Look Out: This Crunch Is Serious." *Washington Post*, 19 August 2007.

Chase, Karen. *Eros and Psyche: The Representation of Personality in Charlotte Brontë, Charles Dickens, and George Eliot*. New York: Methuen, 1984. Print.

Chubb, Hammon. "The Bank Act and the Crisis of 1866." *Journal of the Statistical Society of London* 35, no. 2 (1872): 171–95. Print.

Cohen, Tom, and Barbara Cohen, eds. *Material Events: Paul de Man and the Afterlife of Theory*. Minneapolis: University of Minnesota, 2000. Print.

Cohen, William A. "Manual Conduct in *Great Expectations.*" In *Sex Scandal.* Print.

———. *Sex Scandal: The Private Parts of Victorian Fiction.* Durham: Duke University Press, 1996. Print.

Collini, Stefan. *Public Moralists: Political Thought and Intellectual Life in Britain, 1850–1930.* Oxford: Clarendon Press, 1991. Print.

Collins, Michael. *Banks and Industrial Finance in Britain: 1800–1939.* Hampshire: Macmillan, 1991. Print.

Coovadia, Imran. "George Eliot's Realism and Adam Smith." *Studies in English Literature* 42 (2002): 819–36. Print.

Courtemanche, Eleanor. *The "Invisible Hand" and British Fiction, 1818–1860: Adam Smith, Political Economy, and the Genre of Realism.* Palgrave Macmillan, 2011. Print.

Crosby, Christina. "A Taste for More: Trollope's Addictive Realism." In *The New Economic Criticism,* ed. Osteen and Woodmansee, 251–61. Print.

Crouzet, François. *The Victorian Economy.* London: Methuen, 1982. Print.

Cunningham, W. "Political Economy as a Moral Science." *Mind* 3, no. 11 (1878): 369–83. Print.

Cvetkovich, Ann. *Mixed Feelings: Feminism, Mass Culture, and Victorian Sensationalism.* New Brunswick: Rutgers University Press, 1992. Print.

de Certeau, Michel. *Heterologies: Discourse on the Other.* Minneapolis: University of Minnesota Press, 1986. Print.

Delany, Paul. *Literature, Money, and the Market: From Trollope to Amis.* New York: Palgrave, 2002. Print.

Deleuze, Gilles. *Anti-Oedipus: Capitalism and Schizophrenia.* New York: Viking Press, 1977. Print.

———. "Preface." In *Psychanalyse Et Transversalité.* Paris: Maspero, 1974. Print.

de Man, Paul. *Aesthetic Ideology.* Minneapolis: University of Minnesota Press, 1982. Print.

———. *Allegories of Reading: Figural Language in Rousseau, Nietzsche, Rilke, and Proust.* New Haven: Yale University Press, 1996. Print.

———. *Blindness and Insight: Essays in the Rhetoric of Contemporary Criticism.* Minneapolis: University of Minnesota Press, 1983. Print.

———. "The Concept of Irony." In *Aesthetic Ideology,* 163–84.

———. *Resistance to Theory.* Minneapolis: University of Minnesota Press, 1986. Print.

———. "The Rhetoric of Temporality." In *Blindness and Insight,* 187–228.

Derrida, Jacques. "Freud and the Scene of Writing." *Yale* 48 (1972): 74–117. Print.

———. *Given Time.* Vol. 1, *Counterfeit Money.* Trans. Peggy Kamuf. Chicago: University of Chicago Press, 1994. Print.

———. *The Post Card: From Socrates to Freud and Beyond.* Trans. Alan Bass. Chicago: University of Chicago Press, 1987. Print.

———. *Specters of Marx: The State of the Debt, the Work of Mourning, and the New International.* London: Routledge, 1994. Print.

Dever, Carolyn. *Death and the Mother from Dickens to Freud: Victorian Fiction and the Anxiety of Origins.* Cambridge: Cambridge University Press, 1998. Print.

Dickens, Charles. "Bankruptcy in Six Easy Lessons." *Household Words,* 13 February 1853, 210–12. Print.

———. *Bleak House.* New York: Penguin. 2003. Print.

———. *Great Expectations.* Edited by David Trotter. New York: Penguin, 2002. Print.

———. *The Letters of Charles Dickens: The Pilgrim Edition.* Ed. Graham Storey. Vol. 9. Oxford: Clarendon Press, 1998. Print.

———. *Our Mutual Friend.* New York: Penguin, 1998. Print.

———. "Shadowless Men." *Household Words,* 13 March 1858, 294–99. Print.

Disraeli, Benjamin. *Vivian Grey.* Philadelphia: E. L. Carey, 1837. Print.

"Does Treasury Need $700 Billion All At Once?" *Wall Street Journal,* 24 September 2008.

Doubleday, Thomas. *A Financial, Monetary, and Statistical History of England, from the Revolution of 1688 to the Present Time; Derived Principally from Official Documents.* London: E. Wilson, 1847. Print.

Dumont, Louis. *From Mandeville to Marx: The Genesis and Triumph of Economic Ideology.* Chicago: University of Chicago Press, 1977. Print.

Eden, Emily. *The Semi-Detached House.* London: R. Bentley, 1859. Print.

Eliot, George. *Adam Bede.* Oxford: Oxford University Press, 1998. Print.

———. *Daniel Deronda.* Oxford: Oxford University Press, 1998. Print.

———. "Debasing the Moral Currency." In *Impressions of Theophrastus Such,* 81–87.

———. *Impressions of Theophrastus Such.* Iowa City: University of Iowa Press, 1994. Print.

———. *The Lifted Veil.* Oxford: Oxford University Press, 2009. Print.

———. *Middlemarch.* Ed. David Carroll. Oxford: Oxford University Press, 2008. Print.

———. "The Natural History of German Life." In *Selected Essays, Poems and Other Writings.*

———. *Scenes of Clerical Life.* Ed. Thomas A. Noble. Oxford: Oxford University Press, 2009. Print.

———. *Selected Essays, Poems, and Other Writings.* Ed. Nicholas Warren. New York: Penguin, 1991. Print.

———. "Thomas Carlyle." In *Selected Essays, Poems and Other Writings.*

Ermarth, Elizabeth Deeds. "George Eliot's Conception of Sympathy." *Nineteenth-Century Fiction* (1985): 23–42. Print.

Erwin, Edward. *The Freud Encyclopedia: Theory, Therapy, and Culture.* London: Routledge, 2001. Print.

Evans, David Morier. "Alarming State of Trade." *Charter,* 10 November 1839. Print.

———. *The City.* London: Bailey Bros., 1845. Print.

———. *The Commercial Crisis of 1847–48.* London: Letts, Son and Steer. 1848. Print.

———. *Facts, Failures, and Frauds.* London: Groombridge, 1859. Print.

———. "The Great Banking Forgeries." *Banker's Magazine* February 1857: 105–9. Print.

———. *History of the Commercial Crisis of 1857–1858.* London: Groombridge and Sons, 1859. Print.

———. *Speculative Notes on Speculation: Ideal and Real.* London: Groombridge and Sons, 1864. Print.

"Financial Crisis Illustrates Influence of Emotions, Behavior on Market." *PBS Online News Hour,* 8 October 2008.

Fink, Bruce. *Lacan to the Letter: Reading Écrits Closely.* Minneapolis: University of Minnesota Press, 2004. Print.

Finn, Margot. *The Character of Credit: Personal Debt in English Culture, 1740–1914.* Cambridge: Cambridge University Press, 2003. Print.

Forster, John. *The Life of Charles Dickens.* 2 vols. London: Dent, 1966. Print.

Francis, John. *Chronicles and Characters of the Stock Exchange.* London: Willoughby, 1849. Print.

———. *History of the Bank of England: Its Times and Traditions.* London: Willoughby, 1847. Print.

Freedgood, Elaine. "Banishing Panic: Harriet Martineau and the Popularization of Political Economy." In *The New Economic Criticism,* ed. Osteen and Woodmansee, 180–95. Print.

Freud, Sigmund. *Beyond the Pleasure Principle.* Ed. James Strachey. New York: Norton, 1990. Print.

———. *Briefe an Wilhelm Fliess 1887–1904.* Ed. Jeffrey Masson. Frankfurt am Main: Fischer Verlag, 1986. Print.

———. *Jokes and Their Relation to the Unconscious.* Vol. 8 of Freud, *Standard Edition.*

———. *The Letters of Sigmund Freud.* Ed. Ernst Freud. London: Hogarth Press, 1961. Print.

———. *Standard Edition of the Complete Psychological Works of Sigmund Freud.* Ed. James Strachey. 24 vols. London: Hogarth Press, 1953. Print.

———. *Gesammelte Werke.* London: Imago, 1991.

"From Bagehot to Bernanke." *Wall Street Journal,* 20 August 2007.

Frye, Northrup. *Anatomy of Criticism.* New York: Atheneum, 1970. Print.

Gagnier, Regenia. *The Insatiability of Human Wants: Economics and Aesthetics in Market Society.* Chicago: University of Chicago Press, 2000. Print.

Gallagher, Catherine. "George Eliot: Immanent Victorian." *Representations* 90 (2005): 61–74. Print.

———. *The Body Economic: Life, Death, and Sensation in Political Economy and the Victorian Novel.* Princeton: Princeton University Press, 2008. Print.

Garcha, Amanpal. "Careerist Theory." Conference Presentation, Stanford University, 2007.

Gay, Peter. "Human Nature in History." In *Freud for Historians.* New York: Oxford University Press, 1986, 78–115. Print.

Gayer, Arthur. *Growth and Fluctuation of the British Economy, 1790–1850.* Oxford: Clarendon Press, 1953. Print.

Gellert, Hugo. *Karl Marx's "Capital" in Lithographs.* New York: Ray Long and Richard R. Smith, 1934. Print.

Genette, Gérard. *Narrative Discourse: An Essay in Method.* Reprint. Trans. Jane E. Lewin. Ithaca: Cornell University Press, 1983. Print.

———. *Narrative Discourse Revisited.* Trans. Jane E. Lewin. Ithaca: Cornell University Press, 1990. Print.

Gilbert, Sandra M., and Susan Gubar. *The Madwoman in the Attic: The Woman Writer and the Nineteenth-Century Literary Imagination.* 2nd ed. New Haven: Yale University Press, 2000. Print.

Godden, David. "Psychologism in the Logic of John Stuart Mill." *History and Philosophy of Logic* 26 (2005): 115–43. Print.

Godden, Richard. *Fictions of Capital: The American Novel from James to Mailer.* Cambridge: Cambridge University Press, 2008. Print.

Goux, Jean-Joseph. *The Coiners of Language.* Trans. Jennifer C. Gage. Norman: University of Oklahoma Press, 1996. Print.

———. *Symbolic Economies: After Marx and Freud.* Trans. Jennifer C. Gage. Ithaca: Cornell University Press, 1990. Print.

Grindon, Leo Hartley. *Manchester Banks and Bankers: Historical, Biographical, Anecdotal.* London: Simpkin, Marshall, 1877. Print.

Haight, Gordon S. *The George Eliot Letters.* Vol. 8. New Haven: Yale University Press, 1978. Print.

———. *Selections from George Eliot's Letters.* New Haven: Yale University Press, 1985. Print.

Hall, N. John. *Trollope: A Biography.* Oxford: Oxford University Press, 1991. Print.

Hamacher, Werner. "Lingua Amissa: The Messianism of Commodity Language." In *Ghostly Demarcations: A Sympoisum on Derrida's Specters of Marx,* edited by Michael Sprinker. London: Verso, 1999. Print.

Hardy, Barbara. *Appropriate Form: An Essay on the Novel.* London: Athlone Press, 1964. Print.

Harvey, David. *A Companion to Marx's Capital.* London: Verso, 1964. Print.

———. *The Condition of Postmodernity: An Enquiry into the Origins of Cultural Change.* London: Wiley-Blackwell, 1991. Print.

———. *The Limits to Capital.* Updated. London: Verso, 2007. Print.

———. *The New Imperialism.* New York: Oxford University Press, 2005. Print.

Heinzelman, Kurt. *The Economics of the Imagination.* Amherst: University of Massachusetts Press, 1980. Print.

Henry, Nancy. "'Ladies Do It?' Victorian Women Investors in Fact and Fiction." In *Victorian Literature and Finance,* ed. O'Gorman. Print.

Herbert, Christopher. *Trollope and Comic Pleasure.* Chicago: University of Chicago Press, 1987. Print.

Hertz, Neil. *George Eliot's Pulse.* Stanford: Stanford University Press, 2003. Print.

Hirschman, Albert O. *The Passions and the Interests: Political Arguments for Capitalism Before Its Triumph.* Princeton: Princeton University Press, 1997. Print.

Hollingshead, John. "The City of Unlimited Paper." *Under Bow Bells: A City Book for All Readers.* London: Groombridge and Sons, 1860, 1–15. Print.

"Hope, Greed, and Fear: The Psychology Behind the Financial Crisis." *Knowledge@ Wharton,* 15 April 2009.

Houghton, Walter. *A Victorian Frame of Mind, 1830–1870.* New Haven: Yale University Press, 1957. Print.

Hutton, Richard Holt. 1872. "Review of Middlemarch." *Spectator,* 7 December 1872, 1554–56. Print.

Hyman, Stanley E. *Tangled Bank: Darwin, Marx, Frazer and Freud as Imaginative Writers.* New York: Atheneum, 1962. Print.

"The Interior of the Royal Bank of Liverpool." *Economist,* 16 November 1867, 1294. Print.

"Iron and Coal Trades." *Economist* 12 July 1879, 808. Print.

Jaffe, Audrey. *Scenes of Sympathy: Identity and Representation in Victorian Fiction.* Ithaca: Cornell University Press, 2000. Print.

Jakobson, Roman. *Fundamentals of Language.* Berlin: Mouton de Gruyter, 2002. Print.

James, Harold. "The Literary Financier." *American Scholar* 60 (1991): 251–56. Print.

James, Henry. "Anthony Trollope." In *The Trollope Critics,* edited by N. John Hall. Totowa: Barnes and Noble, 1981. Print.

James, William. *Principles of Psychology.* 2 vols. New York: Henry Holt, 1905. Print.

Jameson, Fredric. "Cognitive Mapping." In *Marxism and the Interpretation of Culture,* edited by Cary Nelson and Lawrence Grossberg, 347–60. London: Macmillan, 1988.

———. *Marxism and Form: Twentieth-Century Dialectical Theories of Literature.* Princeton: Princeton University Press, 1974. Print.

Jennings, Richard. *Natural Elements in Political Economy.* London: Macmillan, 1871. Print.

Jevons, William Stanley. *Theory of Political Economy.* London: Macmillan, 1871. Print.

Johnston, Adrian. *Time Driven: Metapsychology and the Splitting of the Drive.* Evanston: Northwestern University Press, 2005. Print.

Jones, Iva. *Amid Visions and Revisions: Poetry and Criticism on Literature and the Arts.* Baltimore: Morgan State University Press, 1985. Print.

Jumeau, Alain. "The Way We Live Now, or Trollope in Vanity Fair." *Cahiers Victoriennes et Edouardians* 58 (2003): 57–69. Print.

Karatani, Kojin. *Architecture as Metaphor: Language, Number, Money.* Ed. Michael Speaks. Trans. Sabu Kohso. Cambridge, Mass.: MIT Press, 1995. Print.

———. "Capital's Drive." In *Transcritique: On Kant and Marx,* 200–11.

———. *Transcritique: On Kant and Marx.* Trans. Sabu Kohso. Cambridge, Mass.: MIT Press, 2005. Print.

Kendrick, Walter. *The Novel-Machine: The Theory and Fiction of Anthony Trollope.* Baltimore: The Johns Hopkins University Press, 1980. Print.

Keynes, John Maynard. *The General Theory of Employment, Interest, and Money.* London: Macmillan, 1936. Print.

Kincaid, James R. *Novels of Anthony Trollope.* Oxford: Oxford University Press, 1977. Print.

Kordela, A. Kiarina. "Marx Condensed and Displaced." In *The Dreams of Interpretation,* edited by Catherine Liu, 303–20. Minneapolis: University of Minnesota Press, 2007. Print.

———. "Marx's Update of Cultural Theory." *Cultural Critique* 65 (2007): 43–66. Print.

———. "Political Metaphysics: God in Global Capitalism." *Political Theory* 27 (1999): 769–88. Print.

Kucich, John. *Repression in Victorian Fiction: Charlotte Brontë, George Eliot, and Charles Dickens.* Berkeley: University of California Press, 1987. Print.

Kurnick, David. "An Erotics of Detachment: Middlemarch and Novel-Reading as Critical Practice." *ELH* 74 (2007): 583–608. Print.

Kusch, Martin. "Psychologism." Ed. Edward Zalta. *The Stanford Encyclopedia of Philosophy,* Winter 2011.

Lacan, Jacques. *Écrits: The First Complete Edition in English.* Trans. Bruce Fink. New York: W. W. Norton, 2007. Print.

———. *The Ego in Freud's Theory and in the Technique of Psychoanalysis, 1954–1955 (Book II).* Ed. Jacques-Alain Miller. Trans. Sylvana Tomaselli. New York: W. W. Norton, 1991. Print.

———. *The Four Fundamental Concepts of Psychoanalysis.* Ed. Jacques-Alain Miller. Trans. Alan Sheridan. New York: W. W. Norton, 1998. Print.

———. *Le Séminaire Le Livre II: Le Moi dans la theorie de Freud et dans la technique psychanalytique.* Paris: Éditions du Seuil, 1978.

Lafargue, Paul, and William Liebknecht. *Extracts from the Reminiscences of Karl Marx.* London: Lawrence and Wishart, 1942. Print.

Lane, Christopher. *Hatred and Civility: The Antisocial Life in Victorian England.* New York: Columbia University Press, 2004. Print.

Laplanche, Jean. "Psychoanalysis as Anti-Hermeneutics." *Radical Philosophy* 79 (1996): 7–12. Print.

Law, Jules David. "Being There: Gothic Violence and Virtuality in Frankenstein, Dracula, and Strange Days." *ELH* 73, no. 4 (2006): 975–96.

Leatham, William. *Letters on the Currency.* London: Pelham Richardson, 1840. Print.

Levi-Strauss, Claude. *Structural Anthropology.* New York: Basic Books, 1974. Print.

Levine, Caroline. *The Serious Pleasures of Suspense: Victorian Realism and Narrative Doubt.* University of Virginia Press, 2003. Print.

———. "Strategic Formalism: Toward a New Method in Cultural Studies." *Victorian Studies* 48 (2006): 625–57. Print.

Lewes, George Henry. *Literary Criticism of George Henry Lewes.* Ed. Alice Kaminsky. Lincoln: University of Nebraska Press, 1964. Print.

———. *Principles of Success in Literature.* London: Walter Scott, 1865. Print.

———. *Problems of Life and Mind.* London: Trubner, 1874. Print.

Loftus, Donna. "Limited Liability, Market Democracy, and the Social Organization of Production in Mid-Nineteenth-Century Britain." In *Victorian Investments: New Perspectives on Finance and Culture,* edited by Nancy Henry and Cannon Schmitt, 79–97. Bloomington: Indiana University Press, 2008. Print.

Loyd, Samuel Jones. *Reflections Suggested by a Perusal of Mr. J. Horsley Palmer's Pamphlet on the Causes and Consequences of the Pressure on the Money Market.* London: Pelham Richardson, 1837. Print.

Lukacher, Ned. *Primal Scenes: Literature, Philosophy, Psychoanalysis.* Ithaca: Cornell University Press, 1988. Print.

Lukacs, Gyorgy. *Aesthetics and Politics: The Key Texts of the Classic Debate within German Marxism.* London: Verso, 1977.

———. "Art and Objective Truth." In *Writer and Critic,* 25–60.

———. "Critical Realism and Socialist Realism." In *Realism in Our Time,* 93–135.

———. *Essays on Realism.* Cambridge, Mass.: MIT Press, 1981.

———. *A History of the Evolution of Modern Drama.* Budapest: Franklin, 1911. Print.

———. "Realism in the Balance." In *Aesthetics and Politics,* 28–59.

———. *Realism in Our Time.* New York: Harper, 1971. Print.

———. "Reportage or Portrayal." In *Essays on Realism,* 44–75.

———. *Studies in European Realism.* Overland Park: Howard Fertig, 2002. Print.

———. *Writer and Critic, and Other Essays.* Ed., trans. Arthur D. Kahn. London: Merlin, 1970. Print.

Lupton, Julia Reinhard. *Thinking with Shakespeare: Essays on Politics and Life.* Chicago: University of Chicago Press, 2011. Print.

Lynch, Deidre Shauna. *The Economy of Character: Novels, Market Culture, and the Business of Inner Meaning.* Chicago: University of Chicago Press, 1998. Print.

Lyotard, Jean Francois. *Libidinal Economy.* Trans. Iain Hamilton Grant. Bloomington: Indiana University Press, 1993. Print.

Madigan, Brian. "Bagehot's Dictum in Practice: Formulating and Implementing Policies to Combat the Financial Crisis." Federal Reserve Bank of Kansas City's Annual Economic Symposium. Jackson Hole, Wyo.: Federal Reserve Bank, 2009.

Marshall, David. *The Figure of Theater.* New York: Columbia University Press, 1986. Print.

Marx, Karl. *Capital: A Critique of Political Economy.* Vol. 1. Trans. Ben Fowkes. Reprint. New York: Penguin, 1992. Print.

———. *Capital: A Critique of Political Economy.* Vol. 3. Trans. David Fernbach. Reissue. New York: Penguin, 1993. Print.

———. *Grundrisse: Foundations of the Critique of Political Economy.* Trans. Martin Nicolaus. Reprint. New York: Penguin, 1993. Print.

Marx, Karl, and Friedrich Engels. *Marx Engels Collected Works.* Ed. Richard Dixon. 50 vols. New York: International, 1975. Print.

———. *Marx Engels Werke.* 43 vols. Berlin: Dietz Verlag, 1962. Print.

Matthews, R. C. O. *A Study in Trade-Cycle History: Economic Fluctuations in Great Britain, 1833–1842.* Cambridge: Cambridge University Press, 1954. Print.

McGann, Tara. "Literary Realism in the Wake of Business Cycle Theory: The Way We Live Now." In *Victorian Literature and Finance,* ed. O'Gorman, 133–56. Print.

Michaels, Walter Benn. *The Gold Standard and the Logic of Naturalism: American Literature at the Turn of the Century.* Berkeley: University of California Press, 1988. Print.

Michie, Ranald C. *The London Stock Exchange: A History.* New York: Oxford University Press, 2001. Print.

Mieszkowski, Jan. *Labors of Imagination: Aesthetics and Political Economy from Kant to Althusser.* New York: Fordham University Press, 2006. Print.

Mill, John Stuart. *Principles of Political Economy.* London: Longman, Green, 1848. Print.

Miller, Andrew H. *The Burdens of Perfection: On Ethics and Reading in Nineteenth-Century British Literature.* Ithaca: Cornell University Press, 2010. Print.

Miller, J. Hillis. *The Form of Victorian Fiction.* South Bend, Ind.: University of Notre Dame Press, 1968. Print.

———. "Narrative and History." *ELH* 41, no. 3 (1974): 455–73. Print.

———. "Promises, Promises: Speech Act Theory, Literary Theory and Politico-Economic Theory in Marx and de Man." *New Literary History* 33, no. 1 (2002): 1–20. Print.

Mirowski, Philip, ed. *Natural Images in Economic Thought: Markets Read in Tooth and Claw.* Cambridge: Cambridge University Press, 1994. Print.

"Money Market, City, Friday." *Morning Chronicle,* 1 June 1833, 3. Print.

Moretti, Franco. *The Way of the World: The Bildungsroman in European Culture.* Trans. Albert Sbragia. London: Verso, 2000. Print.

Morgan, Victor. *London Stock Exchange: Its History and Fluctuations.* New York: Elek Books, 1962. Print.

Morrison, Alan D., and William J. Wilhelm Jr. *Investment Banking: Institutions, Politics, and Law.* Oxford: Oxford University Press, 2007. Print.

"Mr. Trollope's Last Novel." *Nation,* 19 August 1880, 139. Print.

"The National Debt and the Stock Exchange." *Blackwoods Edinburgh Magazine,* December 1849, 655–78. Print.

Nazar, Hina. "Philosophy in the Bedroom: Middlemarch and the Scandal of Sympathy." *Yale Journal of Criticism* 15 (2002): 293–314. Print.

Nelson, Benjamin. *The Idea of Usury: From Tribal Brotherhood to Universal Otherhood.* Chicago: University of Chicago Press, 1949. Print.

Nobus, Dany. "What Are Words Worth? On Value for Money in the Psychoanalytic Economy." *Keynote Address.* Rutgers University, 2009.

O'Gorman, Francis, ed. *Victorian Literature and Finance.* Oxford: Oxford University Press, 2007. Print.

Oliphant, Laurence. "Autobiography of a Joint Stock Company." In *The Financial System in Nineteenth-Century Britain,* ed. Poovey. Originally published in *Blackwoods Magazine,* July 1876, 96–122. Print.

Ornston, David Gray. "The Invention of 'Cathexis' and Strachey's Strategy." *International Review of Psychoanalysis* 12 (1985): 391–98. Print.

Ortiz-Robles, Mario. *The Novel as Event.* Ann Arbor: University of Michigan Press, 2010. Print.

Osteen, Mark, and Martha Woodmansee, eds. *The New Economic Criticism: Studies at the Interface of Literature and Economics.* New York: Routledge, 1999. Print.

"The Panic in the Money Market." *Examiner,* 12 May 1866, 1. Print.

Pocock, J. G. A. *Virtue, Commerce, and History: Essays on Political Thought and History, Chiefly in the Eighteenth Century.* Cambridge: Cambridge University Press, 1985. Print.

"The Poetry of Banking." *Banker's Magazine,* June 1844, 151. Print.

Poovey, Mary. "Discriminating Reading." *Victorian Review* 31, no. 2 (2005): 10–35. Print.

———. *Genres of the Credit Economy.* Chicago: University of Chicago Press, 2008. Print.

———. "Writing About Finance in Victorian England: Disclosure and Secrecy in the Cultures of Investment." *Victorian Studies* 45, no. 1 (2002): 17–41. Print.

———, ed. *The Financial System in Nineteenth-Century Britain.* New York and Oxford: Oxford University Press, 2002.

Pope, Alexander. "Epilogue to the Satires in Two Dialogues." In *Complete Poetical Works of Alexander Pope.* Cambridge: Cambridge University Press, 1903. Print.

Postone, Moishe. "Theorizing the Contemporary World: David Harvey, Giovanni Arrighi, Robert Brenner." In *Political Economy and Global Capitalism: The 21st Century, Present and Future,* edited by Robert Albritton, Bob Jessop, and Richard Westra, 7–24. London: Anthem Press, 2007. Print.

"Prefatory Words." *Mind* 1, no. 1 (1876): 1–6. Print.

Price, Bonamy. "Credit and Crises." *Fraser's Magazine for Town and Country 1830–1869,* August 1869: 207–22. Print.

Prince, Gerald. *A Dictionary of Narratology.* Lincoln: University of Nebraska Press, 2003. Print.

Purdy, Dwight. " 'The One Poor Word' in Middlemarch." *Studies in English Literature* 44 (2004): 805–21. Print.

Quintilian. *Institutes of Oratory.* London: Haddon Bros., 1856. Print.

Rabinbach, Anson. *The Human Motor: Energy, Fatigue, and the Origins of Modernity.* Berkeley: University of California Press, 1992. Print.

Ray, Isaac. *Mental Hygiene.* Boston: Ticknor and Fields, 1863. Print.

"To Readers and Correspondents." *Economist,* 17 May 1851, 544. Print.

"The Recent Rise in Foreign Securities and the New Turkish Loan." *Economist,* 19 September 1874, 1130. Print.

Redfield, Marc. *Phantom Formations: Aesthetic Ideology and the Bildungsroman.* Ithaca: Cornell University Press, 1996. Print.

Reinhard, Kenneth, and Julia Reinhard Lupton. *After Oedipus: Shakespeare in Psychoanalysis.* Ithaca: Cornell University Press, 1993. Print.

Ringler, Ellen. "Middlemarch: A Feminist Perspective." *Studies in the Novel* 15 (1983): 55–61. Print.

Rivington, F. *The Annual Register, Or A View of the History and Politics of the Year 1846.* London: Longman, 1847. Print.

Robinson, Ken. "The Federal Reserve and Financial Crisis." *Federal Reserve Bank of Dallas,* 2 November 2007.

Ruskin, John. *Modern Painters.* London: Elder, 1843. Print.

———. *Unto This Last and Other Writings.* Ed. Clive Wilmer. New York: Penguin, 1986. Print.

"Ruskin's Remedy for Inundation." *Punch* 1871, 32. Print.

Rylance, Rick. *Victorian Psychology and British Culture 1850–1880.* Oxford: Oxford University Press, 2000. Print.

Sadleir, Michael. *Anthony Trollope: A Commentary.* New York: Houghton Mifflin, 1927. Print.

Said, Edward W. *Culture and Imperialism.* New York: Vintage, 1994. Print.

Scannell, Kara, and Sudeep Reddy. "Greenspan Admits Errors to Hostile House Panel." *Wall Street Journal,* 24 October 2008, A1. Print.

Schabas, Margaret. "Victorian Economics and the Science of Mind." In *Victorian Science in Context,* edited by Bernard Lightman, 72–93. Chicago: University of Chicago Press, 1997. Print.

Searle, John R. *Speech Acts: An Essay in the Philosophy of Language.* Cambridge: Cambridge University Press, 1970. Print.

Seem, Mark. "Introduction." In *Anti-Oedipus: Capitalism and Schizophrenia,* by Gilles Deleuze. New York: Viking Press, 1977. Print.

"Shadowless Men." *Household Words,* 13 March 1858, 294–99.

Shaw, Harry E. *Narrating Reality: Austen, Scott, Eliot.* Ithaca: Cornell University Press, 2004. Print.

Shell, Marc. *Art and Money.* Chicago: University of Chicago Press, 1995. Print.

———. *The Economy of Literature.* Baltimore: The Johns Hopkins University Press, 1993. Print.

———. *Money, Language, and Thought: Literary and Philosophic Economies from the Medieval to the Modern Era.* The Johns Hopkins University Press, 1993. Print.

Sherman, Sandra. *Finance and Fictionality in the Early Eighteenth Century: Accounting for Defoe.* Cambridge: Cambridge University Press, 1996. Print.

Shiller, Robert J. *Irrational Exuberance.* 2nd ed. Crown Business, 2009. Print.

Shrimpton, Nicholas. "Even These Metallic Problems Have Their Melodramatic Side: Money in Victorian Literature." In *Victorian Literature and Finance,* ed. O'Gorman, 17–38. Print.

Skilton, David. *Anthony Trollope and His Contemporaries: A Study in the Theory and Conventions of Mid-Victorian Fiction.* London: Longman, 1972. Print.

Smale, Alison. "Bankers Put Focus on 'Real Economy.'" *New York Times* 1 February 2010.

Small, Ian. *Conditions for Criticism: Authority, Knowledge, and Literature in the Late Nineteenth Century.* Oxford: Oxford University Press, 1991. Print.

Smalley, Donald. *Trollope: The Critical Heritage.* London: Routledge, 1969. Print.

Smiles, Samuel. *Self Help.* London: Murray, 1859. Print.

Smith, Adam. *The Theory of Moral Sentiments.* New York: Prometheus Books, 2000. Print.

———. *The Wealth of Nations.* New York: Bantam Classics, 2003. Print.

Smith, Arthur. *The Bubble of the Age, Or, The Fallacies of Railway Investment.* London: Sherwood, Gilbert, and Piper, 1848. Print.

Smith, Sheila. "Blue Books and Victorian Novelists." *Review of English Studies* 21, no. 81 (1970): 23–40. Print.

Spacks, Patricia Ann Meyer. *Gossip.* Chicago: University of Chicago Press, 1986. Print.

Spencer, Herbert. "The Philosophy of Style." In *Essays Scientific, Political, and Speculative,* 2:333 –69. London: Williams and Norgate, 1891. Print.

———. *Principles of Ethics.* 2 Vols. New York: Liberty Fund, 1978. Print.

———. *Principles of Psychology.* Vol. 2. London: Longmans, Green, 1855. Print.

Stewart, Garrett. *Novel Violence: A Narratography of Victorian Fiction.* Chicago: University of Chicago Press, 2009. Print.

"The Stock Exchange." *The Chambers Journal,* 10 June 1865, 366–68. Print.

Strachey, James. "Obituary for Joan Riviere." *International Journal of Psychoanalysis* 44 (1963): 228–30. Print.

Sutton, Max. "The Affront to Victorian Dignity in the Satire of the Eighteen-Seventies." In *The Nineteenth-Century Writer and His Audience,* edited by Harold Orel, 93–118. Lawrence: University of Kansas, 1969. Print.

Tanner, Tony. "Trollope's *The Way We Live Now:* Its Modern Significance." *Critical Quarterly* 9 (1967): 256–71. Print.

Taylor, Richard, and John Edward Taylor. *The London University Calendar.* London: Red Lion, 1845. Print.

Teichgraeber, Richard. "Rethinking Das Adam Smith Problem." *The Journal of British Studies* 20, no. 2 (1981): 106–23. Print.

"Thackeray's Esmond." *Spectator,* 6 November 1852, 1066–67. Print.

Thomas, Ronald R. *Dreams of Authority: Freud and the Fictions of the Unconscious.* Ithaca: Cornell University Press, 1992. Print.

Thompson, James. *Models of Value: Eighteenth-Century Political Economy and the Novel.* Durham: Duke University Press, 1996. Print.

Trollope, Anthony. *An Autobiography of Anthony Trollope.* Ed. Michael Sadleir. Oxford: Oxford University Press, 1999. Print.

————. *Letters of Anthony Trollope.* Ed. N. John Hall. Vol. 2. Stanford: Stanford University Press, 1983. Print.

————. *The Struggles of Brown, Jones, and Robinson.* Oxford: Oxford University Press, 1993. Print.

————. *The Way We Live Now.* New York: Penguin, 2002. Print.

Trotter, David. "Introduction." *Great Expectations.* New York: Penguin, 2002. Print.

Vernon, John. *Money and Fiction: Literary Realism in the Nineteenth and Early Twentieth Centuries.* Ithaca: Cornell University Press, 1985. Print.

Wagner, Tamara S. *Financial Speculation in Victorian Fiction: Plotting Money and the Novel Genre, 1815–1901.* Columbus: Ohio State University Press, 2010. Print.

Wall, Stephen. "Trollope, Satire, and the Way We Live Now." *Essays in Criticism* 37 (1987): 43–61. Print.

Watt, Ian. *The Rise of the Novel: Studies in Defoe, Richardson and Fielding.* Berkeley: University of California Press, 1957. Print.

————. "Robinson Crusoe, Individualism, and the Novel." In *The Rise of the Novel.* Print.

"What Would Be the Effect of Abolishing All Laws Related to Debtor and Creditor?" *Fraser's Magazine,* May 1838, 545–52. Print.

Wheen, Francis. *Karl Marx: A Life.* London: Fourth Estate, 1999. Print.

Wicksteed, Henry. *Palgrave's Dictionary of Political Economy.* London: Macmillan, 1896. Print.

Wolfson, Susan J. "Reading for Form." *Modern Language Quarterly* 61, no. 1 (2000): 1–16. Print.

Woloch, Alex. "Characterization and Distribution." In *The One Vs. the Many,* 12–42.

————. *The One Vs. the Many: Minor Characters and the Space of the Protagonist in the Novel.* Princeton: Princeton University Press, 2003. Print.

Zaretsky, Eli. *Secrets of the Soul: A Social and Cultural History of Psychoanalysis.* New York: Vintage, 2005. Print.

Žižek, Slavoj. "How Did Marx Invent the Symptom?" In *The Sublime Object of Ideology.* London: Verso, 1989. Print.

————. *The Metastases of Enjoyment: On Women and Causality.* London: Verso, 1996. Print.

————. *The Parallax View.* Cambridge, Mass.: MIT Press, 2006. Print.

————. *The Sublime Object of Ideology.* London: Verso, 1989. Print.

Index